מסורה

ArtScroll Youth Series®

LIBRARY
Manhattan Day School
310 West 75 Street
New York, N.Y. 10023

Rabbi Nosson Scherman / Rabbi Meir Zlotowitz
General Editors

The

by Nechemiah Piontac

translated by
Shaindel Weinbach

illustrated by
Miriam Bardugo

ARIZAL

The Life and Times of Rabbi Yitzchak Luria

Published by

Mesorah Publications, ltd

in conjunction with

HAMESORAH /
Jerusalem

FIRST EDITION
First Impression . . . February, 1988

Published and Distributed by
MESORAH PUBLICATIONS, Ltd.
Brooklyn, New York 11223
in conjunction with
HAMESORAH / Jerusalem

Distributed in Israel by
MESORAH MAFITZIM / J. GROSSMAN
Rechov Harav Uziel 117
Jerusalem, Israel

Distributed in Europe by
J. LEHMANN HEBREW BOOKSELLERS
20 Cambridge Terrace
Gateshead, Tyne and Wear
England NE8 1RP

THE ARTSCROLL YOUTH SERIES ®
THE ARIZAL
© Copyright 1988 by MESORAH PUBLICATIONS, Ltd.
1969 Coney Island Avenue / Brooklyn, N.Y. 11223 / (718) 339-1700

No part of this book may be reproduced
in any form *without* **written** *permission from the copyright holder,*
except by a reviewer who wishes to quote brief passages in connection with a review
written for inclusion in magazines or newspapers.

THE RIGHTS OF THE COPYRIGHT HOLDER WILL BE STRICTLY ENFORCED.

ISBN:
0-89906-835-9 (hard cover)
0-89906-836-7 (paperback)

Printed in the United States of America by Noble Book Press Corp.
Bound by Sefercraft Quality Bookbinders, Ltd., Brooklyn, N.Y.

TABLE OF CONTENTS

	Introduction	7
1	Waiting for Eliyahu Hanavi	11
2	A Sturdy Branch	18
3	Childhood	23
4	In Egypt	35
5	At the Gateway of the Kabbalah	49
6	The Retreat on the Banks of the Nile	60
7	Tsefas and Its Scholars	68
8	The City of Mekubalim	88
9	The 'Lion' Ascends from Egypt	99
10	Chief of the Lions	123
11	Face Reading and Palmistry	135
12	Divine Vision and Divine Powers	149
13	Gilgulim	168
14	Relief and Deliverance for the Jews	179
15	The Rosh Yeshivah	192
16	At the Graves of Tzaddikim	200
17	The Last Years of His Life	215
18	The Book of Wisdom is Buried	233
19	The Lion Cubs	241
20	The Ari's Writings and His Spiritual Legacy	267
21	Locations Tell Their Tales	281

INTRODUCTION

In 5525 (1765), a caravan of Chasidim which had gone up to *Eretz Yisrael* from the Diaspora, reached the Galilee. Riding upon donkeys, they made their way slowly up the winding, dusty road leading to Tsefas. It was late afternoon when the travelers beheld the first houses of the holy city of the *mekubalim*, the mystics. Their hearts beat with excitement mingled with pain when their gaze fell upon an impressive structure built of blocks of hewn stone. It was the famous Sefardic *beis knesses* bearing the name of the Ari Hakadosh. But what a bitter sight! Its dome was in ruins and its walls were full of cracks and breaches. The effects of the earthquake which had shaken Tsefas only a few years before were visible to the eye from afar — ruined houses, islands of rubble and debris. Surviving buildings were few and far between.

The men urged their beasts onward, forcing them to cover the remaining stretch of road quickly so that they might reach the city before sunset. "Our first *minchah* in the very spot which the Arizal chose as his place of prayer!" was the thought which ran through their minds.

This *mikdash me'at*, sanctuary-in-miniature, was unique and splendid. The pilgrims entered it with feelings of joy mingled with awe and trembling. Despite the earthquake, the large, magnificent marble *bimah* still stood, even though it was piled high, with the rubble which had fallen upon it when the roof had collapsed. What most aroused their emotions was a small domed alcove carved out of the eastern wall of the synagogue. "This is where the Ari Hakadosh sat!" they whispered to one another in awe. "This is where Eliyahu Hanavi appeared to him; here he sat and learned!" They peered into the dark recess and noticed a stone pedestal which had been plastered over not long ago. On it burned a *ner tamid*, an eternal light.

Nearby, the pilgrims found *Chacham* R' Binyamin, the *gabbai* of the *beis knesses* and the treasurer of its charity fund, who told them the following amazing tale:

I was ill not too long ago, for my sins, and was bedridden for twelve weeks. I recovered, thanks to the Ari Hakadosh, who appeared to me in a dream.

I dreamt that I came here to the Ari's *beis knesses* to see if the *ner tamid* was burning properly and found the Arizal sitting in his place. I approached him. He was wrapped in his *tallis* and he appeared to be about thirty-three or thirty-four years old; his beard was thick and black and he was very handsome.

"Who are you, honored sir?" I asked him.

"I am the rabbi, R' Yitzchak Luria," he replied.

I then wept and told him how ill I was.

He reproached me: "Why don't you make repairs in the *beis knesses*? Why must the roof and walls leak each time it rains?"

I explained that we were short of funds, but the Arizal insisted that I make the repairs nonetheless.

"But I am ill, honored master."

He continued, "Youngsters come and play in this *beis knesses*. They are unruly and disrespectful. I, therefore, want you to make sure that no one disturbs this niche which I occupied while I was alive."

I said a third time, "But, my master, I am ill."

"Give me your hand," he said to me.

I gave him my hand — I opened my eyes. I looked around me and there I was, in my bed. I asked those who were at my bedside to bring me food, for I suddenly had an appetite and felt much better.

I left my sickbed and had a large pedestal erected and plastered over on the Arizal's place, so that no one would ever be able to stand or sit there. And thus it has remained to this day. I also repaired the roof and walls so that the rain would not leak in.

That *beis knesses*, facing Mount Meron where the *tana* R' Shimon bar Yochai, author of the *Zohar*, is buried, was chosen by the Ari Hakadosh as his place of study and prayer. That is where he learned the secrets of the Torah directly from Eliyahu Hanavi, who always appeared to him to teach him the hidden wonders of *Kabbalah*. There the *Kabbalah* rose and shone forth with renewed glory through the teachings of the Ari, the lion of his peers, the godly and saintly man, who laid the foundations for spreading the teachings of the *Zohar* far and wide.

For many generations the *Zohar* had been the possession of the very few. Then R' Yitzchak Luria, the Ari Hakadosh, appeared and labored to instill the teachings of *Kabbalah* and its practices among the many. His disciples learned from him, and his teachings spread to the people of Tsefas. And from Tsefas the customs rooted in the secrets of the *Zohar* spread further outward and made their way into the communities of the East and the congregations of Western and Eastern Europe.

There was good reason why this holy city, capital of the Galilee, was called "Cradle of the *Mekubalim*". At the time that the Ari Hakadosh lived in Tsefas, it was the home of giants of the Torah, men of unsurpassed knowledge in both the revealed and the mystic Torah, like R' Moshe Cordovero, R' Shlomo Alkabetz, R' Moshe Alshich, R' Yosef Karo, R' Elazar Azkari (author of "*Charedim*") and many such others. To be part of such an elite society — and to be distinguished within it — demanded special stature. And R' Yitzchak Luria possessed that stature. Compared to the other great figures of Tsefas, he was relatively young, yet he stood head and shoulders above them. As soon as they came to know his true measure, they bowed before him and acknowledged him as their teacher and supreme authority in everything that concerned *Kabbalah*. And he has retained that position unchallenged, to this very day.

CHAPTER ONE

WAITING FOR ELIYAHU HANAVI

In the year 5294 (1584), the entire Ashkenazi community in Jerusalem, which numbered some fifteen families, gathered in the small *beis knesses*, dressed in their *Shabbos* best, to celebrate the *bris* of the son of R' Shlomo Luria Ashkenazi.

Everything was ready. The *sandak's* chair stood in place; the *mohel* had arrived and made all his preparations. He glanced towards the *baal hasimchah*, the father, waiting for the signal to commence.

But R' Shlomo appeared to be in a different world. He stood in a corner of the *beis midrash*, a pious, devout figure wrapped in his *tallis*, swaying with fervor, his lips unceasingly murmuring a prayer with deep concentration. From time to time he would cast a look towards his guests and then shut his eyes tightly again to continue his ardent prayer.

"Why doesn't the *mohel* begin?" one man whispered to his neighbor.

"Can't you see that the baby's father is still praying?"

"But the *mohel* is getting impatient. See? He is trying to catch R' Shlomo's attention."

"Ah, now one of the guests has approached and whispered into his ear. He is probably asking why there is a delay. Let's draw near and try to catch their conversation."

"Can you make out what the *baal hasimchah* is saying, friend?"

"He says that a relative who lives far away has not yet arrived."

"That's a strange excuse, isn't it? The father seems confused. I think he is trying to hide something. There is something very odd about all this."

The guests began dispersing. They could not wait indefinitely. Soon, the *beis knesses* which had been packed, emptied and only a few people remained for the ceremony.

Suddenly, someone was heard weeping. All turned their heads towards the sound. It was none other than R' Shlomo. He looked as if his heart was broken. People were about to draw near and comfort him when he raised his eyes, looked around and began beaming. He signaled to the *mohel* to start. People looked around to see if the relative for whom they had been waiting had already arrived, but they did not see any newcomer.

The infant was brought in. The *mohel* recited the blessing aloud and the father intoned his blessing. Then the *bris* was performed with lightning speed. The *mohel* continued with the ritual words, "...preserve this son to his father and his mother, and let his name be called..." He paused, bent an ear to the father's lips and straightened up again to continue, "...Yitzchak ben R' Shlomo." He continued until the end and then wished the

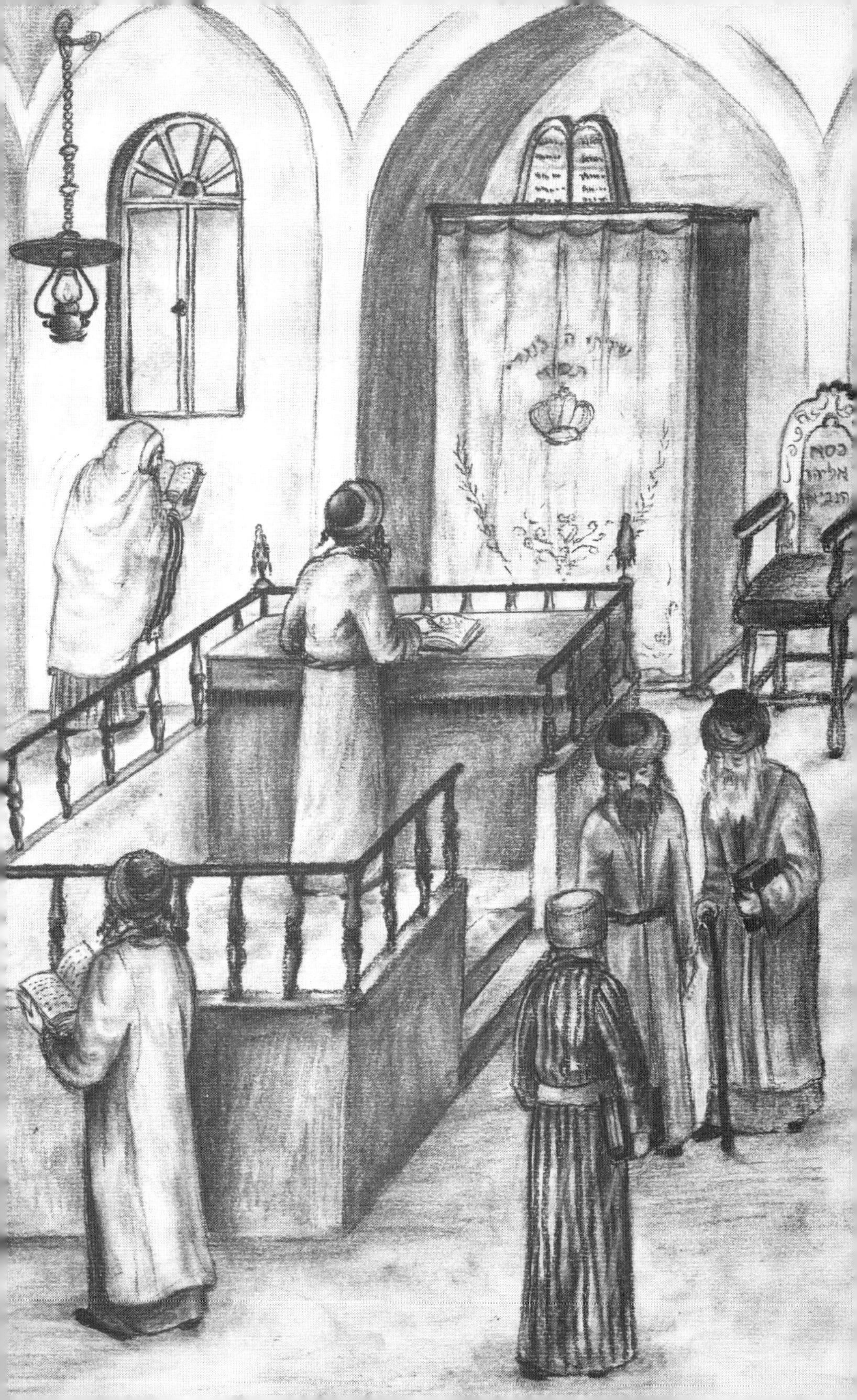
כסא
אליהו
הנביא

father a hearty *mazel tov* and a prayer that he live to raise his son to "Torah, *chupah* and good deeds."

Later, at the *seudas mitzvah*, one of the guests asked his neighbor if he knew why the father had chosen that particular name.

"No," he replied. "I was also wondering about that. I don't think that name is in the family. The mother's father was not called that. But, I'm sure that the merit of his righteous forefathers will stand the infant in good stead and enable him to grow up to be a stalwart tree."

After all the guests had dispersed, the *mohel* went to examine the infant and change the bandages. He removed them and exclaimed in surprise, "I have never seen anything like this! I have circumcised many children in my time and all of them have taken several days to heal. But this little Yitzchak is unusual; he is already completely well. He must have been visited by angels."

The *mohel* could not have known that he had guessed correctly.

A short while before the child's birth, Eliyahu Hanavi had appeared to R' Shlomo and said, "Know that I have been sent to inform you that your wife is about to give birth to a son. You are to name him Yitzchak. He will grow up to reveal the secrets of the Torah and its inner wisdom; through him help will come for his people Israel. But take care that on the day of his *bris* you do not begin the ceremony until you see me among the guests."

R' Shlomo had waited eagerly for the birth of his son. He had been especially careful not to sin and he had increased his hours of learning, fearing lest he prove unworthy of Eliyahu's visit at the *bris*.

When the child had been born the house was filled with light. R' Shlomo's joy knew no bounds. When the child had been eight days old, R' Shlomo had prayed that Eliyahu, the *malach habris*, the angel of the covenant, would, indeed, attend.

But when the clock had ticked away and people had begun leaving, R' Shlomo began to fear that Eliyahu would not come after all. Sad thoughts filled his heart, chasing away his happiness. R' Shlomo had thought to himself, "Perhaps this is not the son I was told about. Perhaps I was trapped by my *yetzer hara* to sin, and was denied the great privilege which should have been my lot. I am probably not worthy enough of becoming the father of a great *tzaddik*, nor am I worthy of beholding Eliyahu at my *simchah*."

At this point, he had begun weeping. He then raised his eyes and saw Eliyahu, who had approached him and said, "You may now begin. I stayed away in order to test you, to see whether you would wait for me or not. Proceed now. You be the *sandak*. I will sit with you and hold the child in my lap but no one will see me."

Eliyahu himself, the *malach habris*, had been the infant's *sandak*. Small wonder, then, that the wound had healed so miraculously![1]

This child whose name had been suggested by Eliyahu Hanavi was R' Yitzchak Luria Ashkenazi who was later to become known as the Ari Hakadosh. ARI — standing for Ashkenazi Rabbi Yitzchak, or *Eloki* (the saintly) R' Yitzchak.

Blessed, She Who Bore Him

Night. Yitzchak lay in his cradle, wailing. "Sh... sh... sh...," his mother whispered to him, rocking him gently to and fro. "Sleep, my son, sleep, my darling." She stroked him gently, trying to calm him. But his wailing did not stop. R' Shlomo, the baby's father, sat by the dim candlelight, exerting his eyes and his mind in trying to fathom a difficult topic. The singsong of his study echoed through the house. This was his lullaby, the chanting which worked wonders in calming his restless infant spirit. Slowly, the wailing subsided, he relaxed and soon fell into a serene sleep. From time to time, a beatific smile would spread over his tiny features. Each night little Yitzchak would fall asleep to the pleasant sound of his father's Torah study. Each morning he would awake from his sweet sleep to the sound of the holy words which his father murmured. They kindled in him a yearning to study and know the entire Torah and to understand all of its secrets.

The infant grew into a child. He was discovered to be blessed with marvelous talents. He absorbed everything that he was taught, mastering the *alef-beis* at a very early age. By three, he was already praying from a *siddur*. When he began studying *chumash*, long before his peers, his teacher discovered that little Yitzchak needed only the barest of explanations in order to grasp a topic. His memory was phenomenal, but even more remarkable were his diligence and perseverance.

It was not long before the boy was ready for *mishnah* and *gemara*. His swift comprehension enabled him to plumb the depths of the most difficult *sugyos* and to debate with much older scholars. The pathways of the Talmud were clear and open to him and his soul thirsted to delve as deeply as possible to get to the very essence of the secrets hidden within the Torah. He aspired to achieve great heights of purity and sanctity.

His father saw that Eliyahu Hanavi's blessing had indeed borne fruit and that his promise — that his son would one day reveal and spread wide the secrets of the Torah — was beginning to take on form. He, therefore, brought him to his own master, R' Klonimus, so that he might benefit from that great man's guidance.

Thus, the Ari, at a very tender age, became the pupil of R' Klonimus, just like his own father.[2]

---

1. Introduction to "Emek Hamelech" (Maase Nisim), Chapter II; Amsterdam 5408; "Shivchei HaArizal" and "Imrei Tzaddikim"
2. "Midbar Kedemos" by the Chida, Maareches 10:15

CHAPTER TWO
A STURDY BRANCH

The Luria family was a unique one which produced many men of great stature over many generations. The first one to adopt the surname Luria was a R' Shimshon who served as the royal physician to the king of France. To show his appreciation for R' Shimshon's having found a cure for his malady, the king awarded him a house on the banks of the Loire River which flows through the province of Orleans; the Jewish doctor adopted the name of the river as his own.

His grandson, who was also called R' Shimshon Luria, served as *av beis din* in the city of Erfurt, and was the head of its *yeshivah* where many noted scholars learned. Even after the death of R' Shimon, these scholars decided not to disband but to continue the *yeshivah* under the leadership of his widow. *Rabbanis* Miriam was one of the most educated and intelligent women in the annals of Jewish history. She is reputed to have been as fluent in the Torah and Talmud as any great rabbi. The scholars stretched a curtain across the *beis midrash* behind which the modest woman sat, hidden from all eyes, expounding profound lectures in *gemara* and *halachah*.

Rabbanis Miriam herself was a member of an illustrious family. Her father was R' Shlomo Shapira, the *av beis din* of Heilbrun. He, in turn, was the grandson of R' Matisyahu Trives, who served as *av beis din* of Paris and was the chief rabbi of all French Jewry. R' Matisyahu traced his lineage back to Rabbenu Yehudah bar Nasan, the Rivan, a son-in-law of Rashi.[1]

The succeeding generations also conferred great honor upon the name 'Luria'. R' Yechiel Luria was the *av beis din* of Brisk; his famous great-grandson was the Maharshal — R' Shlomo Luria, (not to be confused with the Ari's father, who was also called R' Shlomo Luria), who became famous for his important works: *"Chochmas Shlomo"* on the Talmud and *"Yam Shel Shlomo"*. Another distinguished descendant of R' Yechiel Luria was R' Yosef, better known as R' Yoselman of Rosheim, the famous *shtadlan* (mediator) who spoke to government officials on behalf of all German Jewry. R' Yoselman defended his brethren and spared them from many harsh decrees and much suffering.

R' Shlomo, the Arizal's father, was most probably a descendant of R' Yechiel Luria of Brisk, Lithuania,[2] for that is where he grew up. But there are no exact records of his lineage.

"Ashkenazi"

When Jerusalem was captured by Suleiman the Magnificent in 5277 (1517), the Jewish community in Jerusalem numbered six hundred people. Only a few of them were able to boast that their families had lived there for several generations. Most of them were recent immigrants from Spain and Italy; a few had come from Germany. The entire community was supported by charity. R' Yitzchak Sholal, the generous and concerned philanthropist, sent monies from Egypt and funds came from the Jewish communities in Turkey.

This was the *yishuv* which R' Klonimus and his disciples found when they came to the Holy City. The residents of German origin were overjoyed by his arrival and forthwith crowned him as their rabbi.

What brought R' Klonimus from Brisk in Lithuania to Jerusalem? He was noted throughout his land for his knowledge in both the revealed and the hidden Torah and he served as the *av beis din* of Brisk. Before that, he had occupied a similar position in the distinguished congregation of Ostrow and had had many students who were drawn to him from all over the land. However, when his daughter married the Maharshal, he stepped down in favor of his son-in-law and moved to Brisk. Here, too, he attracted many students, among them, R' Shlomo Luria, father of the Arizal.

In 5289 (1529), the Jews of Lithuania fell upon hard times. New tax laws had gone into effect. Although the Jews were a small minority in the country, the taxes collected from them made up one quarter of the entire government budget.

While they were still struggling and sighing over the burden of taxes, they were beset by an additional woe. At that time, it was strictly forbidden for gentiles to convert. Still, some saw the light and the truth in the Torah and became Jews. They converted in secrecy and left the country.

The authorities suspected that the Jews of Lithuania were providing these converts with sanctuary and support. Sigmund, the Duke of Lithuania, was not one to allow such a thing to happen in his domain. He ordered the members of the aristocracy to investigate the matter.

Those corrupt people needed no more. They began to persecute the Jews and torment them. Many Jews were traveling peddlers. While plying their routes they would often be stopped by the local landlords and accused of hiding and supporting converts from Christianity. The blameless peddlers would protest their innocence, but in vain. They were forced to buy their freedom with large bribes. The titled nobility sent their servants to break into Jewish homes and search them. Even if they found no concealed converts, they would extort money from the residents.

The Jews feared to travel the roads. They shut themselves up in their homes, neglected their businesses and became poorer and poorer. And even in their homes they were subjected to threats and blackmail.

Life became unbearable and many Jews wished to leave.

There was good news from the Holy Land. Jerusalem was now in the hands of the benevolent ruler of the Ottoman empire. He allowed the Jewish community to develop and flourish.

It was in those troubled days that the elderly R' Klonimus decided to leave Lithuania. Despite his advanced age, he decided to give up his honored position and go up to Jerusalem. "Nothing stimulates the mind like the air of *Eretz Yisrael*," he thought. "There is no Torah study like the Torah study of *Eretz Yisrael*; there is no sanctity like the sanctity of Jerusalem. I want to live there, near the Western Wall, the relic of our *Mikdash*. There, where the

Shechinah has remained — I will be able to pour out my heart in prayer before my Creator with greater fervor and devotion."

When his *talmidim*, who loved him dearly, heard of his plan, they decided to join him. R' Shlomo Luria was among them. He bid his family a tearful good-bye, knowing that this was the last time he would see them. Although the journey to *Eretz Yisrael* was long, arduous and dangerous, he was not to be put off. He was determined to follow his master wherever he went, especially to the beloved land of the *Avos*.

When they arrived, they found a small, impoverished community. But each member was a devout and pious scholar. Despite their great poverty, they seemed to be content and happy with their lot.

There were so few Ashkenazim in Jerusalem at the time that the description "Ashkenazi" was added to the name of each new immigrant. R' Shlomo Luria became R' Shlomo Luria Ashkenazi.

---

1. "Avos Atara Levanim", Jerusalem 5687, p. 81 ff.
2. "Toldos Chachmei Yerushalayim" by Froumkin, Vol. I, p. 99 footnote

CHAPTER THREE
CHILDHOOD

Yitzchak was a precious son to his father, a delightful child who spent most of his time sitting in the *beis midrash* studying. His only interest in life was Torah. When R' Klonimus gave his profound lectures before the scholars of Jerusalem, the young son of R' Shlomo Ashkenazi would also sit and listen. R' Shlomo would sit by, beaming with *nachas* from his treasure.

But this paradise of the mind was all too brief. A terrible tragedy overtook little Yitzchak; his father, to whom he was so deeply attached, passed away in his prime.[1] In one fell blow, the child lost his dear father, his guide and his teacher. The entire congregation attended the painful funeral. The sages and scholars of Jerusalem came to pay their last respects to the *tzaddik* who had left them. And the elderly R' Klonimus walked behind the bier of his beloved *talmid*, weeping bitterly at his loss.

The young widow would now have to shoulder the burden of supporting her tender orphans and seeing to their education; she must now be more than a mother.

R' Klonimus and his disciples understood the extent of the misfortune. They tried to comfort the widow and spoke to her about the treasure which she possessed. "Wait and see!" they promised her. "This little one will become great! He will bring a new light to the world."

The elderly rabbi began to pay more attention to the orphaned prodigy, to supervise his progress and to encourage him. But all the good words and wishes were not enough to fill the stomachs of the hungry widow and orphans. Her brother, R' Mordechai Francis, who lived in Egypt, undertook the burden of supporting them. He was a wealthy man and lavish with his charity; he agreed to maintain his widowed sister and her tender orphans honorably.

After his father's death, Yitzchak plunged more and more deeply into his studies. The Torah was balm for his broken heart; in it he found comfort and encouragement, counsel and wisdom. He labored with all his might until his body would perspire from his great exertion. Many years later, when he was already teaching others, he would explain, in the light of *Kabbalah*, the reason for his supreme efforts:

"The study of *halachah* breaks off the extraneous shells of *tumah*. One must weaken, crush and slay the power of evil."

With the Torah as his comfort in pain, the young Ari devoted himself to learning and *avodah*. The greater his progress, the greater grew his desire and aspiration. While yet very young, he mastered *shas* and drank deeply from the *poskim*. He became an exceptional scholar and word went out into the world.

A Miracle in Jerusalem

At that time the Jews of Jerusalem enjoyed the benign rule of the Sultan Suleiman the Magnificent. But their enemies, both Arab and Christian, begrudged them their relative freedom and constantly sought to discredit them in the eyes of the local authorities. But the Guardian of Israel neither sleeps nor slumbers; *Hakadosh baruch Hu* always has His eye fixed on Jerusalem. He watched over the Jewish community and protected it from every calamity.

Once a group of Arab residents came to the governor of the city, bowed obsequiously, and said: "Your Excellency, may you rule forever! The Jews do not keep the laws of our sultan. They flout his orders publicly!" And they produced a list of Jewish anti-government acts which was completely fabricated by their fertile minds.

The governor investigated the ways of the Jewish community but found nothing amiss. When the governor saw that the Arabs had tried to dupe him into believing their false tales about fine, upright subjects, he became incensed. He ordered all of the Arabs in the city punished severely so that they might learn a lesson.

But his actions only increased the Arabs' hatred. Now they sought to harm, not only the Jews but the governor himself. They met secretly and plotted to strike at both.

"We will keep an eye on the governor's son," they decided. "When he is alone, we will kidnap him, take him to a deserted spot and kill him. Then we will throw his body into a synagogue. Thus both the governor and the Jews will suffer. For he will surely retaliate against them. We will repay our enemies twofold."

They watched the child and when they saw him all

alone, far from witnesses, they fell upon him, dragged him away to a lonely spot, murdered him and gathered his blood into a jar.

Late that night, while Jerusalem slept the murderers slipped through the streets bearing a large burden. They entered the synagogue, uncovered their load and threw the dead body on the floor. They poured the blood all around and, then, slipped out as silently as they had come.

Earlier that day, as the sun was setting behind the Judean hills, the child's mother turned to her husband and asked anxiously, "Where can the boy be? Why is he dallying? He should have been home long ago. I wonder if anything has happened to him?"

The governor was also worried. He sent out his other sons to inquire at the neighbors' homes. But all returned with the same report: The boy had not visited at all that day. No one had seen him. The parents now became truly concerned.

The governor summoned all of his servants and ordered them to make a thorough search for the lad. They spread out and combed the city. Several hours later they returned. Their search had been fruitless.

Early the next morning a town crier went through the streets of the city, proclaiming:

"Whosoever finds the son of the governor and brings him home alive or dead, will be rewarded with a medal and a prize."

Now everybody joined the search. They went from house to house but were unsuccessful.

That day was a *Shabbos*. The Jews of Jerusalem left their homes, wrapped up in their *talleisim*, to pour out their hearts in prayer and praise to the Creator Who

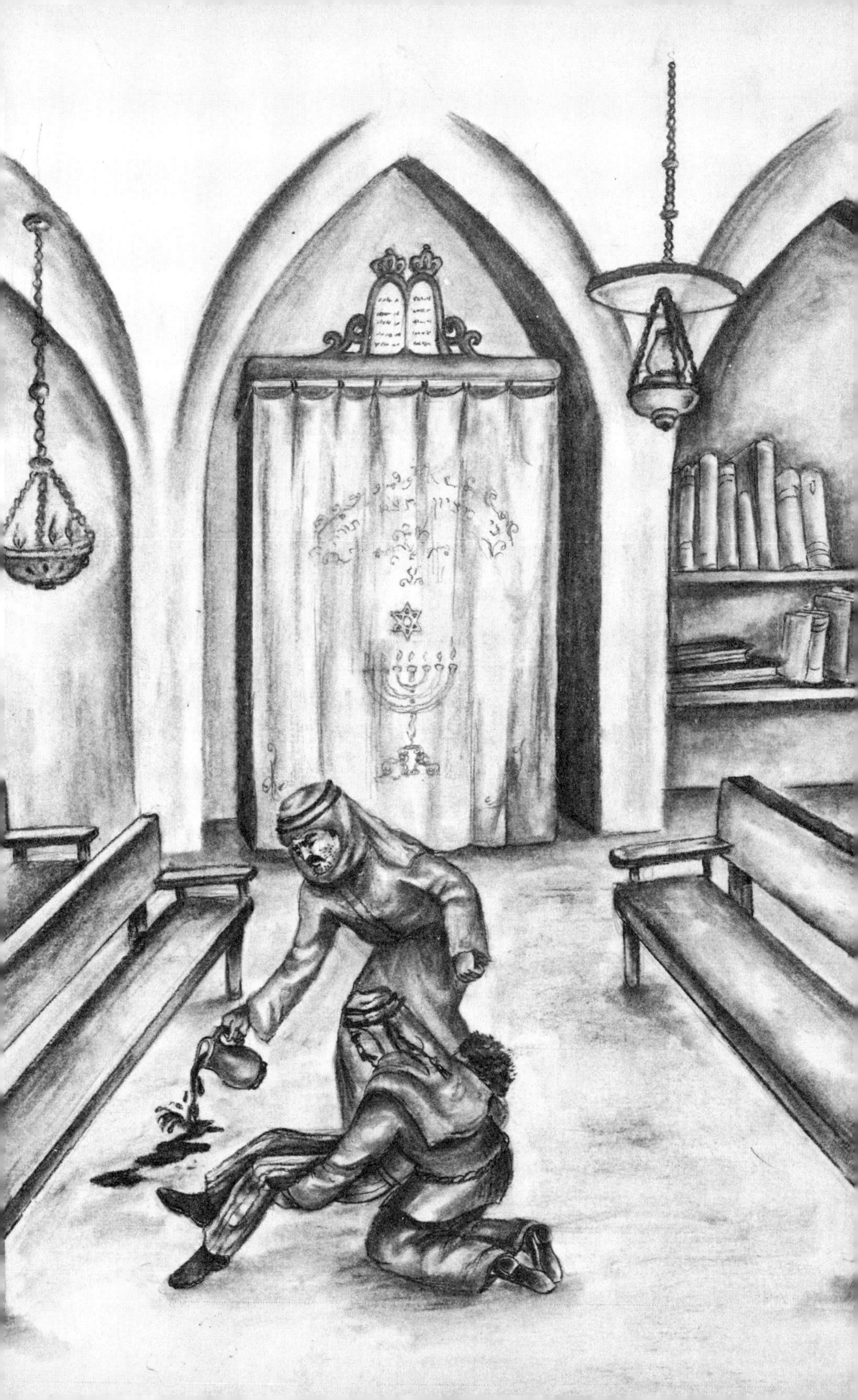

blessed His people with the gift of rest on the seventh day. To their amazement, the door of the synagogue was locked. They looked at one another in surprise, wondering, "The synagoge door locked? Where was the trusted *shammash*, then? Could it be that he had not yet risen that morning?"

They did not know that their loyal *shammash* had already opened the door of the *beis knesses* very early that morning.

When he had discovered the body of the governor's son, his heart had skipped a beat. But he had kept his wits and quickly sped to R' Klonimus's house. There, his heart still pounding with terror, he had told the elderly rabbi exactly what he had seen.

When R' Klonimus heard his story, he cried out, "Alas! What have our enemies done to us! We are all in danger. Go and gather all of the Jews, young and old, to the *beis knesses*. Pray, say *vidui*, repent. Cry out to *Hashem*, perhaps He will have pity on us. Quick! Run! I will remain here and do what I must do."

The first group of worshippers were still standing by the doors of the synagogue, wondering about the locked door, when they saw the *shammash* rushing towards them, weeping hysterically, "Go home and bring your families. Bring everyone here. We are in a terrible plight for the dead body of the governor's son is lying inside on the floor in a pool of blood!"

Stunned and distraught, the people turned around and went back home, to do as they had been told.

Meanwhile, the rest of the city was out looking for the child. The murderers also joined the search. They knew exactly where to go and they headed directly for the synagogue. And lo! They 'discovered' the missing boy.

Pretending to be surprised and shocked, they hurried to the governor to report their discovery. "Your Excellency!" they said. "We found your son's body lying in a pool of blood in the synagogue."

The governor had his carriage harnessed at once and drove to the synagogue at top speed.

The Arab informers rode in the carriage to show the governor exactly where they had found the body. All along the way they filled his ears with abuse against the Jews.

"Now Your Excellency sees that we were justified in censuring the Jews. They are a rebellious, deceitful lot who only have their own interests at heart. You refused to believe us then but now you see how treacherous they really are, how ungrateful and despicable. Instead of appreciating your free hand and benevolence, they turn around and do this terrible thing to you!"

They inflamed his already burning anger against the Jews.

The governor beheld his beloved son lying on the stone floor, his body bruised and bloody. He could no longer contain his hurt and anger and bellowed, "You heartless Jews! I will show you my power! You will yet regret this wanton, brutal murder! I will strike back at you with all my strength. I will avenge the blood of my son." He turned to his guards and said, "Seize the rabbis and trustees. I will liquidate them first."

The members of the congregation were terrified. They could only pray; only their Heavenly Father could help them.

After the *shammash* had left the rabbi's house, R' Klonimus purified himself, immersed himself in a *mikveh* and then secluded himself in a room. There, he began pouring out his broken heart before Hashem. "Hashem!" he wept. "G-d of my fathers, help me to save Your people who are innocent. Strengthen and support me. Put the right words into my mouth when I stand in supplication before the governor and let the merit of the many stand by me."

Although it was *Shabbos*, R' Klonimus dipped his pen into the inkwell and upon a small piece of parchment wrote the holy Name and combinations of letters. Lives were at stake. The entire Jewish community was in danger. The *Shabbos* must be desecrated to save them. R' Klonimus did not hesitate.

Just as he had finished, there was a knock at the door and a loud cry, "Open up, in the name of the governor!" The door was opened and soldiers stood in the entrance. "Where is R' Klonimus?" said one of them. "He is under arrest by order of His Excellency!"

R' Klonimus' wife sank down in a chair. Her eyes did not leave the soldiers. Her husband, R' Klonimus, approached them calmly and said, "Yes. Here I am, ready to come with you. I will be glad to help you discover the murderers."

The guards were somewhat surprised. They were taken aback by R' Klonimus' serenity and poise. With respect, they led the elderly man to the governor's mansion and informed the governor. Although his heart was filled with misery and anger, nevertheless the governor listened with interest when his men told him how R' Klonimus had acted upon being arrested. "Bring him in!" he ordered.

The rabbi entered the chamber and bowed low.

"Your Excellency," he began. "I sympathize with you because of your suffering and pain over the murder of your dear son. I have also heard what you intend to do to us Jews.

"I want to make one thing absolutely clear, Your Excellency. The hands of your Jewish subjects are clean of the blood which was spilled. We regard you very highly and are grateful to you for your kindness towards us. Believe me, all of us sympathize with you in your sorrow from the depths of our hearts.

"I have asked to appear before you because I have something to tell you. I can reveal to you the real murderers of your son, if you only give me the chance. Come with me to the spot where your son is still lying. There, I will point out to you who the true culprits are."

The rabbi's words intrigued the governor. Turning to his soldiers, he ordered them to take him and the rabbi back to the scene of the crime.

The child's body still lay in the synagogue. A small group of soldiers stood guard over it. A large crowd had gathered.

The party arrived — the governor, his retinue and R' Klonimus. The *tzaddik* took out the small parchment which he had prepared and placed it on the forehead of the dead child. Then he spoke in a commanding tone, "Stand up and tell us all exactly how and where you were murdered. Tell us, also, who your murderers were!"

Everyone held their breath, spellbound — all eyes on R' Klonimus and the corpse lying on the ground in a pool of blood.

Slowly, the dead child got to his feet and began to speak. He told how he had been kidnapped and taken to a desolate spot where he had been tortured to death. He testified to his captors' devilish plan to lay the blame of his murder upon the Jewish community and take revenge

CHILDHOOD / 31

on the governor and the Jews with one blow.

When he had finished his story, silence reigned. No one dared move. The son turned to his father and said: "If You don't believe me, father, send one of your soldiers to the barren stretch just east of the Shechem road; that is where I was murdered. There, on one of the large flat stones he will still see bloodstains. That is my blood which spurted from the many wounds which they so cruelly inflicted upon me. Tell your soldier to bring that stone here and you will see whether I told the truth or not."

A soldier was quickly dispatched. He returned a short while later with a large, blood-stained stone. As soon as the stone was set at the governor's feet, the boy fell to the floor, lifeless.

The bereaved father's wrath was dreadful to behold. His face was contorted; his eyes blazed. His voice was hoarse with fury. He ordered: "Seize the villains, murderers of my son, rebels and fiends, and prepare the gallows for them in the central city square!"

The true murderers paid for their crime with their lives. They fulfilled the verse, "He dug a pit and hollowed it, and fell into the ditch which he made." The Jews of Jerusalem breathed with relief. Their *Shabbos* prayer, which had been so cruelly interrupted, was completed with psalms of praise and thanksgiving for the wondrous miracle of their rescue which *Hashem* had sent them through their revered rabbi.

A short while after this incident, in 5308 (1540), R' Klonimus Haberkstein passed away. Before he was buried, his will was opened. It read as follows:

"Since I was forced to desecrate the *Shabbos* and write on that holy day, when the recent disaster threatened the

Jews of Jerusalem, I deserve the punishment of stoning, (*skilah*), for such is the law for anyone who violates the *Shabbos* in public. I, therefore, request of the residents of Jerusalem that whenever they pass by my tombstone — they throw a stone at it. This is to be done for one hundred years after the day of my burial."[3]

All work was called to a halt on the day of R' Klonimus' funeral. All storekeepers left their stores, shoemakers — their workbench; every Jew in the city capable of walking on his own two feet went to accompany the eminent deceased to his eternal rest. The most prominent of Jerusalem's scholars, walked next to the bier. Sounds of weeping and mourning arose from all sides, mingling with the words of eulogy uttered by various communal leaders and scholars.

The Jews of Jerusalem carried out R' Klonimus' will as it was written. His tombstone, on the sides of the Mount of Olives cemetery, became known to all as the "mound of R' Klonimus" because of the many stones which were heaped up on it.

Whenever a local Jew had to leave the country for any mission, he would take along a stone from the pile on R' Klonimus' grave. It was reputed to be a *segulah* (charm) which ensured a safe return home.

This heap of stones was a distinctive landmark for many years, a reminder to all its beholders of the great miracle which had occurred in the time of Sultan Suleiman.

Overnight, the people of Jerusalem, especially the Ashkenazim, were without a leader and father. They felt orphaned.

But one family in particular was stricken by the passing of the elderly rabbi — the Luria family. The rabbi had stood at their side. The widow and her orphans had drawn comfort and spiritual sustenance from him in heaping measure. He had been a second father to them, an understanding soul who had advised them and listened to their troubles and worries. He had done all in his power to soften the pain of their losing R' Shlomo.

With his passing, the family was left doubly orphaned. Once again the young Ari had lost a master and teacher, and his widowed mother felt as if her life had become almost too difficult to bear.

When R' Mordechai Francis, her brother in Egypt, learned of the widow's suffering and her difficult life, he sent for his sister and her children. When they arrived, he gathered them lovingly into his home and heart. He welcomed them, fed them and clothed them and provided their every want. He saw to the education of his nephews; he hired tutors to teach them Torah so that they might continue along the proper path and do credit to their saintly father.

The immigration of the Luria family to Egypt and into the hearts of the Francis family, proved to be a turningpoint in its history. It effected a tremendous change in everyone's lives. For the first time since R' Shlomo's death, they found both material support and a warm family atmosphere to comfort and uplift them. The gateway to a brilliant future now lay before Yitzchak, the child prodigy.[4]

1. "Shivchei HaAri"; "Maase Nisim" and "Shem Hagedolim" on the Arizal
2. "Yosef Ometz" Chapter "Dinei Hanhagas Ha'adam Besha'as Limudo" by R' Yosef Haan
3. "Ose Phele (Jerusalem 5719), p. 204; "Shalmei Chagiga" (506) by R' Yisrael Yaakov Algazi, p. 24 and many others
4. "Shem Hagedolim" on him; "Shivchei HaArizal"

CHAPTER FOUR
IN EGYPT

The Jewish community in Egypt was an ancient one. It had seen many changes of government over the generations. In the half century before the Luria family arrived, there had been bloody battles between the Mamelukes, rulers of this country for the previous two hundred and fifty years, and the Ottoman Turks, who threatened them from the north. After bitter fighting, conquest and rebellion, the Turks succeeded in imposing their rule over the land of the Nile.

In all this turmoil, the Jews were between the hammer and the anvil, forever the scapegoat of the losing side. But, thanks to Heavenly mercy, they were always saved from the pogroms and decrees which fell upon them. They tried to maintain an organized *kehillah* life. Even during the most difficult years, the Jewish community continued to develop and flourish. They were joined by many exiles from Spain who found sanctuary in Egypt, among whom were *gedolim* respected by Jewish communities the world over. They established *yeshivos* which drew brilliant scholars from the four corners of the earth, even from Germany and Italy.

The Uncle's Household

R' Mordechai Francis was one of these immigrants. He was a fabulously weathly man and he leased the franchise to collect custom duties. He possessed a splendid mansion, exquisitely furnished with precious works of art, and a staff of servants. But R' Mordechai was not only esteemed because of his wealth. He was also free with his charity and a *talmid chacham* of standing. His home was a meeting place for scholars and a center for all communal affairs.

Into this home, in which Torah and wealth were joined, came R' Shlomo Luria's widow and orphans. Here, R' Mordechai's nephew, the Ari, grew up.

He was still very young but even then, he was a vessel replete and overflowing. Many times, distinguished scholars who sat in the luxurious reception room, would speak to him in learning. In the give and take of discussion, he impressed them, again and again, with the wealth of his knowledge and with his profundity. They were astounded by his genius and his burning love for Torah. But most of all, they were awed by his character — his modesty, piety and fear of sin — which surpassed and overshadowed his wisdom.

R' Mordechai Francis' guests did not spare their praise for the child prodigy. The master of the house could also see for himself that he had a rare treasure in his home. The praises of his scholarly friends encouraged him to consult his own teacher, R' David ben Zimra (the Radbaz) and beg him to accept his nephew into his *yeshivah*. Not everyone was admitted to this elite circle of students — only exceptional scholars who had spent many years in study were among the privileged few allowed to listen to the *shiurim* of this prince of Torah, the Radbaz.

The Radbaz

R' David Ben Zimra was well along in years at the time that the Ari came to join his select *yeshivah*. Hundreds, perhaps even thousands of noted disciples had passed through his hands. He was world famous for his genius and his generosity.

R' David ben Zimra had been born in Spain, but had left his birthplace even before the Great Expulsion and moved to Fez, Morocco. From there he traveled on to the Land of the Nile where he chose R' Yosef Saragossi, a holy man reputed to perform miracles, as his teacher.[1] Under R' Yosef's guidance, he became a truly great man. After a few years, the Radbaz was offered the position of *dayan* in the court of the noted leader, R' Yitzchak Sholal. With the passing of time, he became the spiritual leader of all Egyptian Jewry and a *halachic* authority for the entire Diaspora. R' David established many beneficial *takkanos* (regulations). Some three thousand of his *halachic* responses were printed in his famous work, "Responses of the Radbaz". He also wrote a commentary on part of the Rambam's *"Yad Hachazakah"* and a commentary on *"Shir HaShirim"* based upon its Kabbalistic interpretation. He called this *"Michtam LeDavid."* He wrote *"Metzudas David"*, explaining the reasons for the *mitzvos* and essays and annotations on the Talmud and the *Zohar*.

Besides being blessed with the crown of Torah, which he earned through tireless effort, he was also endowed with great wealth. It is told that he acquired his fortune when he found a chest with thousands of gold pieces in his home. Much of this treasure was distributed to the scholars of *Eretz Yisrael* — in Jerusalem, Chevron and Tsefas, and part of it to the scholars in Egypt.[2] He invested the remainder in business and was very successful.

He did not use his profits for his personal needs, but to maintain his *yeshivah* which produced scholars of note and distinction, scholars whom he supported.

When he reached the age of eighty-five, the Radbaz cast aside all of his business interests. He wished to spend the remainder of his days in the luxury of Torah study in the palace of *Hashem* — the holy city of Jerusalem. He left Egypt and settled near the very site of the *mikdash*. The Jerusalem community at that time consisted almost entirely of great Torah scholars who had renounced the comforts of this world and whose only interest and goal was to study the holy Torah. When the Radbaz, to whom Eliyahu Hanavi revealed himself, joined this community, they rejoiced over him as if he were a new found treasure. They immediately sought to crown him as their leader and begged him to accept the position of chief rabbi of the city. R' David agreed on the condition that he serve without a salary and only be reimbursed for any losses which he incurred through the position. The Jerusalem community accepted this stipulation and R' David ben Zimra became its rabbi.

They did not enjoy the radiance of his glory for very long, however. Once, several people disobeyed certain rulings of the Jerusalem rabbis. As befit a rabbi of stature and authority, the Radbaz fearlessly ordered them to be punished. They retaliated and went to the authorities, saying that the Radbaz was very wealthy and did not pay taxes in accordance with his full income.

The governor reveled in this bit of information and did not even bother to verify it. He immediately imposed such a stiff fine upon the Radbaz that the latter was unable to pay. He had no choice but to leave his beloved city and move to Tsefas, where he lived out the remainder of his days.

The Radbaz, after a long life filled with Torah study, worthy deeds, riches and a good name, passed away in Tsefas in 5332 (1572), at the ripe age of 110, and was buried there in great honor.[3]

The Yeshivah of the Radbaz

R' Yitzchak Luria Ashkenazi, the child prodigy, joined the select *yeshivah* of the Radbaz. It did not take long for his true worth to be appreciated. Despite his youth, he was admitted into the elite circle of the elder scholars closest to the master.

At about this time, the Radbaz instituted new rulings in the *yeshivah*. The students were required to accept the regulations upon themselves and sign articles of agreement. The historic document contains signatures of giants of the Torah world, and among them, the signature of the then fourteen-year-old Ari.

This document is a very enlightening one, testifying to the high spiritual level of its signers. It states, in part:

> "We, the undersigned, have therefore agreed to accept upon ourselves the decree of our master and teacher to unite as one heart in the service of our Heavenly Father. Every common agreement which is drawn up shall only be approved after all of us have

thoroughly discussed it... and determined the majority opinion, which will also be binding on the minority. Each one in the minority shall embrace the majority opinion with all his might and uphold it firmly... We shall also undertake to treat one another with love and brotherhood, to uphold one another's honor... and if it seems to one of the undersigned that one of the others was disparaging towards him in speech or by act — he must inform him of this within twenty-four hours and rebuke him privately (not publicly). If the accused apologizes, his friend must accept his apology and forgive him. If the accuser sees that the accused did not apologize, he shall tell the others so that they can rebuke him to his face in such a manner that he will never repeat his deed, and he shall also forgive the one who embarrasses him..."

This agreement, written on the 19th of Kislev, 5308 (1548), bears the signatures of: Eliyahu Mizrachi; Yitzchak Modena; Meir Halevi; Bezalel Ashkenazi; Yitzchak Luria (the Ari); Yehuda Massoud; Shmuel Albeli; Meir Ben Chaim; Yitzchak Beirav (son of R' Yaakov Beirav); Yitzchak ben Avraham Beirav; Shmuel Taalta; Zerachya Avraham Halevi; Yaakov Amati and Yeshua Cohen.

Below the signatures of the *talmidim*, the *rav* added the following notation in his own hand:

"It is true that I have thus decreed, and I stand on it — David ben Zimra."[4]

The young lad studied with enthusiasm and application. When the eighty-year-old Radbaz saw his unusual energy, great talents, wealth of knowledge and his pure *yiras shamayim*, he intuitively knew that he was destined for greatness. He began showering him with special personal attention and instructed R' Bezalel Ashkenazi, one of his foremost disciples, to become his mentor. R' Bezalel accepted this responsibility without hesitation.

Marriage

R' Mordechai Francis reaped a full measure of *nachas* from his young nephew. The Ari's name spread and his praises were sung by everyone. Small wonder that many dreamed of marrying off their daughters to this jewel, but no one actually stepped forward to suggest a suitable match. For R' Mordechai had a virtuous daughter, modest, pleasing of character and pleasing in deeds. She was the daughter of a *talmid chacham* and a charitable, good man. It was hardly a secret that R' Mordechai desired R' Yitzchak as his son-in-law. Who, then, would dream of suggesting any other match for the Ari?

When the Ari neared marriageable age, fifteen (in those times), his uncle took him aside and asked him if he was willing to marry his daughter. The Ari did not hesitate for a moment. His cousin had all the virtues necessary for a wife to be a crown to her husband. He considered it a privilege and pleasure to accept.

The girl was asked. She also knew his worth. In her modesty, she nodded and said a simple "Yes." Her heart overflowed with pride and thanks to *Hashem* Who had sent her such a worthy *chasan* who embodied all the virtues.

Shortly afterwards, the wedding between R' Yitzchak and his cousin was celebrated in grand style. All the notables of the community were present; nobility and members of the royal court attended as well.

R' Mordechai's joy knew no bounds. He gladly assumed the support of the young couple while encouraging his son-in-law-nephew to continue his studies as before.

Together with the Author of Shitah Mekubetzes

In 5309 (1549), after his marriage, the Ari began studying together with R' Bezalel Ashkenazi, by the request of the Radbaz. R' Bezalel was already acknowledged as one of the great rabbis of Egypt and his spiritual impact upon its Jews was considerable. Who was this man whom the Radbaz had appointed to guide the promising young Ari?

R' Bezalel was born in *Eretz Yisrael* to R' Avraham in 5280 (1520). His distinguished family hailed from Germany, and when they settled in the East, they added the "Ashkenazi", to their name, as was customary.

This family boasted world-famous leaders. His uncle was called "the great rabbi of all Germany, *Moreinu haRav Yitzchak Bezalel*". R' Bezalel Ashkenazi's cousin married the father of the Taz (*Turei Zahav*) and one of the uncle's granddaughters married the Maharshal.

R' Bezalel spent most of his childhood in *Eretz Yisrael*. R' Yisrael Nag'ara, the saintly poet and Kabbalist, was his childhood friend. While R' Bezalel was still young, his family moved to Egypt. There, he studied under R' Yisrael de Koral together with his friend, R' Shimon Castillatz. The two continued studying together in the Radbaz's *yeshivah*. R' Shimon, R' Bezalel and the Ari were the only non-Sefardic students there. Later, they were to lead the small Ashkenazi *kehillah* in Egypt and answer all *halachic* queries.

R' Bezalel Ashkenazi wrote two famous works, the first: "R' Bezalel's Responsa", consisting of the questions referred to him as one of the leading authorities in Egypt and "*Shitah Mekubetzes*" which has become one of the basic texts for every Talmudic scholar. This work is a compilation of the opinions of the *Rishonim* in their study of *gemara* and is arranged according to the tractates in *shas*. R' Bezalel did not merely quote from the *Rishonim*; he also explained them thoroughly. He amended the texts where errors had crept in.

We possess the "*Shitah Mekubetzes*" on the tractates *Berachos, Beitzah, Nedarim, Sotah* and, the more famous ones, on *Kesubos, Bava Kamma, Bava Metzia* and *Bava Basra*. R' Bezalel also compiled similar works on *Shevuos, Chulin, Gittin, Seder Kodshim, Sotah* and *Nazir*, but these have not been published to date. They remain as yet in manuscript form.[5]

As a student, R' Bezalel showed remarkable diligence. His love for Torah was so great that he denied himself sleep and food, begrudging every minute away from study. This, then, was the Torah giant whom the Radbaz chose as the Ari's new mentor.

The young Ari followed in the ways of his new guide. They sat together, apart from worldly cares, abstaining from bodily needs while satisfying the spirit. The Torah was their life. The Ari was freed from financial cares, thanks to his rich uncle-father-in-law. R' Mordechai undertook to support R' Bezalel Ashkenazi and his family as well, so that he might continue to teach R' Yitzchak undisturbed.[6]

The Ari studied *shas* and *poskim* together with his mentor for seven years. He embraced his teacher's approach, succeeded in widening and deepening his knowledge in both the revealed and the mystic Torah and slowly, made his way into the *pardes* of *Kabbalah*.

The Ari was not the only one to benefit from this partnership; he was a student who stimulated his teacher and R' Bezalel gained from his student likewise. They worked together on the *"Shitah Mekubetzes"* on *Zevachim*, a work which was not published. The Chida, in his *"Shem Hagedolim"*, notes that he found R' Aharon Alfandari's copy, which he studied from. It indicates whether the author of each *chiddush*, was R' Bezalel or the Arizal. Unfortunately, this copy went up in smoke together with all of R' Aharon Alfandari's treasures in the great fire that struck Izmir, Turkey.

Aside from this work, they collaborated on emendations to the works of the Rif (R' Yitzchak Alfasi) and the commentaries of the Ran (Rabbenu Nissim).[7]

The Nagid-Turned Chilbi

During these seven good years, when they were learning together, the Radbaz left Egypt and went to settle in *Eretz Yisrael*. R' Bezalel, his most prominent disciple, took his place. But, despite his new responsibilities, R' Bezalel would have continued studying with R' Yitzchak had it not been for the hand of Providence which steered events in a different direction.

In 5316 (1556), the *nagid*, the wealthy R' Tagier passed away.

For centuries the Jews of Egypt had had a communal leader called a *nagid*, or as the Arabs called him, *"rais (rosh) al Yahud."* He was the representative of Jewish interests to the government. He was also responsible for communal affairs; he appointed rabbis and judges, collected taxes from the congregation and supervised expenditures of public funds.

The office of *nagid* in Egypt had existed from the times of the *Gaonim* (the Jewish leaders after the codification of the Talmud).

The *nagid* was elected by the Jews of the land but officially received his authority through a directive from the ruler.

The position was maintained even after Egypt was taken over by the Turks. But, now, the *nagid* was no longer chosen by his fellow Jews; he was appointed by the authorities in distant Constantinople, the capital of the Ottoman Empire, and sent to Egypt.

R' Tagier had carried out his duties well and he had respected the rabbis of Egypt. When he died, he was replaced by R' Yaakov Ben Chaim who was appointed and sent from Constantinople.

Upon the first *Shabbos* after his arrival, immediately after the *musaf* prayer, a delegation of *dayanim, rabbanim and parnasim* of the community, led by the chief rabbi, R' Bezalel Ashkenazi, made its way to the official quarters of the *nagid*. They wished to present themselves to him and inform him of the rules and regulations of the community.

Yaakov Ben Chaim, attired in his official clothing, disappointed the members of this distinguished delegation. He met them with marked disdain which was in total contrast to the attitude of former *negidim*. He wished to impose his authority and will upon the men who had come to pay their respects.

R' Bezalel took serious affront. He was unable to overlook the new *nagid*'s condescending attitude and rebuked him for belittling men of learning. The *nagid* took offense and insulted the rabbi. R' Bezalel, shocked by Yaakov's disrespect towards the Torah and its scholars, put the new *nagid* into *cherem* and left his presence in anger, with the rest of the delegation following in his footsteps.

Yaakov Ben Chaim felt that he had been degraded and decided to avenge his wounded pride upon the Jews of Egypt, and against R' Bezalel in particular. He went to the *pasha*, ruler, and described the event, vividly slanted in his own favor, and accused the rabbi of insulting the government and rejecting its authority. He went so far as to charge R' Bezalel with inciting the Jews of Egypt against the government. Since he, the *nagid*, was a government official, any insult to him was, in effect, an act of treason.

When R' Bezalel learned about the slander against him, he decided to take action. On that very Sunday he went to the *pasha*'s palace, a *Tanach* tucked under his arm.

R' Bezalel came before the *pasha* and said: "You surely know that from the day that our Temple was destroyed, our government was disbanded and we Jews were exiled among the nations of the world. We were warned not to seize power for ourselves: no one is allowed to call himself 'king' for we must remain subservient to the rulers of our different lands of exile and be loyal to them. The official who was sent to us from Constantinople, Yaakov Ben Chaim, has seized undue power. He calls himself *nagid*, a prince, which is almost synonymous with king or ruler. This is a title used in the ancient days for our kings."

R' Bezalel opened up the Bible under his arm and showed the ruler the passage where King Shaul's coronation is described; there he is referred to as *nagid*: 'Has *Hashem* not anointed you over His possessions as a *nagid*?'

And he continued, "Your Excellency, I would like you to know that when I stood before the new official, together with the rest of the delegation representing all the Jews of Egypt and saw that he had seized more power than was his due, I explained to him that it was forbidden to do so, but he brazenly insulted me. My only recourse was to excommunicate him."

The *pasha* was convinced of R' Bezalel's innocence and forthwith abolished the title of *nagid* which had been conferred upon Yaakov Ben Chaim.[9]

He was, henceforth, to be called the *chilbi* and his power was limited to financial matters only. The community's spiritual matters were to be in the hands of the *beis din*.

Yaakov Ben Chaim burned with a desire for revenge against R' Bezalel Ashkenazi and harassed him at every turn. R' Bezalel also felt the displeasure of the heads of the community who resented the abolishment of the centuries-old office of *nagid*. They realized that he had acted to uphold their honor. Still, they found it difficult to forgive him. Their longstanding historic tradition had been abruptly broken.

The strained atmosphere in the *kehillah* and the maliciousness of the *chilbi* forced R' Bezalel Ashkenazi to leave Egypt and resettle in Jerusalem.

R' Bezalel had gone; R' Yitzchak Luria had lost his friend and teacher.

1. "Shem Hagedolim" Os Yud, Siman 156
2. "Koreh Hadoros" on him
3. "Otzar Hagedolim", a treasury of Jewish leaders, on the Radbaz
4. Ibid
5. "Shem Hagedolim", on him, Os Beis, Siman 28
6. "Shivchei HaArizal" page 5 and "Maase Nisim"
7. "Toldos Chachmei Yerushalayim" I, p. 103, footnotes 3-4
8. Ibid, p. 29
9. "Divrei Yosef" by R' Yosef Sambari and "Toldos Chachmei Yerushalayim" p. 117

CHAPTER FIVE
AT THE GATEWAY OF THE KABBALAH

For the seven years in which the Ari sat and learned with his master R' Bezalel, he studied the revealed Torah in depth — the six *sidrei mishnah, Talmud Bavli* and *Yerushalmi, Sifri, Sifra* and similar works. He also gained vast knowledge of *poskim* like the Rif, the Rambam, Baal Haturim and others. But his soul yearned to know and understand the hidden Torah as well, to get closer to its Creator.

There were few who studied that area of wisdom. It was secret and arcane, meant only for those who were ready to renounce worldly matters, to strive towards holiness and purity. One who wished to approach the mystic, first had to acquire the quality of *zehirus* (care), and *zerizus* (diligence) in his service to G-d. He had to be thoroughly familiar with the revealed Torah.

Kabbalah was called "*Toras haCheN*" that is, *Chochmah Nisteres* (hidden knowledge). The great scholars who studied it, did so in secret and only revealed its hidden mysteries to someone fitting, to someone who had undergone the necessary preparation. *Kabbalah* was transmitted from master to pupil and never recorded lest it fall into the hands of someone unworthy.

When the ancient sages saw that few suitable people were pursuing this branch of knowledge, and that it was beyond the comprehension of most, they did record some of the principles and gave their students the introduction which was necessary to understand them. This is why it is called *Kabbalah* which means 'transmission' from the select sages of one generation to those of the succeeding generation.

Among those who study *Toras haCheN*, there are some who dwell upon matters which are beyond nature. They are able, through their knowledge, to effect changes in the laws of nature and produce real miracles; all of the secrets of Creation are open to them. This aspect of *Kabbalah* is called "practical *Kabbalah*".

A Treasure More Precious than Gold

The basic work of *Kabbalah* is the *Zohar*. It is a compilation of all the secrets of the Torah which the saintly R' Shimon bar Yochai and his son, R' Elazar, revealed to their disciples. These two *tanaim* hid in a cave for thirteen years to avoid being seized by the Roman conquerers who sought their lives. They were sustained by the fruit of a carob tree which had miraculously sprouted near the cave and from a gushing spring inside it. They spent their time studying the mystic secrets of the Torah, and recorded the major points. After their passing, their disciples gathered up their notes and added the important teachings which they had learned directly from them. This compilation was called the "*Zohar*".[1]

Over the generations, the scholars of *Chen (Chochmas Nisteres)* became few and far between. The *Zohar* disappeared and was forgotten. But the ways of Providence are wondrous. *Hashem*, the Prime Mover, Who wills things to happen, did not want this branch of Torah to be forgotten and brought about its rediscovery.

In an eastern city there was a rumor that a treasure of gold, silver and precious gems was buried in a particular place. When the king heard this he sent his servants to dig up the buried treasure and bring it to him. The servants dug up the entire area and then dug again, deeper. Suddenly, their spades clanged against an iron chest. Shouts of joy went up from the group. "Hurrah! We have found it," they exclaimed to one another. They tugged at the heavy chest, raised it and quickly brought it to the palace.

The guardian of the royal vaults had it delivered before the king. He bowed low and said, "Your Majesty, may your kingdom flourish forever! We have fulfilled your royal command. Here is the chest which we have uncovered. It is locked; shall we open it for you?"

The king nodded. A locksmith was brought to open the iron chest. Everyone in the court held his breath. When the top of the sealed chest was finally lifted and its contents revealed, a cry of disappointment rose up from the spectators. There was no buried treasure inside, no sign of gold, silver or jewels. Only a weathered parchment bearing strange, unknown characters.

The king summoned his advisors and wise men to unravel the secret of the ancient writing. They turned it from side to side, passed it from hand to hand but in the end, shrugged their shoulders and shamefacedly said,

"Your Majesty, we cannot understand this writing."

The king sent the scroll to the wise men of Rome.

They studied the parchment and knew enough to determine that the writing was Hebraic. The experts in ancient Hebrew tried their hand at deciphering the manuscript and while they were able to read the words, they could not understand their meaning. "The writer must have been a Jewish scholar, for the meaning is very profound and beyond our comprehension," they said.

The king ordered Jewish scholars to be brought before him. They studied the manuscript and were equally confused by it. They had no trouble reading the words but could not comprehend the meaning. "Perhaps Jewish scholars in Spain, some of whom are students of *Kabbalah* and philosophy, will succeed in explaining the secrets hidden here," they suggested.

The king had the manuscript sent to the scholars of Spain. They read it, pondered over every word and succeeded in understanding its meaning. It was the *Zohar*! They were overjoyed at the discovery and begged the king to sell it to them. As a sign of their appreciation to the king for having discovered this scroll, they sent him many costly gifts.

The king had, indeed, discovered a treasure — the gold and silver, the gifts of the Spanish scholars. But the true treasure which was priceless, was the find itself, the *Zohar*, which had been rediscovered in such an amazing manner.[2]

The Spanish scholars guarded this manuscript for many years. They cherished it lovingly. But when the Jews were exiled from Spain, it once again, fell into gentile hands.

While it was in Jewish possession, only a few scholars

who were fluent in *Kabbalah* were permitted to study it. They wrote commentaries to it based on the knowledge that they had received from their teachers and on their own understanding. These works were copied and entrusted to saintly men who studied them in purity and holiness.

A Strange Siddur

In those early years when the Ari had lived in Jerusalem, he had made the acquaintance of great *mekubalim* such as R' Klonimus Haberkstein. But R' Yitzchak had concerned himself for the most part with the study of *nigleh* (the revealed). Yet, it had been Eliyahu Hanavi himself who had informed his father that R' Yitzchak was destined by Providence to study *Kabbalah* and to spread its hidden light abroad. When the time was ripe, Providence put the writings of *Kabbalah* directly into the Ari's hands.

It was *Shabbos*. R' Yitzchak, the young nephew of R' Mordechai Francis, was sitting in his usual place in the *beis knesses*. His seat was not to be found on the *mizrach* wall, among the wealthy and prominent men as befitted a scholar such as he. His seat was at the far western end, where the poor common folk and the traveling beggars sat. He chose to pray among those who did not have the means to buy a better seat. There he felt more at ease, away from inquisitive eyes. He was able to pour out his heart in peace and quiet.

On this particular *Shabbos* a stranger came and sat down next to the young Ari. He seemed to be a traveler from abroad, for he looked confused, as if the local *nusach* (order of prayers) and synagogue customs were foreign to him.

R' Yitzchak saw that the visitor was bewildered and tried to put him at ease. He took the stranger's *siddur* and began leafing through it, but realized, to his astonishment, that this was not a *siddur* at all; it was an ancient manuscript!

He fetched one of the *siddurim* from the synagogue and showed the stranger where the *chazzan* was up to. When the prayers were over he asked to borrow the book the visitor had brought, since he wished to study it. The stranger gladly obliged.

The Ari looked through the book and discovered that it contained profound, esoteric secrets which required much deeper study. Its owner, he thought, must be a great *mekubal*, proficient in the secrets of the mystic. But, when he tried to engage him in conversation, the stranger lowered his eyes in embarrassment and muttered some words under his breath. R' Yitzchak did not press him but changed the subject. "Where do you come from?" he asked. "How did this book come into your possession?"

It became clear that the visitor was a simple unlearned Jew. He admitted that he actually did not know how to read Hebrew. His parents had been Marranos in Spain and he had been educated as a Christian, since his parents had been deathly afraid of the dreadful Inquisition. Only as an adult had he learned that he was a Jew. After building up a thriving business, he had succeeded in leaving the land of bloodshed and terror, taking along with him a small part of his wealth and a few manuscripts which he had found among his family belongings.

He had come to Egypt, now, on business and desired to

get closer to his brethren. But he was too ashamed to admit that he was unfamiliar with Jewish customs and prayers and, therefore, always took along these Hebrew manuscripts and pretended to pray from them.

The Ari listened to this strange tale in amazement and when the man finished, asked him whether he would be willing to sell the manuscript. He could name any price, the Ari assured him. The man laughed and said, "Are you making fun of me, young man? Look at me: do I look like I lack money? I am a prosperous businessman, thank G-d. I have no need to sell these writings."

Undaunted, R' Yitzchak persisted, "Please, you cannot read them and they serve you no purpose. Even though they are a family heirloom and you are sentimentally attached to them, they are not fulfilling their purpose in your possession. These scholarly works were meant to be studied. That is what I would do, if they were in my possession!"

The Ari was so insistent that the stranger finally gave in and said, "If you put it that way, I will give these writings to you as a gift, for I see how highly you value them, but on one condition — try to get your father-in-law, R' Mordechai Francis, the customs inspector, to waive the duty put on my merchandise.

R' Yitzchak was so determined to possess those rare writings that he spoke to his father-in-law. To his joy, R' Mordechai Francis agreed and the Ari acquired the coveted manuscripts.[3]

The Ari began to study the works in depth and was captivated by the wonderful things he learned. He suddenly realized that his soul had been thirsting for this type of knowledge, for *Kabbalah*. His soul found true satisfaction and serenity in its teachings. He feared, however, that perhaps he was unworthy; he might not be sufficiently fluent in the revealed Torah. Were his ways holy enough? He decided to lay all of his doubts and thoughts before the Radbaz to learn if he was suited for such study or not.

The young scholar waited for the right moment to present his request to his master. And soon that opportunity arrived.

Three Named Yitzchak

One day, after R' David ben Zimra had given the *shiur* to his select group of students, the Ari felt that the time had come to consult with his rabbi on the question that had been pecking away at his heart for some time now. The lesson was over and most of the disciples had gone. R' Bezalel, the close friend and teacher of the Ari, was busy gathering up his *seforim* before leaving for the house, which he shared with R' Yitzchak.

Only three students remained in the room, clarifying a difficult point in the lesson they had just heard. These were R' Yitzchak Apomado, R' Yitzchak Fasi and R' Yitzchak Luria Ashkenazi. After they finished their discussion, the Ari turned to the Radbaz and said cryptically: "There are three here whose names are Yitzchak." His master was puzzled. True, and what of it? "What are you trying to say, my son?" he asked.

"We three are identical in name," the Ari said. "We are all called Yitzchak. But our natures are very different; each of us has strengths in different areas. I, for example, am drawn to the study of the *Kabbalah*. My friend, Morenu HaRav Yitzchak Apomado's strength lies in reflection. He is destined to become a scholar of repute because of his incisive mind and vast knowledge in the Talmud. R' Yitzchak Fasi, will become famous for something else: he has the ability of directing an issue in any course of his choosing."[4]

And all turned out as the Ari had foresaw. He himself was to become responsible for the widespread knowledge of *Kabbalah*. Much is told about R' Yitzchak Fasi and R' Yitzchak Apomado which justified the Ari's prediction concerning them.

Refining His Character

When the Arizal asked the Radbaz if he was worthy of embarking upon the study of *Kabbalah*, or not, the latter outlined the requirements of perfecting one's character, *tikkun hamiddos*, needed in preparation for safely entering upon such study.

R' Yitzchak took his master's words to heart. He intensified his efforts in directing and improving his character. He strove to reach the heights of sanctity and purity which were necessary to acquire the spiritual powers to understand the secrets of Torah. R' Bezalel, his teacher and friend in study and seclusion, assisted and encouraged him greatly. The Ari felt his understanding and perception increasing from day to day. He sensed a constant improvement; he was truly getting nearer his goal.

Through study and *hisbodedus* (seclusion), the Ari Hakadosh gained twenty-one praiseworthy traits. As he expresses it himself: "*Ach (alef-chaf)* (numerically 21) *tov leYisrael*" *(Tehillim 73:1)* Twenty-one is good for Israel. —

These are the twenty-one aspects which sanctify a person. Among them he enumerates: "Humility and lowliness before *Hashem;* fear of sin, keeping one's distance from pride, anger and irritation with regard to others; steering clear of forbidden food and *lashon hara;* avoiding lies, lightheadedness and foul language..." All the guidelines which he set for others were first adopted by him; he practiced what he preached. He was particularly careful to concentrate upon the words of the blessings before and after eating; he wished to be sincere in expressing his thanks for the bounty which *Hashem* showered upon mankind. He was strict in regularly saying the *tikkun chatzos;* each midnight he would rise, sit on the floor and mourn over the destruction of the *Beis Hamikdash* and the exile of the *Shechinah*. He also urged a careful study of *halachah* in order to practice the laws properly. He also advocated studying Torah while wearing one's *tallis* and *tefillin* all day. Among the things which he was strict about was putting on Rabbenu Tam's *tefillin*. He urged regular purification in a *mikveh* and tried to be one of the first ten men to come to synagogue, to show how dearly he loved the *mitzvos*.

The *Shulchan Aruch HaArizal*, which describes his holy practices, also speaks of the profound love he bore for every *mitzvah*. When he had to buy a *lulav* and *esrog*, for example, he never bargained the price down; he always paid the price which was quoted. He sometimes even went further than that by laying down his purse on the stand and telling the seller to take whatever he wanted, noting that one must not bargain when it came to a *mitzvah*.[5]

His love for the *mitzvos* matched his love for the Torah; both were unbounded. He cherished the joy of *Hashem*,

His Torah and His commandments more than any treasure in the world. He once confided to a close friend that everything that he had achieved — in having the gates of wisdom and *ruach hakodesh* opened before him — was his reward for always finding more joy in performing each *mitzvah* than in any other pleasure in the world. They meant more to him than gold and jewels.[6]

The Ari inspected all of his actions throughout his life. He examined the innermost chambers of his heart to see if, G-d forbid, he had overlooked any aspect of self-improvement or had regressed in anything. He always prayed to his Creator and begged that He help him to continue achieving higher levels of purification. It is said that even upon the threshold of death, he was heard murmuring, "Spare me from pride."[7]

1. "Seder Hadoros" Tanaim and Amoraim on Rashbi
2. "Shem Hagedolim", sefarim, Letter Zayin 8:8
3. "Imrei Tzaddikim" end, and "Divrei Yosef"
4. "Shem Hagedolim" on the Arizal, as quoted from "Midrash Eliyahu" p. 12
5. "Taamei Haminhagim" footnote to 927
6. "Reishis Chochmah", Shaar HaAhava 7:34; "Charedim" (Jerusalem 5741) p. 17
7. "Taamei Haminhagim" para. 10, footnote to last essay

CHAPTER SIX
THE RETREAT ON THE BANKS OF THE NILE

In order to attain the virtues to which he aspired, the Ari decided to break all contact with the vanities of this world and all of its cares. He went off with his *sefarim* to a secluded spot where he would not be disturbed. Throughout the week he studied the *Kabbalah* and returned home on Fridays.

The more he immersed himself in the writings of *Kabbalah*, the more he understood its teachings and the more he found it necessary to purify himself to become worthier.

In the first years of his isolation, he already attained great heights in the esoteric knowledge of the mystic. He recorded much of his thinking from that period. These writings include his commentary on *Sifra d'Tsniyusa*.[1]

Sifra d'Tsniyusa is one of the first Kabbalistic writings. Even the *Zohar* quotes from it at the end of *Parashas Terumah*. This work is attributed to Yaakov Avinu and its teachings are arcane and profound. Precisely because of its difficulty, the Ari labored over it arduously when he first began studying *pardes* and wished to explain it so that others might find it easier to understand.

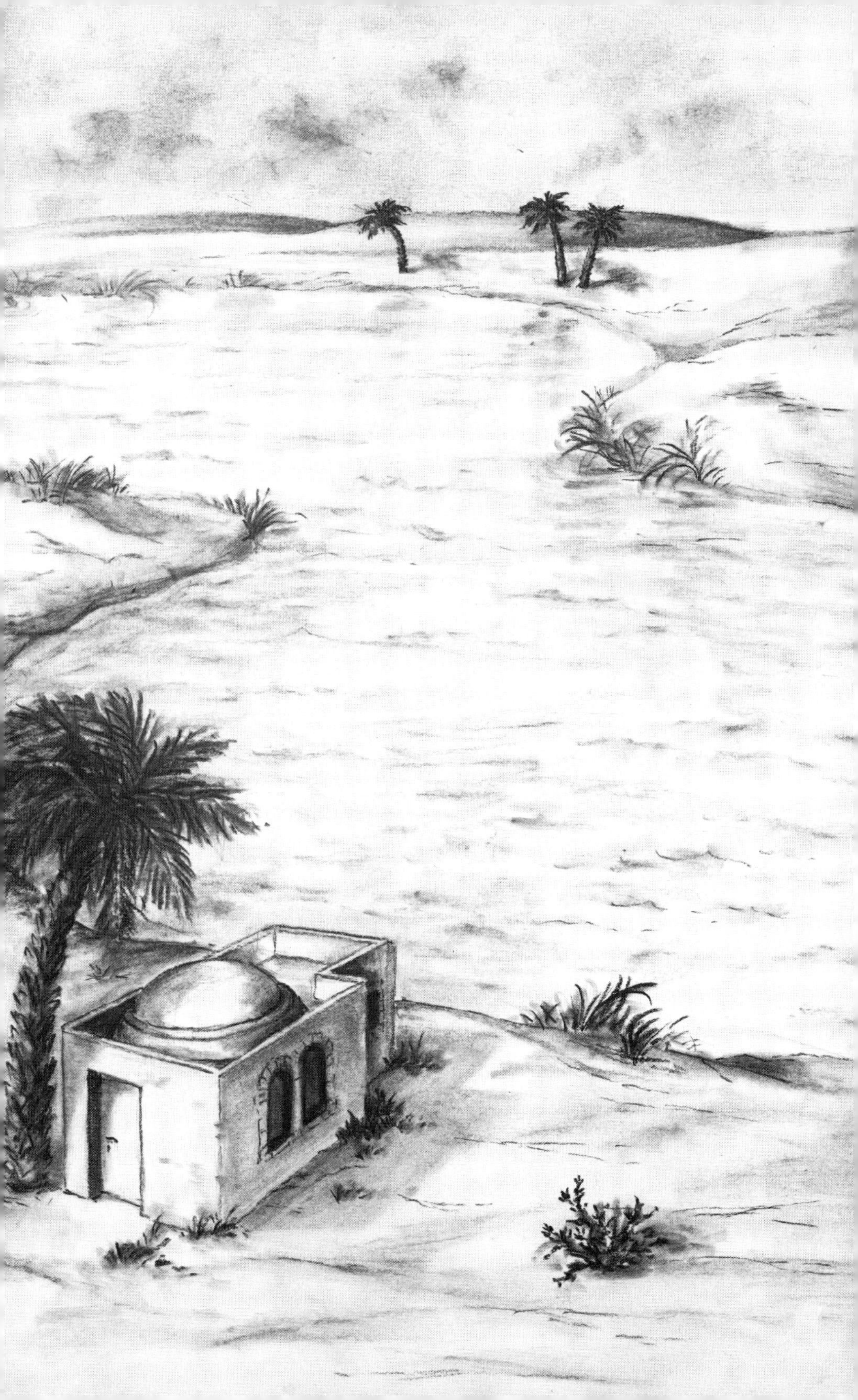

Rising Ever Higher in Sanctity

At the end of seven years of retreat, the Ari was still not satisfied. He wanted to increase his *kedushah* even more until he reached the level of *ruach hakodesh*. He found himself an isolated hut, even more removed than his first retreat, on the banks of the Nile, far away from all civilization. Here he lived, not speaking to another soul until he returned home on Fridays for a short visit. But even in his home he refrained from speaking unless the matter was extremely urgent and then — only in Hebrew and as tersely as possible. He returned to his hut on the Nile on Friday night. This retreat was in an area called 'ancient Egypt' while his wife and children lived in 'modern Egypt' which was just within the permitted walking distance of *Shabbos*.

His hut was not too far from a customs depot. His father-in-law, who rented the franchise for customs collection, employed twenty clerks to process the transactions and entrusted them with the additional responsibility of providing the Ari with his needs. Thus, freed of all bothersome cares, the Ari was able to devote himself entirely, body and soul, to his studies.

On Friday night, after his brief stay home, the Ari would resume his hermit's life with its minimum of contact with the outside world. When the time came for prayer, the customs clerks would come and knock on his door and join with him in a *minyan*. The Ari's soul, which was otherwise soaring in lofty spheres, had to constrict itself in order to participate in the prayers with the others, but immediately afterwards, he returned to his exalted thoughts; he had no words at all with any of his father-in-law's clerks.[2]

The Ari knew that without assistance from Heaven, he would be unable to achieve the heights which he sought. He, therefore, fasted much and prayed fervently that Heaven would help him.

Eliyahu Reveals Himself

After all of his preparations in study, prayer and self improvement, the Arizal was rewarded. The fountains of knowledge were opened and Eliyahu Hanavi was sent by Heaven to reveal himself to him regularly and teach him the most exalted and hidden secrets of the Torah. Moreover, while he slept, his soul soared to the upper spheres until it reached the *mesivta d'rekiya*, the heavenly *beis midrash*. There, the guardian angel at the doorway would ask him with whom he wished to study. Sometimes, he chose the *yeshivah* of the writers of the *Zohar*, the *tanaim* R' Yeiva Sava or R' Hamnuna Sava. They would explain various passages in the *Zohar* which he had studied that day but had not thoroughly understood. At other times, he preferred to attend the *yeshivah* of Bezalel ben Uri ben Chur, who had built the *Mishkan*, or Aharon Hakohen. There he would learn all the secrets alluded to in the structure of the *Mishkan* and the *avodah*, its holy service. Upon different occasions he elected to study under the prophets. Here he would ponder the secrets concealed within their visions. The Ari had only to say the word and the angel would lead him to the teacher of his choice. Thus, he succeeded in gaining that which is beyond human grasp and understanding.

The Ari confided to his students that if they were

worthy, he would be able to bring their souls to perfection to such a degree that they, too, would be able to study Torah in the *mesivta d'rekiya*. He also told them that eighty years of human life was not enough to even record what he learned in one night.[3]

In these years of seclusion, Eliyahu Hanavi revealed to him the innermost secrets of Torah which had been buried for centuries, from the time of R' Shimon bar Yochai.

After Eliyahu Hanavi began to appear to him and teach him the secrets of the Torah, he continued to live in isolation for another seven years. By then, he had spent twenty years in isolation and retreat from worldly matters. At the age of sixteen, he had closeted himself with R' Bezalel Ashkenazi for seven years. Afterwards, when R' Bezalel had been forced to leave Egypt, he had continued to study in seclusion until he had become worthy of Divine revelation.

During these twenty years, he occasionally helped his father-in-law. Sometimes he tried his hand at business on his own. We find, for example, a bill of sale signed by him, dated Tuesday, the second of *Elul*, 5319 (1559). It notes that R' Yitzchak Luria Ashkenazi sold a large amount of pepper belonging to him and located at the time in Alexandria. The amount of the sale was one hundred and fifty gold florins (a type of currency in use in Egypt at the time).

During this long period of twenty years, the Ari left Egypt once with his family and went to *Eretz Yisrael* to give his three-year-old son his first haircut at the grave of R' Shimon bar Yochai. R' Chaim Vital, his disciple, describes the event in his *Shaar Hakavanos*, as follows:

"He remained there for the first three days of that

week. This was the first time that they came from Egypt. But I do not know if he was then as learned in the marvelous study of the mystic as he was later."

The Time Has Come

In his twentieth year of seclusion, when he was thirty-six years old, a vessel filled with knowledge of *Kabbalah*, Heaven decreed that he reveal himself and spread his knowledge far and wide among other scholars. At that time Eliyahu appeared to him and said:

"Know that the time when you must leave this world is drawing near. You must leave the land of Egypt and go up to *Eretz Yisrael*. Go to Tsefas, settle there and reveal your knowledge to those who seek *Hashem*. There, your name will go forth to the rest of the world."[4]

The Ari was not overjoyed by this revelation. He was loathe to leave his high plane to descend to the level of his students. He was to express this many times later in life.

Besides, he found difficulty in transmitting his ideas. It is told that once, when he was seated with a group of scholars in Tsefas, they asked him why he did not record his knowledge in writing so that it would not be forgotten in the coming generations. He replied, "Were all the oceans ink and all the heavens parchment and all the reeds pens, they still would not suffice to write down all that I know."

Often he told his disciples, "When I begin to reveal to you even one secret from the Torah, I am flooded by such an outpouring of knowledge, like a gushing stream. I seek ways to develop a small pipeline, a narrow channel for a single secret of the Torah, which you will be able to grasp and assimilate. I make great efforts not to go above your heads, lest you lose everything you have acquired already."

Thus, while he did not write down his teachings, he urged his students to do so, that their writings might remain a record for them and also for succeeding generations.[5]

Now, when Eliyahu Hanavi came to inform the Ari that he must reveal himself in the city of Tsefas, and saw how grieved he was about it, he comforted him and explained, "True, it is difficult for you to begin to impart to others the secret knowledge you have gained. But in Tsefas you will find R' Chaim Vital. You can transmit your knowledge to him. Know that he will be your successor; he will write down your teachings and will spread them. Your very coming to this world was only for R' Chaim's sake. His is a very precious soul and through you he will be worthy to understand and to delve even deeper into the teachings of the mystic so that he can diffuse it far and wide, throughout the land."

R' Yitzchak still could not make peace with the decree. His soul still yearned to study. He was well aware that the rigors of the journey and the concern for his students' cares would rob him of precious time for personal study and he would have to devote many hours to preparing lessons. Besides, here, in Egypt, he was free from any financial burden, for he was supported by his devoted father-in-law. But in *Eretz Yisrael* he would be forced to support himself. This, too, would steal time from his precious hours of study.

Eliyahu had to persuade him further. He promised the Ari that in Tsefas, as in Egypt, he would continue to appear to him. He would reveal more secrets of the Torah concerning the workings of Heaven and earth. And besides, Egypt was an impure land while in Tsefas, he would be on holy soil. There he would be thought worthier of grasping even deeper secrets.[6]

R' Yitzchak Luria was appeased. He began to make his preparations for going up to *Eretz Yisrael*, to Tsefas.

1. "Shem Hagedolim", on the Ari, Os Yud, Siman 332
2. "Shivchei HaAri" p. 30; "Maaseh Nisim" chapter 4
3. Ibid
4. "Shivchei HaAri" p. 7; "Maaseh Nisim" chapter 3; Introduction to "Etz Chaim" 5. "Shivchei HaAri" p. 6
6. Ibid p. 8; "Maaseh Nisim" chapter 8

CHAPTER SEVEN
TSEFAS AND ITS SCHOLARS

The Ottoman conquest blew a refreshing new wind over the desolate cities of *Eretz Yisrael*; they flourished once again. Thanks to this, the city of Tsefas was transformed into one of the most illustrious of Jewish communities. It attracted many great Torah scholars who glorified its name and made it known throughout the world. They left a priceless spiritual legacy for generations to come. Their teachings were a beacon in the darkness of the bitter exile, lighting the way for our trouble-blinded people so that they would not stumble.

The Turkish government designated Tsefas as the capital of the entire Galilee because it lies at the crossroads leading to Damascus and to Acco and Sidon — at that time the northern ports of *Eretz Yisrael*. Its accessibility to these port-cities encouraged the merchants of Tsefas to develop commercial ties with many countries and trade expanded. The flocks of sheep grazing upon the lush fields of the Galilee provided wool for workshops which spun the wool into yarn. This was then woven into high-quality fabrics. These same sheep provided milk and its by products, among them the famous Tsefas cheese celebrated for its delicate flavor and richness. The olives that grew in abundance provided plentiful oil for food, soaps and cosmetics. The manufactured goods of Tsefas acquired an excellent reputation and enjoyed a widespread demand.

Jews began flocking to it from all over the globe. A combination of many factors brought them there; the economic opportunities promised prosperity; the local ruler was benevolent and protected the Jews of the district; the air was clear, the climate wholesome. But more than anything else, people were drawn to the aura of sanctity which enveloped the city and its environs. Here, were to be found the graves of many Jewish leaders of past generations, dating as far back as the Talmudic era, of *tanaim* and *amoraim*. Among them were the tombs of R' Shimon bar Yochai and his son, R' Elazar, in nearby Meron.

The exiles of Spain and Portugal also heard of this upsurge of development in *Eretz Yisrael*. They had not as yet found a permanent haven and rejoiced at the opportunity of finding sanctuary and a new lease on life on this holy soil. They longed to rebuild their lives in peace and tranquility upon the foundations of Torah and sanctity. The city grew by giant leaps with their arrival and there were great improvements made in all spheres of living.

An anonymous traveler who visited the land during the years 5292-3 (1532-33), described the holy sites in and about Tsefas. He had this to say about the city itself:

"Tsefas is situated in the Upper Galilee in the

portion of Naftali. There is a massive fortress at the west of the mountain and four other mountains surrounding it. Two of these are inhabited by Ishmaelites while the slopes of the other two mountains are dotted by Jewish cottages, housing more than three hundred families. The Jewish community has three synagogues: one belonging to the Sefardim, another to the Muriskim (this was the description given to the local Jewish population then) and the Mugrabi synagogue (for Jews of African descent). This last one is called *Knesses* Eliyahu Hanavi, for it is the most ancient. Tradition has it that Eliyahu himself prayed here.

Tsefas does not lack anything. It has fine food. Grain and wine are to be found in abundance and are cheap. Everything can be had in season. These are so plentiful that were it not for their export value — the products are sent to Damascus and other cities — they would be negligible in price. Tsefas has all kinds of good fruits and what it lacks is imported from Damascus. The land is spacious with plenty of opportunities for trade. Jewish merchants deal in all sorts of goods, which they import from Damascus to Tsefas. Whoever lacks the capital to invest in trade can make a living as a craftsman. (*Otzar Masaos*, Eisenstein, p. 132)

In the work of responsa *Avkas Rochel* by R' Yosef Karo, we find written (*Siman I*):

"And *Hashem* saw the affliction of His people Israel who had been in exile from their homeland for nearly one and a half millennia, driven from one country to another, from one government to another, persecuted and rejected. He recalled the covenant of their forefathers... And they settled in the city of Tsefas, the coveted one of the lands. And its leaders and trustees ruled it properly, shouldering the burden of the poor amongst them and of the scholars... And thus, the vineyard of *Hashem*, pleasant and comely, flourished. The vines throve and the pomegranate trees blossomed. The *roshei yeshivah* and their disciples pursued their studies, firmly entrenched in their place, free from evil forces and disturbances, safe from the sound of the oppressor."

The city attracted so many new residents that it soon became congested. Plans were laid for extensive construction to fill the need for new housing. This is reflected in the introduction to one of the *halachic* questions of that period, appearing in *Avkas Rochel*, mentioned above (*Siman 159*). It notes that since the existent housing is not sufficient for the Jews of Tsefas, the residents thought of demanding that the government erect the necessary housing. They sent a messenger to a person of influence in Constantinople, the capital of the Ottoman Empire. They wished him to speak to the authorities on their behalf. However, he demanded one thousand florins for his efforts, a huge sum. The Jews involved thought that the sum was impossibly high and washed their hands of the entire affair.

A few years later, a new governor came to Damascus. He became convinced that the situation in Tsefas was, indeed, unbearable, and decided to build a residential neighborhood, expecting this to be a profitable venture since he would be able to collect rents. The heads of the Jewish community appointed R' Moshe Tabas to buy up all the fields on the mounain peak. He gave them all to the *pasha* as an outright gift and the latter built the long awaited development.

Many famous scholars were among those who came to live there.

The Tzaddik of the Roosters

R' Yosef Saragosi was an exile from Sicily. At first, he settled in Egypt where he established a major *yeshivah*. He left Egypt and went to settle in Tsefas where he devoted himself to the study of *Kabbalah* and was one of the chosen few to whom Eliyahu Hanavi revealed himself.

Aside from his greatness in Torah, he was also renowned for his character which was like that of Aharon Hakohen. He settled arguments between neighbors and between husband and wife. He offered his help not only to the Jews of Tsefas but also to the Arabs, who came to him with their quarrels. They implicitly trusted him to arrive at a true and just settlement.

Before R' Yosef passed away, he left instructions to be buried on the very spot where Eliyahu had revealed himself to him. His request was honored and his grave was dug in Kfar Ein Zeisim, not far from the tomb of the *tana*, R' Yehuda bar Ilai.[1]

R' Yosef was a holy man, who performed miracles. He gained his various titles from those miracles. He was called "*Tzaddik* of the Roosters" because of an interesting event which occurred after his death.

The governor of Tsefas at that time was an evil, hard-

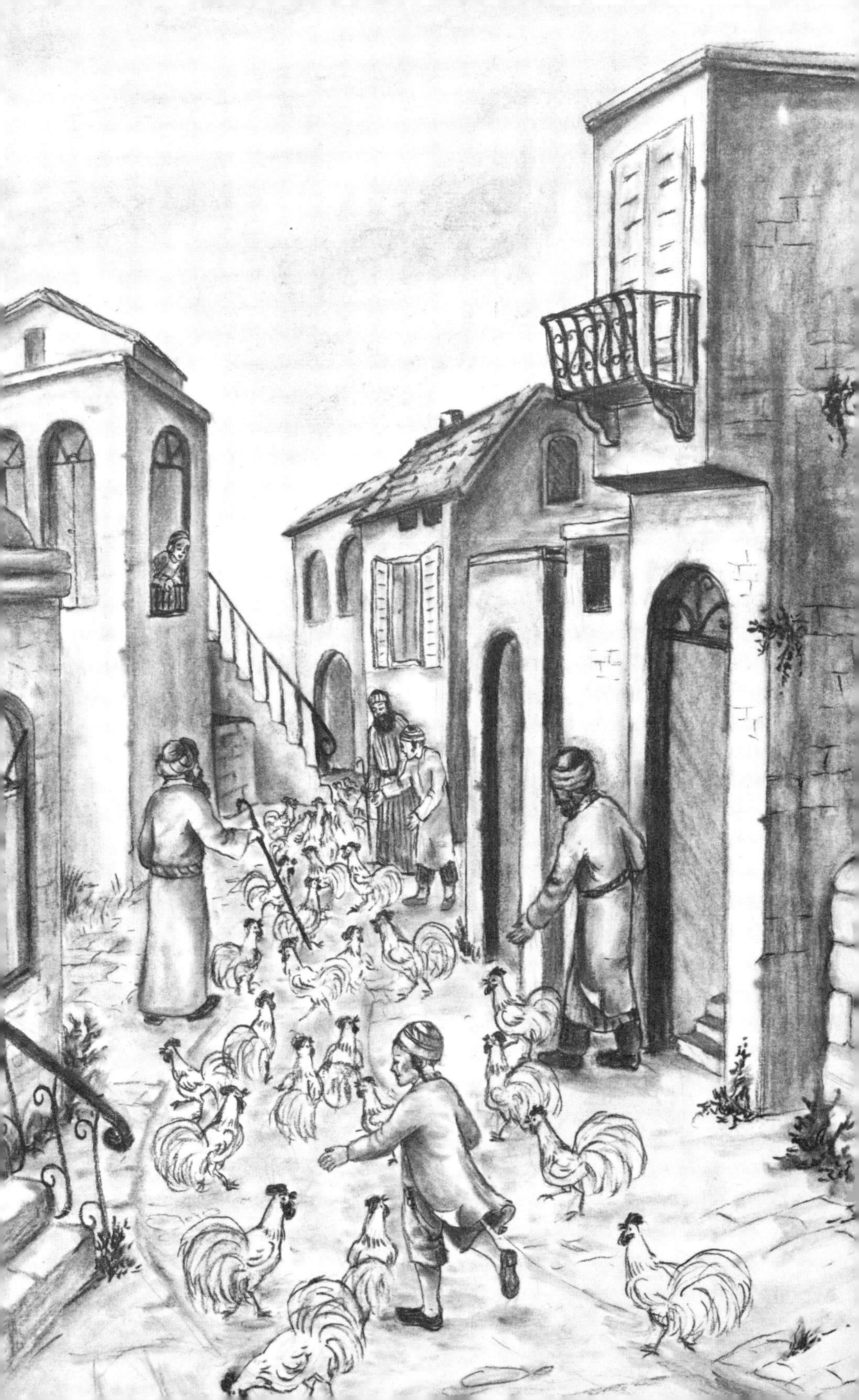

hearted person who despised the Jews and was jealous of their financial success. He had designs on their money. Once, he decreed that the Jews bring him a large number of pure white roosters, knowing very well that they would never be able to find such a large number in all of the surrounding area. And if they were unable to fufill his decree, he would be free to punish them as he pleased.

The Jews of Tsefas gathered in the *beis knesses*. They poured out their hearts and prayed for heavenly assistance. And then, they went to the graves of the many holy men who were buried nearby and prayed that the merit of the *tzaddikim* protect them and save them from the evil-doer.

That night, the head of the community had a dream in which R' Yosef Saragosi informed him that *Hashem* had heard their prayers at his graveside. He then instructed him to tell the Jews of Tsefas to gather all the roosters they could obtain, regardless of color, and to bring them to a certain place.

When he awoke, the man was very excited. He told his dream to the members of the community. They immediately went off to gather all the roosters which they could find. They brought them to the required place and a miracle occurred. The yellow, brown, black, reddish, spotted fowl, all suddenly turned a pure white!

The Jews of Tsefas were overwhelmed with joy. They quickly led the crowing chorus to the governor's house. The leader of the *kehilla* was at the head of the procession and informed the governor that his request had been fulfilled. The governor looked at the snowy white crowing birds and understood that the Jews had wrought a miracle. From that time on, he was careful to treat his Jewish subjects fairly and to offer them his protection. And from that time, the byname *"Tzaddik* of the Roosters" clung to R' Yosef Saragosi; others called him "The White *Tzaddik"*. The *beis knesses* where he had been accustomed to study and pray during his lifetime has been preserved to this very day and is referred to by the Jews of Tsefas as "The *Beis Knesses* of R' Yosef the White".[2]

R' Yaakov Beirav

The successor to R' Yosef Saragosi as chief rabbi of Tsefas was R' Yaakov Beirav, an exile from Spain. He was eighteen when he arrived in Morocco and was already well-known as a G-d-fearing scholar. The community of Fez welcomed him with open arms and, although he was young in age and as yet unmarried, begged that he serve as their spiritual leader. This was an esteemed position in an illustrious community, numbering in the thousands.

After some time, R' Yaakov moved on to Egypt where he had many students before going up to *Eretz Yisrael* and Tsefas.

Upon settling in Tsefas he was taken with the idea of renewing the practice of *semichah*. This is the official granting of rabbinical authority to men who are expert in all branches of *halachah*. This authority was vested only in judges who had received *semichah*, and *semichah* could only be granted by judges who themselves had *semichah*. This continuing chain of *semichah* went back all the way to Moshe Rabbenu. During the period of Roman rule, however, the chain was broken.

R' Yaakov Beirav relied on Rambam who suggested that there was a possibility of renewing the *semichah*, even in the absence of authorized judges. If all the sages living in *Eretz Yisrael* at a given time were to come to an agreement, appoint judges and grant them *semichah*, then *semichah* could be renewed. Hopefully, all the scholars in *Eretz Yisrael* would agree and perhaps they would even form a *Sanhedrin*.

R' Yaakov Beirav gave voice to this idea which beat in his heart and brought it before the sages of the Holy Land. The rabbi of Jerusalem, R' Levi ibn Chaviv (the Ralbach), opposed the plan most forcefully and as a result it was abandoned.

R' Yaakov Beirav had many famous students, to some of whom he gave *semichah*. Among them were R' Moshe of Trani (the Elder), R' Elazar Azcari and R' Yosef Karo.

R' Moshe of Trani, the Elder maintained a *yeshivah* in Tsefas which attracted many great scholars. Among his published works are: *Kiryas Sefer* on the Rambam, *Beis Elokim* on the topic of faith and a compilation of responsa in *halachah* which is called *She'elos Uteshuvos Hamabit*.

R' Elazar Azkari, was the author of *Charedim*, a *musar* work reflecting the greatness of its author. This work enumerates the commandments according to the parts of the body to which they apply. The Chida, in his *Shem Hagedolim*, describes its author: "We have heard of his greatness and the wonders which occurred to him in Costantinople."

R' Yosef Karo

R' Yosef Karo was born to R' Efraim Karo in Toledo in 5248 (1488). Before he was five years old, Yosef, his family and all of the Jewish community were banished from the country. The family first found refuge in Portugal, but their sojourn there was brief, for that government too expelled all of the Jews in 5256 (1496), some four years after their arrival. They wandered from place to place and, after much pain and deprivation, they finally reached Constantinople. R' Efraim Karo settled down and remained there until the day of his death.[3]

It was then that R' Yosef Karo, at the age of thirty, decided to move to Adrianople, some two hundred kilometers from Constantinople. There he married the daughter of R' Chaim ben Elbalag, but his young wife became mortally ill and died a short while after. R' Yosef was overcome with grief. He mourned his wife deeply, but, following the dictum of the sages that a scholar should not be without a wife, he remarried, this time, to the daughter of R' Yitzchak Saba.

In Adrianople R' Yosef made the acquaintance of many scholars and began writing down his Torah *chiddushim* on the *Arba'ah Turim*. He called the work *Beis Yosef*. It aroused much interest immediately upon its publication.

Just at this time he was asked to serve as *rosh yeshivah* in Nikopol, Bulgaria. The rabbi of this city, an elderly Sefardic sage, often disagreed with R' Yosef and would often jibe at him, although he was by now a celebrated scholar, highly esteemed in the various Jewish communities all over the world. Jews from places far and wide turned to him in Nikopol with their questions which he answered. But, he was primarily occupied with his teaching. He found solace in the stimulating challenge of preparing and delivering his *shiurim* and would forget the humiliation which was heaped upon him by the local rabbi. So troubled was he during this period that when he signed his name to *halachic* responsa, he added the words "the preoccupied and the wretched".

He left Nikopol in 5295 (1535) for Tsefas, where he hoped to settle permanently. But getting there was not at all easy. He traveled through Constantinople and Adrianopol; from there he sailed to Egypt. He stayed in Egypt for a year until finally, in *Elul* of 5296 (1536) he finally succeeded in fulfilling his dream when his feet trod on the holy soil of Tsefas.

He got to know R' Yaakov Beirav and forthwith became his disciple. But R' Yosef had many disciples of his own, great scholars in their own right, who flocked to drink of his Torah wisdom. In Tsefas, he divided his time between teaching and writing. And as always, he had to reply to the many questions which were sent to him from all over the world.

A first son was born to R' Yosef and to his wife in Tsefas. They called him Shlomo. The young infant filled the house with joy but again, it was short-lived, for the young mother passed away, leaving R' Yosef a widower for the second time, now with a young child on his hands who needed a mother. R' Yosef remarried, this time to the daughter of R' Zecharya Zabshil Ashkenazi. As the name denotes, this family belonged to the Ashkenazic community in Tsefas. This wife bore R' Yosef his second son, whom they named Yehudah.

Upon completing the work on his book, the *Beis Yosef*, the author set his hand to a new labor, a compilation of the *halachic* decisions of the *rishonim*. He gathered these in his *Shulchan Aruch*, which followed the same format as the *Arba'ah Turim*. This soon became a widely accepted and basic text. Rabbis everywhere began to rule in matters of *halachah* in accordance with its decisions. And since then,

R' Yosef Karo has acquired the title *Maran*, our master.

To be sure, the *Shulchan Aruch* was not without its critics. His detractors claimed that his decisions were based only upon Sefardic and Eastern customs and not those of the communities of Ashkenazic Europe. Thus, R' Moshe Isserlish, the Rama, added his own marginal comments and thoughts upon the *Shulchan Aruch*, which point out the varying customs as practiced in European communities. His addenda were called, by others, the *Mapah*, that is, the "tablecloth" for the "set table", the *Shulchan Aruch*.

After only a few years of residence, the community of Tsefas decided to crown R' Yosef Karo as its rabbi after the death of R' Yaakov Beirav. During his tenure the city flourished, reaching the peak of its development. Tsefas' reputation spread far and wide and it became a source of pride and yearning for every Jew.

In 5335 (1575), old and full of years, the *Beis Yosef* passed away at the age of eighty-seven.

Aside from the *Beis Yosef* and *Shulchan Aruch*, which we have already noted, he also left behind the *Kesef Mishneh* — his commentary on the Rambam's *HaYad HaChazakah*, *Avkas Rochel* — a work of *halachic* responsa arranged according to the *Orach Chaim*, *Yoreh Daia* and *Choshen Mishpat* sections of the *Shulchan Aruch*, *Kelalei HaTalmud*, a collection of the sermons he delivered on the weekly portion and on *Shir HaShirim* — a work called *Or Tzaddikim*. The other manuscripts which he wrote were never published. He mentions that he wrote a commentary on the *mishnah*, on Rashi and on Ramban on the Torah.

R' Yosef Karo was not only a learned scholar; he was also a pure and holy man to such a degree that when he studied *Kabbalah* he was taught by a special angel called a *maggid* who descended from heaven to reveal to him the innermost secrets of the Torah and to disclose the future to him. Few are the great men who were thus privileged to have their own *maggid* to instruct them! *Maran*, the *Beis Yosef*, wrote down the revelations which he heard from this angel and called the work *Maggid Meisharim*. This contains not only Torah concepts but also exhortation, *musar*. We learn from this work that the angel told him that his writings would have widespread acceptance throughout the Diaspora and would become a fundamental text for determining the *halachah* for Jewry throughout the ages. He would become *Rabban shel Yisrael*, the master and teacher of all Jewry.

The Heavenly Retinue Listens

R' Moshe Alshich was one of the *Beis Yosef*'s outstanding disciples, one who received his *semichah* from R' Yosef. R' Moshe hailed from Spain and he, too, had many of his own followers in Tsefas, among them R' Chaim Vital. The Arizal, who was R' Chaim's master in *Kabbalah*, thought highly of the Alshich. He often said that his sermons grasped the essential truth of the Torah and he frequently attended them. It is told that the Ari once left the *beis midrash* in the middle of a *drashah*. When asked later why he had done so, R' Yitzchak replied, "I always go to hear the Alshich's *drashos* because I know that the Heavenly retinue also descends to hear his holy words. This time I saw them leave the *beis midrash* in the middle because, even though the concept he was expounding was dazzling, because of his modesty he did not evaluate his own words highly enough. When I saw the Heavenly retinue leaving I joined them."

The Alshich served as the rabbi of Tsefas after R' Yosef Karo and replied to many questions. His responses were compiled but the work was never published.[4]

R' Moshe Alshich is most famous for his *drashos* and his marvelous commentary on the *Tanach* which have been reprinted again and again.

The Brilliant One

After the Ari's death, the elderly R' Moshe Galanti became the next rabbi of Tsefas. He, too, was a disciple of R' Yosef Karo and was ordained by him. When he was twenty-two years old, his master already entrusted him with complicated cases of marriage and divorce. His voluminous *halachic* correspondence was compiled and printed.

R' Moshe was born in Italy; his family name was Engel but because of his handsome appearance and aristocratic bearing, he earned the description of Galanti, which in Italian (as in English) means gallant, noble, gracious. Over the years, the name Engel was forgotten and the adjective Galanti became the new surname.[5]

Two Pennies — And No More

Once, after the Ari had been living in Tsefas for some time, he was visited by R' Moshe Galanti who asked him to study his forehead. "Tell me what my blemish is," he begged. He wished to know whether he had a spiritual fault. If the Ari did see one, he would show R' Moshe how to do *teshuvah*. R' Yitzchak knew how upright and righteous a *tzaddik* R' Moshe was and he demurred. "I am not worthy of prescribing a *tikkun*, corrective, for one as great as you," he said.

But R' Moshe persisted. "Please, consider it as if you were fulfilling the commandment of *tochachah*, admonishment, of a fellow Jew, which is in the Torah. How can you refuse me? All you need do is to look at my forehead and I am sure that all my sins will be clearly revealed to you for you know everything that is hidden in a person's soul. Indicate where I have failed and show me how I can mend my ways. Save me from perdition, from *gehinnom*, Rebbe, for I feel that I have sinned."

The Ari was unable to withstand his pleas. It would be improper to do so. And so he answered, "I do see a tiny smudge. It signifies a hint of the sin of theft."

R' Moshe Galanti almost fainted when he heard this pronouncement. He began examining his deeds, trying to remember where and how he had committed such a terrible sin as theft.

R' Moshe was a very wealthy man. He owned both a spinning and a weaving mill which employed many workers. "Perhaps," he thought, "I have underpaid some worker, or not paid someone on time."

The elderly rabbi gathered all of his employees together and said, "My dear workers, I want each one of you to think back and remember if I owe any of you money. If so, stand up and tell me what that sum is at once for I wish to pay up anything I owe."

The workers looked at one another in surprise. R' Moshe owe someone money? Why, he was the most scrupulous of employers! He always paid on time! They replied unanimously, "Oh, no! You are very generous in your salary. The wages you pay us are a source of blessing; they always suffice for the needs of our families. We never even keep a strict reckoning of our wages or overtime because it is such a privilege and a pleasure to work for you!"

"My dear friends," he continued, his voice pleading and gentle, "I want you to be especially careful in counting your wages for if I do owe anyone money, it is considered *gezel*, theft, a sin which is not atoned for on *Yom Kippur* and which will follow me to the grave! You must all promise me that from now on you will keep careful account of the money I owe you, be it the smallest sum. For if you refuse, I will have to shut down the shop even if it involves a heavy loss! As for the past, here is a sack of coins. If anyone feels that money is due him, let him come up and claim it."

R' Moshe laid a heavy sack of coins on the table and opened it to make it all the more accessible to his workers.

The people squirmed in their places, feeling very uncomfortable at their employer's distress. No one dreamed of taking any money from the open sack. "How can we take," they asked one another, "if we do not know whether he owes us money or not? Why should *we* be guilty of taking money that is not rightfully ours?"

The righteous rabbi smiled at them encouragingly, "Take, take! Fill your palms with coins. And if you are afraid that you are taking more than your due, I hereby announce that I willingly forego any claim to that surplus. Take it, and G-d bless you! It is a gift!"

They were still not convinced. "None of us have claims against you," they murmured. "You are fair and just and far more than that — you are very generous. And even if any of us has the slightest claim, we forgive you."

The whispers and murmurs died down. Then, suddenly, one woman separated herself from the group of workers and went over to the sack of coins. She selected two copper pennies and took these — no more. She turned to rejoin the group but R' Moshe stopped her. "Please, take more!" he urged. "No!" the elderly worker stated firmly. "Only this is due to me." She returned to her place.

Seeing that no one else was ready to take any money, R' Moshe gathered up the sack and returned to the Ari. He begged him to scan his forehead once more. R' Yitzchak looked at the visitor and said, "The sin has been erased; your forehead is completely clear."

The elderly rabbi told R' Yitzchak exactly what had happened and asked for an explanation. The Ari said, "The worker who took the two pennies is one of your oldest workers, the most skilled in your employ. She truly deserves higher wages than the rest but you always paid her the same wages that the others were getting. That was considered marginal theft. But now that she has taken her due, your sin is erased."[6]

Tsefas did not only have Spanish Jews; it also had an Ashkenazic community which boasted great scholars equally conversant in the revealed and the mystic. Among them were R' Zecharya Zabshil Ashkenazi, R' Yosef Karo's father-in-law. Another famous figure is R' Yosef Ashkenazi who first served as rabbi in an illustrious community but left it to settle in *Eretz Yisrael*. He spent much much time learning *mishnayos* with a *niggun*. People would refer to him as the *tana*, for he was especially knowledgeable in the various readings in the text of the *mishnah* and its explanations. His teachings are mentioned in the commentaries on the *mishnah* of Torah giants of later generations.

The Candle Flame Speaks

Each *Shabbos* evening R' Yosef Ashkenazi would study *mishnah* in his home together with the Ari. Once, they were studying from memory, reciting the *mishnayos* in order, and explaining each one according to the four different approaches of *pardes* (the direct, allusive, homiletic and kabbalistic). The candle which gave them light started sputtering and flickering, as if it had fallen into water. The flame faltered for a quarter of an hour before it resumed burning normally. R' Yosef paid no attention and continued with his study.

When the Ari rose to leave, he turned to R' Yosef's son, R' Avigdor, and asked if he would accompany him home, a request he had never made before. As soon as the two left the house, the Ari turned to his companion and asked, "You have a younger brother. How is he? Is he well?" R' Avigdor looked at the Ari in surprise. "Why do you ask? He is sleeping peacefully in bed, as usual."

The Ari then revealed that he understood the language of candles and the secrets which they knew. The flickering candle had told him that this week the young child would pass away.

As so it was: that very week R' Yosef's young son unexpectedly passed away.[8]

There were many other scholars of Ashkenazic origin in and around Tsefas, among them R' Avraham Ashkenazi who lived nearby, in Biriya. R' Avraham ran a press and printed, among other works, the *Orach Chaim* part of R' Yosef Karo's famous *Shulchan Aruch* in 5315 (1555).

Another renowned scholar and *mekubal* was R' Yechiel Ashkenazi Luria, a relative of the Ari. His *chiddushim* in *Kabbalah* appear in his book *Heichal Hashem* which was printed in Venice in 5381 (1621). R' Yechiel was a saintly, ascetic man who was very careful in his speech. He tried to avoid everyday talk on *Shabbos* and would speak only *divrei Torah*. Many turned to him with their questions on the mystic; he was able to satisfy them all with clear and cogent answers. Part of these can be found in the various works of other scholars. His responsa in *halachah* have also been published separately.

After living in Tsefas for several years, R' Yechiel went up to Jerusalem. Here, too, his personality shone forth and he was numbered among the rabbis of the city.

In the course of his travels abroad, which were necessary in order for him to publish his writings, he also issued R' Elazar Azkari's *Charedim* in Venice in 5361 (1601).[9]

The names enumerated above give only a sample of the wealth of scholars and scribes; men of vast learning, of piety and holiness, who enriched the city of Tsefas by their presence and their holy labors. But they serve to show us the greatness of the city and the remarkable figures who inhabited it.

1. "Shem Hagedolim", Os Yud, Siman 156
2. "Chibas Yerushalayim" and "Eden Tzion" by R' Yeshayah Halevi Horowitz (Jerusalem 5716), Os Yud, Siman Mem
3. "Divrei Yosef" (Sambari)
4. "Shem Hagedolim", on him, Os Mem, Siman 101
5. Ibid, Siman 111
6. "Toldos HaAri"; "Oseh Pele" II p. 299
7. "Shem Hagedolim" on him, Os Yud, Siman 112; Introduction to the commentary "Meleches Shlomo" on Mishnah
8. "Shivchei HaAri p. 30 and other works
9. "Toldos Chachmei Yerushalayim" I, p. 108, footnote 3

CHAPTER EIGHT

THE CITY OF MEKUBALIM

Tsefas contained many great kabbalists even before the Ari arrived.

R' Shlomo Alkabetz

Who is not familiar with *Lechah Dodi* with which we greet the *Shabbos* Queen? The combination of the first letter of each stanza spells out Shlomo Halevi; this refers to the author, R' Shlomo Alkabetz, the famous poet and *mekubal* whose songs have been incorporated into our *siddur*.

R' Shlomo was born to R' Moshe Halevi Alkabetz and grew up in Salonika. He studied in the *yeshivah* of R' Yosef Taitatzak, of whom many unusual stories are told. R' Yosef did not sleep in a bed for forty years but on top of a chest with his feet dangling over the edge for fear of having comfort or pleasure from this world.[1] At midnight he would arise to study Torah. During most of the day he would teach his students.

From Salonika R' Shlomo went to Adrianopol where he settled among the scholars living there and became very friendly with them. As soon as they became aware of his stature, they flocked to him. When he was planning to leave and go up to Tsefas, he and the scholars of Adrianopol made a pact of friendship. As his parting gift to them, he wrote *Bris Halevi*, a commentary on the *Haggadah* in which he explains the Exodus according to *Kabbalah*.

His other famous works are *Ayeles Ahavim* on *Shir HaShirim* and *Shoresh Yishai* on *Megillas Ruth*.

He lived to a ripe old age in Tsefas and studied Torah in purity and sanctity. Here, too, many students came to learn the secrets of Torah at his feet.[2]

The Revelation on Shavuos Night

On the eve of *Shavuos* R' Shlomo Alkabetz was granted *ruach hakodesh* and heard the secrets of *Kabbalah* which were revealed to R' Yosef Karo by his angel *maggid*.

The *mekubalim* of Tsefas, with R' Yosef Karo at their head and R' Shlomo in their midst, assembled to study together throughout this night of *kabbolas haTorah*. They devoted themselves to a *Tikkun Leil Shavuos*, which R' Shlomo had compiled. They recited it with a *niggun* and felt themselves becoming more exalted, rising and soaring beyond human limits. When they had completed the *Tikkun*, they turned to *mishnayos*, explaining their mystical significance. Then, suddenly, they heard the voice of the *maggid* issuing forth from the throat of the *Beis Yosef*, clear and resonant. There were other people present in the *beis midrash* but only that group heard the voice. They were so overcome by awe that they could not even lift their heads or move.

The *maggid* told the members of that group that their devotion to the *Tikkun* caused great pleasure in Heaven. From the time of the Destruction of the *Beis Hamikdash*, nothing had been as gratifying in the upper spheres. "Rejoice in your endeavor," the angel said, "and in the knowledge that all the angels in Heaven stand and listen to your voice. Be strong and continue, for your Torah is sweet to *Hakadosh baruch Hu*. Rise, now, and declare aloud, as on *Yom Kippur*: '*Baruch Shem kevod malchuso le'olam va'ed.*'"

When they heard this, all the members of the group rose as one and cried out feelingly and strongly, "*Baruch Shem kevod malchuso le'olam va'ed.*" And then the voice of the angel reached their ears again, calling upon them to resume their study, promising them a shower of blessing and guaranteeing them the best that *Gan Eden* has to offer in the World-to-Come.

They sat down and continued their study on into the next day and into the next night, which is the second night of *Shavuos* outside of *Eretz Yisrael*. Again, they said *Tikkun* and again at midnight they heard the voice of the *maggid* issuing forth. The angel revealed to them Heavenly secrets which they had never heard before and he blessed and praised them once again, telling them how much their efforts were commended by Heaven.

The secrets which they learned during those two nights were such that few mortals in all history had been privileged to hear. But, the men who composed this group were indeed worthy of such a sublime revelation.[3]

90 / THE ARIZAL

The Fig Tree Takes Revenge

R' Shlomo Halevi remained in Tsefas for many years, adored and honored. The Arabs were envious that the Jews had so wise and esteemed a leader and schemed to do away with him.

"How can we murder him without being discovered?" they asked one another in their councils. "If the governor learns that we murdered the Jewish rabbi, he will surely punish us severely."

Then one of the evil plotters rose and said, "I know! The rabbi is accustomed to go out to the mountains seeking solitude for his meditations. One of us will follow him and murder him with no fear of any witnesses."

The plan was received with enthusiasm. Immediately, one of the gang volunteered to stalk R' Shlomo and ambush him. And so, one day when R' Shlomo was all alone far beyond the city and his mind was wandering among the heavenly spheres, the Arab fell upon him and murdered him. He then carried the corpse to his home and buried it under a fig tree in his yard.

Tsefas was in fear and confusion. R' Shlomo Alkabetz had been missing for several days. Had something happened to him? Had a loose boulder fallen upon him, G-d forbid, or had a wild beast attacked him? Perhaps he was lying somewhere, wounded, in dire need of help. Groups of Jews combed the surrounding mountains. They searched caves and crevices, highways and byways — but in vain. There was no trace of their beloved rabbi.

The Jewish community was still anxious and fearful when an amazing report flew threw the city. The fig tree in Achmed the Arab's garden had suddenly begun to bloom out of season, producing the finest, most delectable fruits that anyone had ever tasted. And this, at a time when all the other fig trees were still bare! The people of Tsefas thought that Achmed was a sorcerer to have been able to effect such a miracle.

Word of the strange phenomenon reached the ears of the local governor, who refused to believe the report. "Do you think I am softheaded to be taken in by such foolishness? No fig tree bears fruit at this time of year! And you claim that the tree is bowed down by its load of ripe fruit. Impossible!" But when more reports arrived of this untimely harvest, the *pasha* decided to see for himself.

When Achmed saw the governor approaching his house, he ran out and bowed obsequiously before him, then led him into his courtyard where the miraculous fig tree stood, its branches heavy with luscious fruit. The governor looked at it unbelievingly and thought, "If only I knew the secret of this tree, I could have an orchard full of all kinds of fruits, ready for eating at any time I chose. I would be the envy of the entire area. And I could sell these fruits and become fabulously rich!"

Turning to the fawning Achmed, he said, "Listen here, I see that you must have a secret formula. You must share it with me for I wish to produce similar fruit in my own gardens. Well, then, what is it?"

Achmed stood there, dumbstruck.

The governor grew impatient. "Tell me at once! I demand that you reveal your secret," he thundered at the quaking Arab peasant, his bushy mustache bristling. "Do you think that you can keep your knowledge to yourself and get rich quick? No! Oh no! Speak, or I will order that you be given ninety lashes on your bare soles! And if you continue to keep your silence, your end will be bitter,

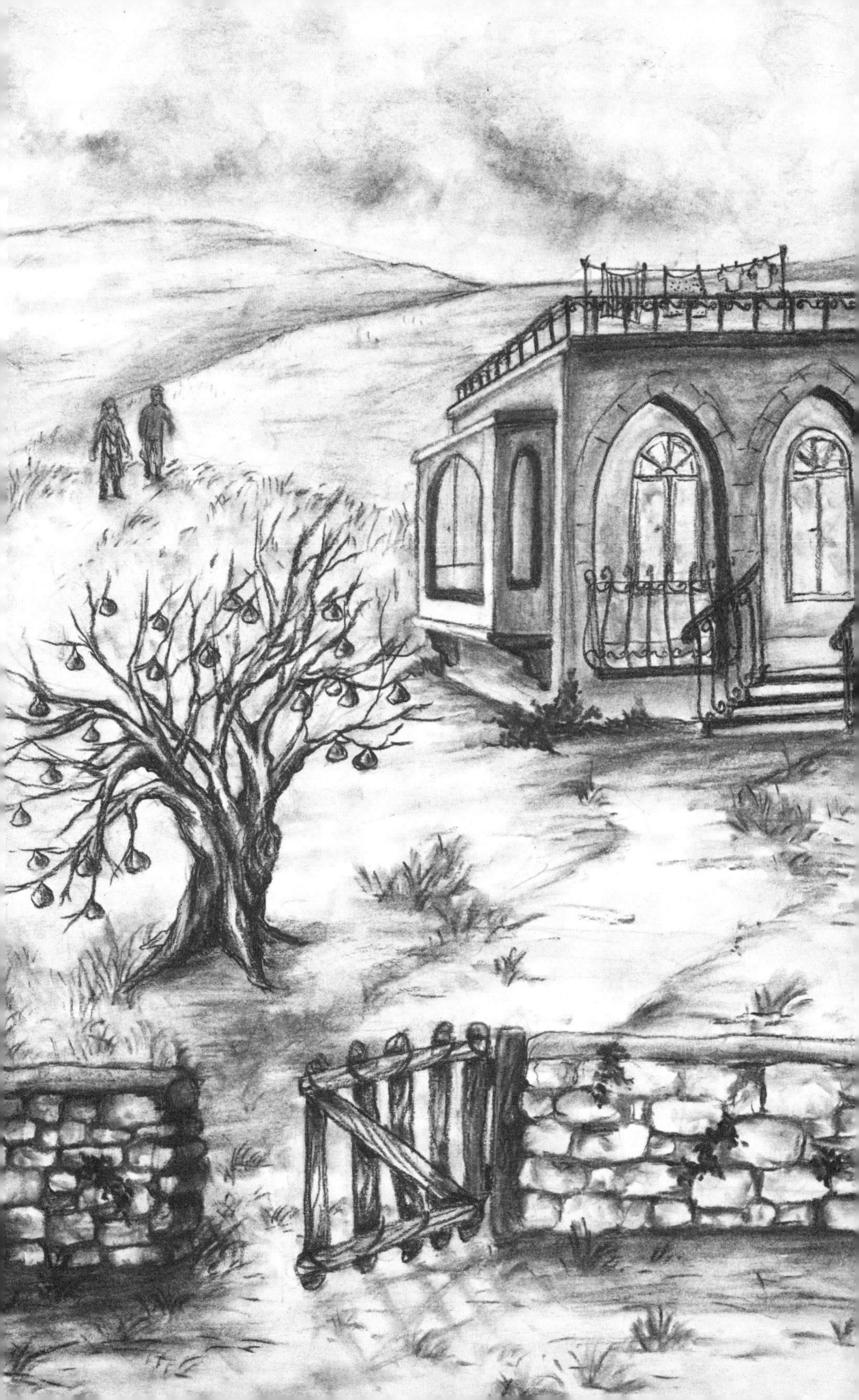

indeed!"

Achmed's eyes grew round with terror and he began shaking like a leaf. But he was unable to utter a word. The governor turned to his bodyguard and told him to tie the Arab up for the flogging. After two or three lashes, Achmed broke down and told the governor the truth — how he had laid ambush to the Jewish sage and murderered him in cold blood. He described how he had dragged the body home to his yard and buried it under the fig tree where he was sure that no one would discover it. Only a short while later, that tree had begun producing the strange fruit.

This solved the mystery of the rabbi's disappearance. Deep mourning settled down upon the entire Jewish population. Nor was their sorrow tempered by the fact that Achmed was duly punished; he was hanged upon the very tree which had borne witness against him, the fig tree under which R' Shlomo Alkabetz lay buried.

This posthumous miracle showed the Jews how great their beloved rabbi had been, for he had succeeded in pointing the accusing finger at his murderer even after his death.[4]

R' Moshe Cordovero

One of R' Shlomo's most prominent disciples was R' Moshe ben R' Yaakov Cordovero, who eventually married his master's sister and become his brother-in-law.

R' Moshe was born in Tsefas in 5282 (1522) and lived for a brief forty-eight years. He acquired his knowledge in the revealed Torah from R' Yosef Karo and studied with extreme dedication and fervor, thus gaining his master's high esteem and favor. R' Yosef showed this in speaking about his *talmid*, "My son, if your heart is wise, I am all the more happy myself" (*Avkas Rochel, Siman 91*).

After he was filled with the knowledge of the revealed Torah, his master, the *Beis Yosef*, introduced him to the study of *Kabbalah*. But his most important teacher in the knowledge of the mystic was his brother-in-law, R' Shlomo Alkabetz.

With time, R' Moshe Cordovero, the student, became Ramak the teacher and many disciples gathered about him. Aside from being their master and teacher, he was also a *dayan* and a mediator of personal arguments.[5]

It is said that Eliyahu revealed himself to him, also.

In his brief forty-eight years, the Ramak succeeded in enriching Jewish Torah literature with many works, most of them dealing with *Kabbalah*. He wrote, among other things, *Pardes Rimonim*; a commentary on the *Zohar* called *Or Yakar*; *Gerushin*, which received this title because it was written when he assumed a self-imposed exile and considered himself 'banished' for the sake of the *Shechinah*; *Tomer Devorah*, a *musar* work arranged according to the Thirteen Attributes of Mercy (*yud-gimmel middos*), and other works on the *siddur* and *Yom Kippur machzor*. These display his creative ideas in *Kabbalah*.

However, this did not come to him easily. His disciple, R' Chaim Vital, writes that when R' Moshe Cordovero used to study the *Zohar* during his periods of retreat, after midnight, Satan would employ his wiles through all kinds of disturbances to divert his attention from his holy study. The Ramak would have to concentrate intently in order to overcome these distractions and when he saw that he was succumbing, he would pray, invoking holy Names of *Hashem* to protect him and banish the evil forces.

In 5330 (1570), when he was led to his final rest, he was eulogized by his master in the revealed, R' Yosef Karo, who said: "Here lies buried the ark of the Torah!"

Like sheep gather around a well to drink, so had his students, the great rabbis of Tsefas, flocked to the Ramak to drink of his fountain of knowledge in *Kabbalah*. His most outstanding disciple was R' Chaim Vital, and the rest of the Ramak's students now drew about him as their leader.

The Dream and the Notebook

Heaven chose to reveal sublime secrets to R' Chaim in his dreams and he recorded them. One such dream shows the greatness of the disciples of the Ramak and how they sanctified and purified themselves.

In 5300 (1570), the year that the Ramak passed away, the elite of Tsefas' scholars gathered and made up to meet each Friday night in the *beis knesses* where one of them, in turn, would relate what he had done during the past week. They thought that if someone had committed a sin or had not been careful enough in his deeds, he would become ashamed of himself through this public confession and this shame would serve as part of his atonement. And, from then on he would be sure to avoid evil acts.

R' Chaim was opposed to this. He thought that the members of the group would not be open; they would refrain from confessing their shortcomings and if they did, they would eventually stop being embarrassed, which would cause more harm than good. Hence, R' Chaim kept away from those meetings.

On the Friday evening of the first meeting, R' Chaim had a dream. He saw himself walking down the road, leading to the butchers' market. When he came to a fork in the road he suddenly noticed that his deceased father was coming towards him from one direction while from the other side, on the road ascending from the cemetery to the city, the Ramak and R' Moshe Sagis were approaching, followed by the souls of many Jews long departed. These souls were descending from heaven. The Ramak and R' Moshe held a notebook in their arms listing the names of many of the sages of Tsefas. They read off the names in a whisper: the first was that of R' Shlomo Sagis, the second, R' Chaim Vital and, then, all the *talmidei chachamim* of the city.

When R' Chaim saw this, he was frightened. Was this, perhaps, a list of the people who would die that year?

When the Ramak and his friend had drawn closer, R' Chaim begged his master to tell him what the names in his notebooks signified and if the list was, as he suspected, that of the men destined to die shortly. If that was so, he begged that his teacher tell him how to conduct himself so that he might repent properly before his death.

When his teacher heard his fears, he reassured him, "Those listed in this notebook are the scholars to whom Heaven has granted special assistance in repenting. This very evening they are gathered in the *beis knesses*, examining their deeds and repenting." His tone became accusing, "But you refuse to participate in such a worthwhile gathering!"

R' Chaim tried to justify himself and explain why he had stayed away, but his master refused to accept his excuses. R' Chaim then asked, "Why did the name of R'

Shlomo Sagis appear at the head of the list when I am your chief disciple and the leader of the inner circle of *talmidim*? What has he done to deserve that honor?"

"You are right in assuming that you are my favorite disciple, my dear Chaim. But R' Shlomo has earned the privilege of heading the list of the people this time since it was his father, R' Moshe, who thought of the original idea of gathering for *teshuvah* and he has brought it into being and organized tonight's gathering in the *beis knesses*.[6]

---

1. "Reishis Chochmah", Shaar Hekedushah, chap. 7 2. "Shem Hagedolim" on him, Os 300, Siman 26
3. "Shnei Luchos Habris" Maseches Shevuous; "Uleheraos"
4. "Kav Yayashar" chap. 86
5. Introduction to the Rama of Pano's "Pelach Harimon"
6. "Shivchei R' Chaim Vital" (Jerusalem 5718) p.32

CHAPTER NINE

THE 'LION' ASCENDS FROM EGYPT

It was to this large, vibrant, flourishing city, rich in its spirit and its great scholars, that the Ari and his family came in 5330 (1570) — he, his wife, his sons and his widowed mother.

They came without fanfare, without arousing any interest. The Ari did not wish to draw any attention to his stature in either the revealed or the mystic. He rejoiced in the reunion with his teachers from Egypt, among them the Radbaz, and they were equally glad to see him. Little did they know how much their gifted student had accomplished and what heights he had reached.

The Ari had realized while yet in Egypt that in his new home he would have to find some means of livelihood. Even there, under the wing of his benevolent uncle and father-in-law, R' Mordechai Francis, he had, now and then, had business dealings and so, he was not altogether inexperienced. Upon his arrival, he opened up a business where he spent most of his daytime hours.[1] His many affairs, at times, took him out of the city.

The Ari made the acquaintance of the grandson of R' Yaakov Beirav, R' Yaakov Abulafya, who was an erudite scholar; he bore the title *Chacham Hakahal.*[2] Yaakov had been born in Egypt and often revisited it. He, possibly, served as a link between the Ari and the merchants with whom he dealt.

Mysterious Herds in the Desert

Once, as R' Yaakov was preparing for another of his trips to Egypt, he approached the Ari. Before he even had a chance to open his mouth, the Ari said to him, "I know all about your forthcoming journey; I know that you have come to ask me for a letter of recommendation to the leaders in Egypt. In fact, I have already prepared such a letter for you which should open all gates to you. Here, take it and go in peace." The Ari gave the letter to R' Yaakov, adding, "Your trip has an additional importance and urgency about which you will find out on your way back. Go there and hurry back, even though your mission has no ostensible purpose connected with a *mitzvah*."

R' Yaakov took the letter which the Ari had prepared even before he had asked for it. He finished his preparations hastily and set out.

R' Yaakov successfully accomplished all that he had set out to do in Egypt. R' Yitzchak Luria's letter of recommendation was like a magic wand, opening all doors before him. People helped him in every way imaginable, so that he was able to efficiently discharge all of his duties. It was not long before he was ready to pack his belongings and return home.

R' Yaakov went out to look for a camel caravan which he could join in his journey across the Sinai desert. But his acquaintances told him that he should buy a donkey and join a train of horses which was about to set out for *Eretz Yisrael*. This was a far more comfortable way of travelling than by camel.

R' Yaakov agreed. He bought a sturdy beast which would be able to carry him and his belongings. Then he signed up with the caravan, paying the fee which entitled him to passage and protection across the desert.

The journey was most exhausting. Desert in all directions — sand and more sand. The caravan stopped at the occasional oases. The travelers would water their thirsty animals, rest under the palm trees and taste of the dates, gifts from heaven in the midst of the desolation. R' Yaakov truly appreciated the fruit and recited the blessings before and after eating with great fervor.

At one such oasis, R' Yaakov gratefully got off his donkey's back and found himself a shady spot to rest. He put his saddlebag under his head for a pillow and was soon fast asleep. He was so exhausted by the traveling that he fell into a deep slumber and did not hear his companions preparing to continue on. Nor did they notice him, so busy were they with their own activities.

R' Yaakov slept on for a few hours before awakening.

He opened his eyes and looked all around. "What is this?" he asked himself in surprise. "Where is everyone? Where is the caravan?" There was nothing in sight but the monotonous yellow sand and the cloudless blue sky — no trace of man or beast. "I must have slept for a long time," he concluded. "Long enough for them to have disappeared from sight."

He saddled his donkey and prodded it to trot forward at top speed. R' Yaakov hoped to overtake the caravan. At first, he was able to follow the way they had traveled because the tracks were still fresh but as he went on, the evening wind began blowing, erasing all traces of the caravan. R' Yaakov was lost.

What could he do? How would he ever find his way in this desolate wilderness which had no landmarks? He knew nothing about desert lore. R' Yaakov put his trust in *Hashem* and prayed that He would bring him safely to some settlement. "Even though I walk through the valley of the shadow of death," he prayed in the words of *Tehillim*, "I will fear no evil for You are with me."

The sun was setting. R' Yaakov still wandered aimlessly. With no shelter or defense against wild beasts, he felt utterly helpless. Then he looked around and saw a herd of cattle being led by a herdsman. "At last!" he breathed a sigh of relief. "I will surely be able to spend the night with him and find shelter from the dangers of the desert. When morning comes, the herdsman will direct me to the nearest town." He urged his donkey on so that he might reach the herd before nightfall.

When he drew near, he saw the strangest sight. The cattle were plowing the earth. The man was beating them mercilessly when suddenly, he turned into one of the bullocks while another of the animals turned into a man and he now began beating the rest of the animals viciously.

R' Yaakov did not believe his eyes. Was this a dream, a desert mirage? But he saw it so clearly. Again and again the herdsman turned into a beast and a beast became a herdsman who beat the others brutally.

What did this all mean? R' Yaakov was petrified.

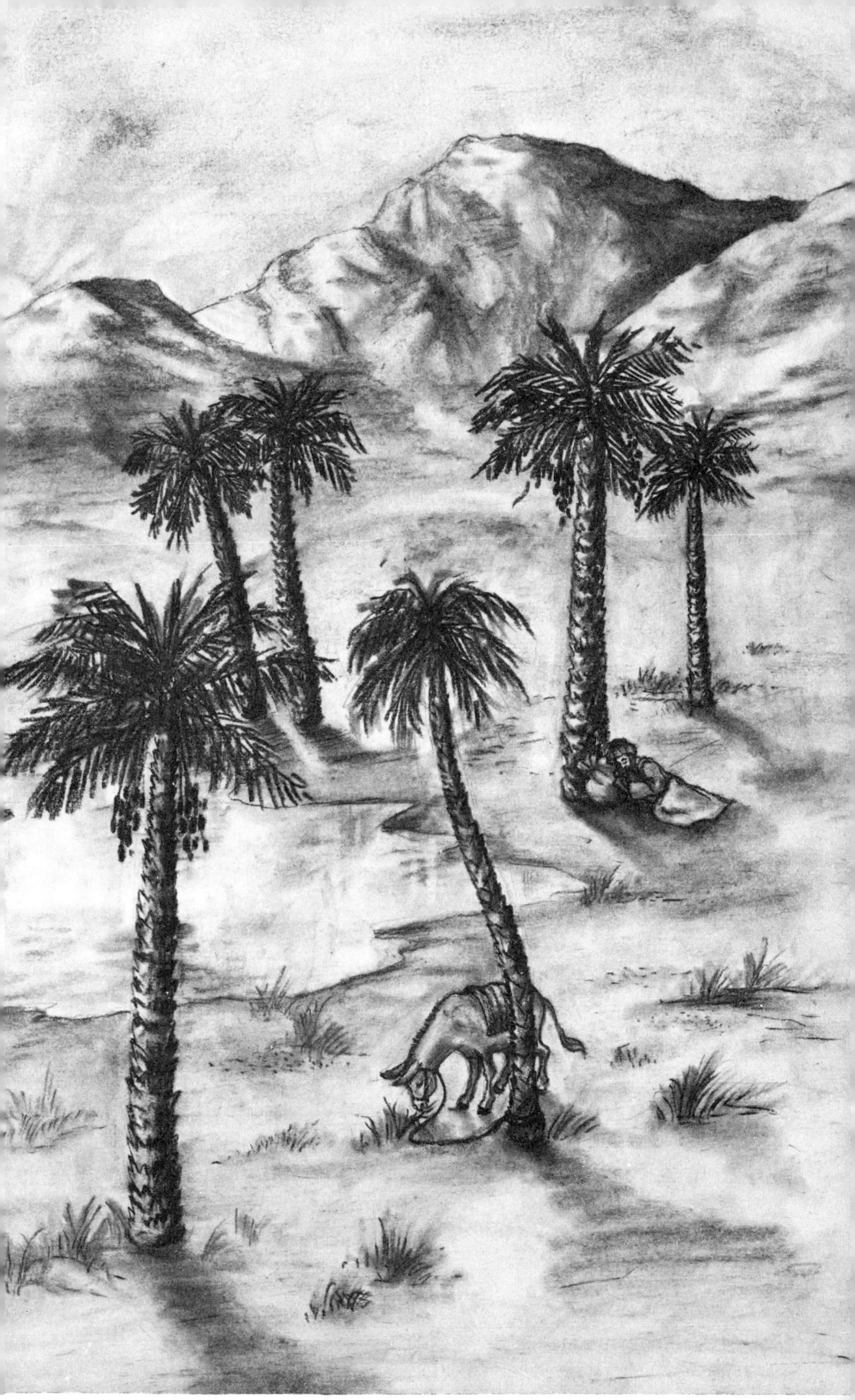

Meanwhile, the sun had set and the moon now rose from the east, round and full. By its eerie silvery light he saw that the entire herd had taken on human form. They faced him and wept bitterly, "Rebbe! By your appearance and clothing, you must be a Jew from Tsefas." R' Yaakov nodded, spellbound. "Do you know R' Yitzchak Luria Ashkenazi of Tsefas?" they implored hopelessly.

"Yes, I know him! I was on my way back to Tsefas upon a mission for him when I lost my way in the desert. When I saw you from afar, I came to ask you for directions to *Eretz Yisrael*."

When the oxen-men heard his words, they threw themselves at his feet. "You have seen how we are suffering," they wept. "There is no one who can help us except the Ari in Tsefas. We beg of you: when you return there, tell him of our plight. Tell him that we can no longer bear our terrible torture and that he give us a *tikkun* for our souls so that we may find some peace!"

R' Yaakov's tender heart melted in sympathy. He sincerely promised to do what they had asked. The strange creatures then led him to the road and accompanied him until he caught up with his caravan. Now he could continue on with them.

As soon as he returned to Tsefas, R' Yaakov immediately went to the Ari. R' Yitzchak greeted the weary traveler and before the latter even had a chance to open his mouth, the Ari recounted exactly what had happened to him. He explained to the astonished R' Yaakov that those creatures had, in their lifetime, shaved with a razor, which is forbidden by the Torah, and had been sentenced to their punishment by the Heavenly court. "The time has now come to save them," the Ari concluded. He told R' Yaakov exactly what he must do in order for those souls to have their *tikkun*.

R' Yaakov fulfilled the Ari's instructions to the letter: he prayed for the lost souls, fasted the number of required fasts and mortified himself with the necessary *sigufim* (torments) in order to redeem them. When he had done all that he should, those people appeared to him in a dream and told him that they had finally been released from their terrible fate, thanks to his efforts."[3]

Who Shall Succeed the Ramak?

The Ari had been told in Egypt that R' Chaim Vital would be the one to record his teachings and spread them throughout the world. R' Yitzchak waited for the suitable opportunity to tell him this. But, when the Ari came to Tsefas, R' Chaim was studying under the Ramak.

And after R' Yitzchak settled in Tsefas, he also drew close to the Ramak and began studying *Kabbalah* with him.

The great *mekubal* saw at once that the Ari was concealing his greatness. The Ramak regarded the Ari as the most suitable candidate to succeed him and began grooming him for the difficult task of both guiding his flock and teaching *Kabbalah*.

But, the two giants were not destined to have much time together. In 5300 (1570), the very year in which the Ari settled in Tsefas, R' Moshe Cordovero passed away.

It was the 23rd day of *Tammuz*. The city of Tsefas was devastated by the terrible news — their saintly rabbi was on his deathbed. Everyone rushed to the *beis knesses* to pour out his heart in prayer to the Healer of all flesh that He send R' Moshe a speedy recovery. Those closest to him, the heads of the community and his intimate disciples, rushed to R' Moshe's home to be at his side. There, they sobbingly prayed that their master recover and not end his fruitful life at such a young age (he was only forty-eight). But the Ramak lay in bed, pale and motionless, seemingly lifeless.

Suddenly, he opened his eyes and indicated to his disciples that he wished to tell them something. All ears were attuned. Hearts fluttered, knowing that R' Moshe was about to impart his last words to them.

With a weak but clear voice, he slowly began, "I want you to know, my dear colleagues and students, that today I am leaving you and going to my eternal rest. Heaven has informed me that one of you, a wise man from Tsefas, will open your eyes to the light of *Kabbalah*. His way and my way are different, but they do not conflict. Know, my dear students, that when I began to teach you *Toras hanistar*, the channels through which the secrets of the Torah pass were still closed. The people worthy of knowing them, the great leaders of the previous generations, were unable to absorb many concepts without exerting themselves to the utmost. After my death, however, these channels of blessing will be opened and the *tzaddikim* of this generation will be able to fathom many hidden secrets. The man to whom I have alluded has already grasped them and will reveal them to you. His teachings are more profound that those you learned from me and so, you must not suspect him of challenging my teachings or negating them for his Torah is true."

R' Moshe's tremulous voice was silent. The students surrounding his bed did not know how to interpret his words. Till now, they had thought that the greatest among them, R' Chaim Vital, was the leader whom he had groomed all along to replace him, for he had been closest to R' Moshe and had best understood his teachings. But from R' Moshe's words it was apparent that some anonymous, unnamed wise man would fill his place and would show them a different approach to *Kabbalah*. "Who could he be?" they wondered. And what innovations would he introduce?

One of the great men present broke the silence that had gripped them until now. His eyes damp with tears, he approached the deathbed and whispered pleadingly, "I beseech you, reveal to us who that man is? To whom is the master referring?"

The Ramak summoned the remainder of his strength and in a faint whisper said, "I will not divulge his name. But I will give you a sign by which you can recognize him when the time comes. The one who will see the pillar of cloud rising before my bier — he is destined to carry on my work."[4]

These were R' Moshe's final words. He closed his eyes for the last time and a thunderous *"Shema Yisrael..."* which shook the very walls of the building burst forth unanimously from the throats of those present.

The weeping and wailing were heard from within the house and told everyone in Tsefas the bitter news. Deep mourning descended upon the city and its surrounding villages. Multitudes of weeping people streamed to the home of the departed to take part in his funeral. All the shops and businesses were shut and many of the Arabs, including the *pasha* himself, came to pay their respects to the Jewish sage.

The funeral bier was taken out of the house, borne by the disciples of the Ramak. The rabbis of Tsefas and its great scholars followed, reciting *Tehillim* in heart-broken tones. And behind them came the huge crowd with bowed heads and tearful eyes.

The procession advanced slowly towards the cemetery at the outskirts of the city. Each time it reached a *beis knesses*, it stopped and one of the students recited *kaddish*.

The grave was closed. Little Gedalyah, the Ramak's son, now said the *kaddish* in his childish treble. People could hardly answer the *amen* and when he had finished, they burst into unabashed wailing.

Maran R' Yosef Karo, the rabbi of Tsefas and R' Moshe's teacher, eulogized him as did other great figures of Tsefas.

When they had finished, one of the *talmidim* of the Ramak asked R' Yitzchak Ashkenazi to say a few words.

There were a few raised eyebrows and questioning glances. Why had he been singled out with such a privilege? He had come to Tsefas only a short while ago and, even though it had been apparent, at once, that he was learned and had even studied briefly with the Ramak — still, he did not yet deserve to be numbered among the foremost of the city.

Without hesitation, R' Yitzchak drew near to speak. He first emphasized that the *tzaddik*'s death was not a punishment for his deeds. On the contrary, the Ramak had been whole and perfect in all his ways. He explained the verse, "If a man commits a sin deserving of death and he is put to death, you shall hang him on a tree (*Devarim* 21:22)" in the following manner. The word *chet* is to be taken as 'a lack', rather than in its conventional meaning of 'sin'. And this was to be how the verse was interpreted: If a man shall lack a reason to die — that is, if he is altogether worthy — and dies nevertheless, you must 'hang' — attribute — his death to the tree — the

Tree of Knowledge, the fruit of which Adam tasted and brought death to the world. The *tzaddik* R' Moshe was perfect. The only reason he had died was because of Adam's sin which brought death to the entire world."[5]

The *hespedim* were over; the crowd had dispersed. Only a few devoted disciples remained behind at the grave, not ready to part from their beloved master. As they stood there, broken-hearted, a member of the *chevrah kadishah* came up to them. It was the man who had called upon the Ari to speak.

"Did you wonder why I called upon the Ari?" he asked. "I will tell you. When we were about to dig a grave for our master, we went to that section of the cemetery where the most distinguished sages of Tsefas are buried. But R' Yitzchak approached us and said that we had not chosen the right site. He said that the pillar of cloud which preceded our master's bier did not stop there but had gone on to a different place. And that is where we buried the Ramak. When I heard his words, I could not help but remember our leader's last message. Do you remember it?"

The small group nodded as one. They were stunned by this revelation. "Our master said that whoever saw the pillar of cloud preceding his stretcher was the one destined to assume his position as master and leader! We must now wait for R' Yitzchak to reveal himself to us so that we can sit before him and drink from his wisdom."

Some were impatient and turned then and there to the Ari and begged him to teach them.

"We want you to become our master," they pleaded. "We will obey you in all that you command us, as devoted *talmidim*."

At first he shied away, explaining that his method of

THE 'LION' ASCENDS FROM EGYPT / 109

study in *Kabbalah* was different from the one to which they had become accustomed, but when they persisted repeatedly, he finally gave in and began to teach them.

Three Times 'Ashrei'

When the sages of Tsefas heard that the Ari had become the teacher of the Ramak's students, they had doubts as to whether or not this was proper. For, until now, the Ari had concealed his light. Even his former teachers from Egypt, who were now living in Tsefas, were unaware of the Ari's true stature.

The Radbaz, the most elderly of them, also feared that the Ari was not a proper successor to the Ramak in the field of *Kabbalah*. He sent for him and said: "I beg of you, my dear disciple, do not teach mysticism for you are not yet ready for it."

The Ari listened to his master respectfully but made no definite commitment.

The Ramak's students continued to beg him to show them the true path of study and he felt obliged to satisfy their thirst. He remembered the words of Eliyahu Hanavi who had told him that his years were numbered and that in Tsefas he would have to reveal himself and spread his teachings abroad. Time was short and there was so much to teach! He could not possibly give in to his master's warning not to teach yet, especially since the Radbaz was mistaken.

When R' David ben Zimra saw that R' Yitzchak Luria was ignoring his explicit request, he decided to clearly prove to the Ari himself that he was not yet fit to teach such advanced students. He sent R' Bezalel Ashkenazi, the great *mekubal* who had studied with the Ari in Egypt, to listen in on one of R' Yitzchak's *shiurim* and to demolish its very foundations.

R' Bezalel dutifully went. When he arrived at the *beis midrash* he discovered, to his amazement, that the Radbaz himself was listening, spellbound, to the Ari. R' Bezalel sat down and began to listen intently himself. His awe and wonder grew by the moment.

When he went to report to the Radbaz, he could not contain his amazement for R' David asked him, "Did you follow through on what we talked about? Did you challenge him?"

"How could I do such a thing?" he asked. "Did I not see you yourself, my master and teacher, sitting there in the audience, enthralled by the wisdom flowing from the Ari's mouth? And I will not deny that I, too, was captivated by the truth of his teachings and the depth of his thinking."

The Radbaz understood that Eliyahu Hanavi must have assumed his form and come to protect the honor of the Arizal. From then on he no longer opposed the Ari's teaching *Kabbalah*.

R' Yaakov David of Slutzk (the Ridbaz) used to tell the above story in the name of the *Gaon* of Vilna, adding that when the *Gra* related it, he would conclude thus: "*Ashrei! Ashrei! Ashrei* (Fortunate!)" Fortunate was the Arizal that Eliyahu Hanavi attended his lecture; fortunate was the Radbaz, whose form Eliyahu assumed and fortunate was R' Bezalel who had the privilege of seeing him![6]

R' Chaim Vital Tests

During this time, R' Chaim Vital was in Damascus, continuing the life work of his master, the Ramak — a commentary on the *Zohar*. When he heard rumors that the young Ari was teaching *Kabbalah* to the Ramak's students in Tsefas, he was very displeased. He had not been present when R' Moshe Cordovero, on his deathbed, spoke about his successor and he knew nothing about the sign which he had given them. He did know, however, that the Ari's method of study differed substantially from the Ramak's approach; he could not understand how so many of his own friends, students of R' Moshe, could change their *derech* in study. R' Yitzchak Luria, he maintained, was very young and had not yet proven himself worthy of the prestigious mantle which he had assumed.

The Ari was very sorely grieved by R' Chaim Vital's attitude. He had come to Tsefas, specifically, to teach R' Chaim who was to carry on his vital work after he passed away. But he did not turn directly to R' Chaim and beg him to come and hear his *shiurim*. His divine intuition told him that R' Chaim must come of his own initiative and be won over. Throughout his stay in Damascus, R' Chaim was haunted by dreams and visions, urging him to seek out the Ari and accept him as his teacher. But as soon as he awoke, he would belittle those dreams as disturbing but inconsequential thoughts.

Once, while he was still laboring over the work on the *Zohar*, he found himself involved in a deep *sugyah* which he could not understand. As soon as he thought he had mastered the difficulty by answering one set of questions, another set surfaced to refute them, more difficult than the first. He wrote and erased, wrote and once more erased, again and again. He had to admit that he had reached an impasse. R' Chaim was deeply troubled. He fasted and mortified himself, pouring tearful prayers before G-d, Who grants man understanding, to enable him to solve the problem. One night, as he was sleeping, he dreamt that he was told as follows, "If you return to Tsefas and study under the Ari, this difficult passage in the *Zohar* will become clear to you."

When he awoke this time, he did not dismiss the dream as before. He decided to do what he had been told and to present his questions to the Ari. This would be the determining test. This would show him whether the Ari was worthy of becoming his master or not.

R' Chaim gathered up his belongings, his books and his writings and set out for the capital of the Galilee. When he reached the city, he sought out the home of R' Yitzchak Luria. Following the directions which he was given, he descended to the lower part of town and turned into a narrow alley by the slaughterhouse. There, near the Sefardi *beis knesses* known as the 'Eliyahu Hanavi Synagogue', not far from the cemetery, he found the home of the saintly man he was seeking. He knocked at the door and asked if he could see R' Yitzchak.

"R' Yitzchak?" said the person at the door. "He is never home at this time of day. If you wish to find him, you must go to his store."

R' Chaim found the store without much difficulty. From the doorway he could see the Ari bent over his account books. He felt a bitter distaste. Was this the person he had traveled so many miles to meet? "I see I was right in the first place in laughing at my dreams. Dreams are not worth a fig," he thought. "How could such a man, who is so engrossed in the empty affairs of this world, mundane matters such as columns of figures in an account book — how could such a man know the most complex of hidden secrets? One who wishes to study *Kabbalah* must devote his entire life to it and not dabble in it after business hours!"

R' Chaim was filled with disappointment and turned to leave the building without even having spoken to the Ari. R' Yitzchak had known immediately who he was and even knew that R' Chaim had come to test him. Now, he had that golden opportunity to win him over. He went over to him in a friendly manner and said, "And how can I help you, sir? What would you like to buy?"

R' Chaim looked at him morosely and said wearily, "I have not come here to purchase goods of this world but to seek truth in Torah. I see, however, that this is not the proper time. You are involved in business matters."

The Ari smiled indulgently. "I know exactly why you have come. You are troubled by a complex matter in the *Zohar* which deals with..."

R' Chaim now realized that it was not a simple businessman who stood before him but a man of divine intuition. He allowed himself to be led aside to a small room and began speaking with the Ari. R' Yitzchak divulged to him sublime secrets which he had never heard before. R' Chaim listened avidly, drinking in every precious word and his soul thirsted for more.

"R' Yitzchak," he finally turned to him, deeply moved, "I have heard marvelous things fall from your holy lips just now. But you still have not answered the difficulty which has brought me all the way here. Can you explain that?"

"All that I have spoken to you just now is what

Heaven allowed me to reveal. Anything beyond that must, as yet, remain sealed to you."

R' Chaim left. His soul was not satisfied. He went to the nearby *beis knesses,* opened the *aron kodesh* and poured out his heart before his Creator, begging Him to permit the Ari to divulge more of his secret knowledge. When he returned home, he resumed his fasting and prayed in the hope that *Hashem* would deem him worthy of studying under the Ari.

Early the next morning, he returned to the narrow alley that led past the 'Eliyahu Hanavi Synagogue' to R' Yitzchak's house. He hoped to catch him before he went to work. When he saw him, he fell at his feet and kissed them. R' Chaim wept and pleaded that the Ari allow him to join the group of his *talmidim* which heard his lectures in *Kabbalah.*

The Ari raised him to his feet and said, "Know that your prayers yesterday opened up the channels of bountiful blessing for you." He went on to tell R' Chaim how, back in Egypt, Eliyahu Hanavi had informed him that he, R' Chaim, was destined to carry on his work and disseminate his teachings. At this meeting he also solved the difficulties which had so puzzled R' Chaim and brought him all the way to Tsefas. He won R' Chaim's undivided admiration and loyalty forever more.

From then on, R' Chaim sat among the disciples of the Ari. He served the Ari faithfully and became his most devoted follower. And he took care to record every precious word.[7]

R' Chaim writes of his spiritual development. He tells us how he once made an *aliyas neshamah* — his soul separated itself from his body and wept soaring up to Heaven and asked for divine assistance in study. What must he do to be able to grasp even deeper concepts in Torah and *Kabbalah*? He was told that if he fasted for forty consecutive days in sackcloth and ashes and then continued to fast every Monday and Thursday for another two and a half years, he would attain a purity of thought which was totally devoid of any influence from the powers of evil. He was also told that at the end of the first month of fasting he would already be purged from the sin of lightheadedness. Three days of humility and modesty would bring him to the level of *ruach hakodesh*.

R' Chaim followed these instructions. Throughout this period he consulted his master, the Ari, and received his blessing that he be able to accomplish what he was striving for. "My master promised," he writes, "that a soul of a departed *tzaddik* would assist me to increase my *yiras shamayim* and especially my humility. These two qualities would enable me to see a great light and grasp the most hidden secrets of the Torah."

The Ramak Confirms

"Our Master said that at the point where philosophy ends *Kabbalah* begins. And, at the point where the *Kabbalistic* teachings of the Ramak end, the teachings of the Ari begin."

R' Chaim of Volozhin wrote the above words in the name of his teacher, the *Gaon* of Vilna.[8] The Ramak himself said as much when, three months after his death, he appeared to R' Chaim Vital in a dream. He then told him that the *Kabbalistic* teachings of the Arizal were more fundamental than his own, adding that in the World of Truth he himself studied *Kabbalah* according to the Ari's approach.⁹

R' Moshe Cordovero's fears, expressed upon his deathbed, were realized. As soon as word went out that the Ari's approach differed radically from his predecessor's, many of the *mekubalim* of Tsefas arose in opposition. They sought to test the Ari and show him that he was misguided.

Late one night, R' Yitzchak was lecturing to his students. In his audience sat one of the *talmidim* of the Ramak who refused to accept the Ari's school of thought. In the midst of the lecture he commented that what he had just been said directly contradicted the Ramak's teachings. R' Yitzchak ignored his remark and continued as if nothing had happened.

That scholar thought that the Ari had not reacted because he had no answer to the challenge. He interrupted again with further criticism. R' Yitzchak was forced to react now, and said, "Have you come to uphold the honor of your teacher? Well then, know that he is also listening to this *shiur* in Heaven. And when he heard your remarks he said, 'A pity on my disciple who did not undertand what I said. Otherwise he would not have said that the Ari was contradicting me.'"

The man was not yet satisfied and demanded, "R' Yitzchak Ashkenazi, bring proof that what you just said about the Ramak is true! If not, I will conclude that you made it all up."

The Ari addressed the rest of his audience and said, "Wait a moment while I ask R' Moshe Cordovero to give me a sign that this *talmid* is in the wrong." He then became silent, sunk in deep thought; his eyes were tightly shut and his face aflame. Everyone sat motionless, waiting for the sign. They gazed upon the Ari and it appeared to them as if his soul was disembodied and soaring up to a different world.

After a short while, the Ari opened his eyes and fixed them upon his critic. "Your master gave me a sign; this is it. Go to his widow, and ask her to show you the bundle of his manuscripts of *chiddushim*. Study them at such and such a place, on such and such a page and you will find confirmation to what I have just taught."

The *talmid* did as instructed and had to admit that the Ari had been right all along. From that time on he revered the Ari with all his heart and related this incident at every suitable opportunity to convince others how worthy the Ari was.[10]

During another of the Ari's lectures, a different *talmid* of the Ramak attempted to interrupt him. He cut the Ari short and announced that he had many questions to ask about what the Ari had just taught. Before he even had a chance to elaborate, the Ari replied, "Wait until the end of this lesson and I will answer all of your problems."

The man was quiet. He waited impatiently for the *shiur* to end. In his mind, he reviewed what he would ask, confident that the Ari would not be able to reply. This time he would show him! To his amazement, at the end of the lecture, the Ari listed all of his questions, one by one. Not one question was missing! And then he said, "All of your questions stem from one misconception. If you study the teachings of *Kabbalah* on this certain *parashah*, the questions will fall away of themselves." He then gave an explanation of that *parashah* and was so thorough that the scholar gaped in amazement. And he no longer had any questions..."

Among the Ten Appointees

Tsefas, during that period in history, was a unique city. It was filled with men of spirit — sages, scribes and scholars. Even its common folk — the laborers, shopkeepers and craftsmen — were men who strove to improve their deeds and to emulate the paragons of virtue whom they so revered. The city's rabbis and leaders also labored to preserve the sanctity of Tsefas and to guide the people along the right path. To this end, they appointed a committee of ten devout, G-d fearing men. They were to visit the market-places and alleyways and, if something was amiss, to make the necessary regulations to improve the moral quality of the community. The Ari was one of these ten.

One morning, one of the ten inspectors rose early and prepared to go to the *beis knesses*. It was still dark and he kept looking out from time to time to see if dawn had already broken. In the faint light of daybreak he discerned the figure of a woman leaving his neighbor's house and recognized her to be the wife of someone else. "What is she doing leaving a strange house so early in the morning?" he wondered. His neighbor was known to be a coarse, idle fellow who spent his days and nights in worthless pursuits and rowdy merrymaking. The inspector was horrified. The time had come to put a stop to his neighbor's evil ways.

Immediately after prayers he gathered the members of the committee, the Ari among them, and, his voice trembling with anger, told them what he had seen that morning. He demanded that the neighbor and the woman give an account of themselves.

The *memunim*, appointees, were shocked and started to

suggest what steps should be taken. But, the Ari silenced them. Turning to the accuser, he said, "Why did you immediately jump to evil conclusions? Just because you saw the woman leaving a strange house before daybreak? Did you try to find any justification for her? Perhaps she is a good woman and innocent of anything that you suspect. I know, without any shadow of a doubt, that the woman in question is a fine, upright person and not to be suspected of anything wrong. She surely had her own reason for being at that particular place. In fact, I can tell you what it is. A visitor from far off in the west is lodging in the same courtyard. Before the visitor came here, the woman's husband, who is now in that far off country on business, gave him some money to deliver to his wife and a list of things which he needed. The wife knew that the visitor was leaving early this morning and hastened to bring her husband's things to him. And now, my friend, let this be a lesson. Bear in mind what our Sages taught — 'Always judge a person favorably.'"

When the *memuneh* heard this explanation, he felt guilty because he had misjudged an innocent person. Later that day, he made inquiries and learned that everything that the Ari had said was true. He was so upset at having suspected a decent woman that he went to the Ari and apologized. The Ari looked at him in wonder. "Are you asking for *my* forgiveness? Did you insult me? It was the innocent woman whom you falsely suspected. Go and ask her to forgive you."[12] And so he did.

The man marveled at the Ari's power in knowing all hidden things and told the story to all his acquaintances but some of them refused to believe that the young man, the Ari, truly had divine vision. However, witnesses verified the story. The doubters decided to keep a watchful eye on the Ari and his ways.

The Ari sensed that he was under observation and concealed his ways, for he was not yet ready to reveal his holiness publicly. A few men decided to approach the Ari and speak to him. They met him one day on his way home and asked him outright if what the *memuneh* had told them was true and that he was able to see hidden things. The Ari changed the topic and did not give them a straight answer. They continued to converse with him in the hope that he might inadvertently reveal some hint of his marvelous powers.

As they were standing there, talking, a man came by. As soon as the Ari saw him, he cringed and flattened himself against the wall to avoid any contact when he passed them by, but the alley was very narrow and the man could not help brushing against the Ari. R' Yitzchak shuddered and said, "May *Hashem* forgive you for touching me. Now I will have to purify myself in a *mikveh* because of you."

They left the Ari and hurried after the man who had brushed against him. When asked about the meaning of the Ari's words, he, at first, shrugged his shoulders, and said that he had no idea. But they persisted, sensing that he was concealing something. They threatened to put him into *cherem* (excommunication). The man finally confessed that he had eaten non-kosher food in privacy. "But no one knows about it," he said. "R' Yitzchak must be a prophet to have guessed my secret!"[13]

1. In the name of R' Yedidyah Galanti who heard it from R' Yaakov Abulafya, the Ari's friend
2. "Shem Hagedolim" Os Yud, Siman 202; "Shivchei Rabbenu Chaim Vital" p. 46
3. "Shivchei HaArizal" (Jerusalem 5245) p. 13
4. "Divrei Yosef" by R' Yosef Sambari (Jerusalem 5741) p. 194
5. "Taamei Haminhagim" (Eshkol Pub., Jerusalem) p. 494 in a footnote from "Divrei Shaul"
6. "Eden Zion" by R' Yeshayahu Halevi Horowitz who heard it from the Ridbaz in Tsefas, entry on the Arizal, Os Mem, Siman 53 7. "Shivchei HaAri" p. 26; "Divrei Yosef" p. 199
8. "Orchos Chaim" in the "Siddur HaGra", Os 61
9. "Shem Hagedolim" II, Os Alef, Siman 57; "Shivchei Rabbenu Chaim Vital"
10. "Divrei Yosef" P. 208
11. Ibid p. 209
12. "Yalkut Me'am Lo'ez" Bamidbar, p. 146 quoted from "Shivchei HaAri"
13. "Divrei Yosef" p. 198

CHAPTER TEN
CHIEF OF THE LIONS

It happened just as Eliyahu Hanavi had prophesied. As soon as R' Chaim Vital joined the students of the Ari, he became accepted and widely acclaimed by the other wise men of his generation. The sages of Tsefas learned about the measure of the Ari's greatness from his *talmid*, R' Chaim, for R' Chaim never stopped praising this young master from Egypt. R' Yitzchak preferred to remain obscure and begged his student not to praise him to others, but to no avail. Other scholars came, their curiosity aroused, and once they met the Ari and heard his lectures, they were won over and begged to be allowed to join his circle of disciples.

'Maran' and the Ari

Maran R' Yosef Karo had been the chief rabbi of Tsefas for many years and the entire Diaspora accepted his *halachic* authority. He assessed the Ari's true value correctly and would refer to him as the "wise, perfect mekubal (hechacham hashalem hamekubal)." R' Yitzchak accepted *Maran*'s authority in the area of *halachah* and we even find a question of his which the *Beis Yosef* answered in *Avkas Rochel*. The topic is handled at length in deference to the questioner whom *Maran* esteemed highly and held dear.[1]

As we have already noted, R' Yosef Karo was very learned himself in *Kabbalah*. But in this, he acknowledged the Ari's superiority and sought to join his circle of disciples. The Ari felt that the *Maran*'s line of thinking followed that of the Ramak, which differed radically from his own, and was reluctant to accept this 'student', as he rejected everyone whose approach in *Kabbalah* was different from his own.

R' Yosef Karo did not understand the Ari's attitude and repeatedly begged to be allowed to sit in on his lectures but the Ari was firm. When he could no longer withstand the pressure, he explained his reasons to the rabbi of Tsefas but the latter was still not satisfied. Finally, the Ari had to yield, since R' Yosef was, after all, the figure of authority in the city. He began teaching him. And whenever the Ari began to lecture, a deep slumber would steal over R' Yosef. No matter how fiercely he fought against the angel of sleep, he was always defeated; his eyelids dropped with a will of their own. R' Yosef realized that this was a sign that the Ari was right in having initially refused to teach him. He gave up the battle and no longer asked the Ari to teach him.[2]

One *Shabbos* afternoon, the congregation praying together with R' Yosef Karo felt that a cloud of gloom had fallen upon their rabbi. The *Shabbos* serenity which rested upon him was marred and his forehead was furrowed with anxiety. "Something is disturbing R' Yosef," people whispered to one another. "Let us go over to him after the prayers and ask him what troubles him."

Before they could even approach him, the Ari, who had also prayed in that synagogue, went over to *Maran* and whispered something in his ear. R' Yosef's eyes immediately lit up and his face assumed its usual *Shabbos* glow. He grasped the Ari's hand warmly and thanked him.

R' Yosef left the synagogue, followed by many guests and *yeshivah* students who had come to Tsefas from all over the land. They used to eat *seudah shlishis* in the soup kitchen maintained in the courtyard, near his home. This 'restaurant' had been established by the community of Tsefas, headed by the rabbi. He made sure that it functioned smoothly. He possessed the keys to the place and was the one who opened and closed it each time. On this *Shabbos*, after leaving the *beis knesses* he walked first, followed by the large crowd of guests. Upon reaching his courtyard, he asked them to wait while he fetched the keys. He returned shortly with the large ring of keys.

When they were seated at the table, he turned to all the guests and said, "Do you know, my friends, that you owe thanks to the angel dwelling in our midst, the Ari, for being able to sit peacefully at this table now, as you always do?" In reply to the incredulous looks, he continued, "Before I went to *minchah* this afternoon, I noticed that my ring of keys had disappeared. I searched for it all over the house, high and low, in all the nooks and crannies, but it was gone. As you can guess, I was sorely distressed. What was I to do with all the guests who expected to eat the third *Shabbos* meal after prayers? I searched again but was forced to leave for the *beis knesses*. And yet, I was unable to leave my worries behind; even my prayers were confused and troubled.

"While I was wondering what to do, R' Yitzchak Luria approached me after prayers and said, 'Why does a misplaced ring of keys disturb you so greatly that you cannot even concentrate properly upon your prayers? Is a bunch of keys resting under a pillow cause for such anxiety?' At that moment I remembered that after locking up the dining room after the morning meal, I went to bed for a short nap and laid the keys under my pillow. I breathed in relief. Is it not wonderful that even in our days we have prophets from whom nothing is concealed? This is none other than R' Yitzchak Luria, who is a veritable angel! May *Hashem* preserve him and give him a full measure of days!"[3]

A similar incident occurred upon a different occasion:

In the same *beis knesses* where they both prayed there were other great personalities: the author of *Reishis Chochmah*; the Alshich; the author of *Charedim*, who was the *gabbai* and others. The custom was for the *baal tefillah* to wait for R' Yosef Karo to finish the *shemoneh esreh* before starting the repeat prayer aloud, but he would not wait for any others. The Ari prolonged his prayer since he filled it with intense *kavanos* (concentrated thought) based on *Kabbalah*.

It happened once that all the members of the congregation finished their silent prayer, and even the Ari, who was always among the last, had already taken his three steps backwards. But *Maran* was still standing and praying.

The prominent members were perplexed. What should they do? They were always accustomed to wait for the rabbi but this was unusual; the worshippers were growing restless. While they stood there, glancing at one another, wondering what to do, the Ari gave the sign for the *shaliach tzibbur* to begin.

Some of the people were shocked and demanded an explanation. The Ari said, "We are commanded to show respect to our rabbi while he is praying but we are not obligated to wait for him to finish his study!"

When they heard this, people were both puzzled and amazed. They were not satisfied by this explanation. Even the *gabbai*, R' Azcari, author of *Charedim* remarked to the Ari that it was disrespectful to the rabbi of Tsefas. The Ari repeated his statement, "We are not obliged to wait until Rabbenu finishes his study." He even sent the *shammash* to R' Yosef to tell him that the matter he was pondering could be found in a *mishnah* at such-and-such a place in *shas*...

The *shammash* did as he was told. R' Yosef finished his *shemoneh esreh* at once and turned to the *shammash* excitedly. "We are unable to fully appreciate the degree of *ruach hakodesh* which the Ari possesses! Today, when I was judging a case, the two sides presented their arguments. I had not yet come to any decision and the matter weighed heavily on my mind so that I was unable to concentrate upon my prayers as usual. I kept thinking about the matter of the law involved. And lo! R' Yitzchak Luria both saw, in his divine vision, what was bothering me, and sent me the answer — the *mishnah* which had eluded me!"[4]

"With the Grapes of the Vine"

R' Yitzchak Luria's respect for the *Beis Yosef* was no less than R' Yosef's for the Ari. Each of these giants of the spirit appreciated the greatness of the other. Small wonder, then, that the worthy son of R' Yosef, a gifted scholar, should be married to the virtuous daughter of the Ari. The two illustrious families joined, and the Ari and the *Beis Yosef* became related by marriage.

The marriage was celebrated in the *kallah*'s home at a regal banquet. The great rabbis of Tsefas gathered to rejoice with the two revered leaders. There were many speeches and the *kallah*'s father, the Ari, also spoke and his words were most elevated. R' Yosef Karo could not stop marveling at the pearls which he heard and upon his return home, he turned to his wife and said, "What shall I tell you? How shall I describe the profundity of the secrets of Torah which I heard today from the bride's father! How much knowledge and understanding I gained from his talk! Truly, the Ari knows more than an angel! He must have the soul of one of the prophets for even the *tanaim* could not have expressed what he did." *Maran* paused and sighed sadly. "Our generation is too puny for him. We cannot grasp what he teaches or appreciate the measure of his greatness. Alas! Who knows if our generation can even bear his powerful holiness. I fear that because of our sins we will lose this priceless pearl. If only he would live out a full life and not die young!"[5]

The Alshich Pleads His Cause

It is interesting that the great men of Tsefas, who were acclaimed throughout the Diaspora did not consider it demeaning to come to the Ari and beg to study under him, even though he was younger than they. They were not embarrassed to ask him to teach them. Like R' Yosef Karo, the Alshich — one of the most revered figures of Tsefas and the master of R' Chaim Vital in the revealed Torah — also yearned to sit in the Ari's shadow and hear the Torah secrets which he expounded. But the Ari rejected him, too.

During one of their meetings, R' Moshe Alshich turned to R' Yitzchak bitterly and said, "What is my sin that you refuse to befriend me and accept me as a student? My own disciples — R' Chaim Vital and Rav Falcon — have become your *talmidim*. Why should you discriminate against me?" Tears streamed down his cheeks as he spoke.

The Ari saw his pain and tried to calm him. "What you say is true, I do refuse you. This is not because your comprehension is poor, G-d forbid, but because you have a different purpose in life. Your task is to explain the Torah through *pshat* (the direct meaning), as you do in your excellent lectures which even the Heavenly retinue attends. I see in your soul a spark of the soul of R' Chutzpis HaMeturgeman, the translator. In its previous *gilgul*, however, your soul did have a powerful grasp of *Kabbalah*."

The Alshich, however, was not appeased. He was still depressed and full of complaints.

"I know," the Ari continued, "that you suspect that I simply do not wish to teach you. Let me, therefore, give you a sign to show you that the reason I gave you before is true. As you know, we are accustomed to going out on *erev Shabbos* at sunset to greet the *Shabbos* Queen as she descends upon the hills of Tsefas. Come and wait for us this week on the road leaving the city. If you see me on the road, you will know that I have simply been putting you off. But, if you fail to see us, that will be a sign that you have not descended to earth this time around to study *Kabbalah*."

R' Moshe Alshich nodded. That Friday morning he made all of his *Shabbos* preparations early so that he would be free. After noon he changed his weekday clothing to his *Shabbos* garments and went to the road which the Ari always took when he went forth to greet the Queen.

He stood there for a long time, waiting, until he became tired. Leaning against a tree trunk, he peered in the distance to see if the Ari, the Lion, and his 'cubs' were approaching, but no one was in sight. His limbs suddenly felt very heavy. R' Moshe sank down on the ground and his eyelids closed. Soon, he was in a deep sleep.

The Ari and his *talmidim*, dressed in their special white robes, their faces glowing with holiness, came down the road with the Ari looking like an angel. They passed the sleeping figure. The *talmidim* wished to wake the Alshich up but, to their surprise, the Ari restrained them and they continued on. They reached the place where they always stopped and recited the songs greeting the Queen. Their concentration was intense and fervent; even the mountains and the grasses listened in awe. They, too, seemed to feel the aura of majesty that had come to rest upon the entire creation in these moments of sublime holiness.

The Ari and his group came upon the sleeping R' Moshe again on their way back. The Ari now told his *talmidim* to awaken him. It was already late and it was not

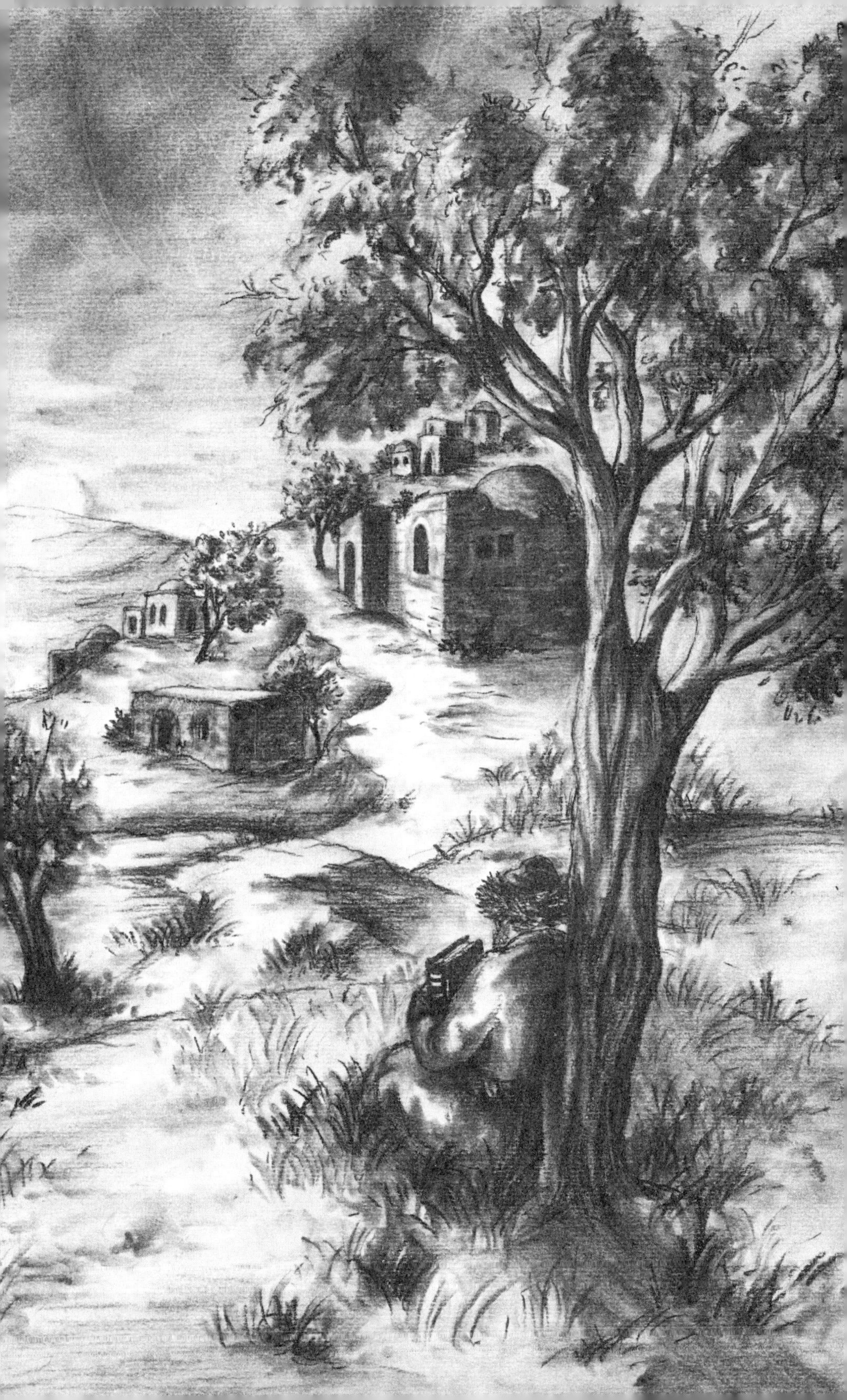

right to leave a man alone in the field at night. There were dangers. An Arab villager might murder him or wild beasts might attack him.

When R' Moshe opened his eyes, he realized at once that it was too late; he had missed his chance. The group must have passed him coming and was on its way back for *maariv*. He was bitterly disappointed and told the Ari how he had prepared himself early in the day in order to see them greet the *Shabbos*. But the Ari had been right; he was not destined to join him. His soul was not destined to study *Kabbalah*; he must adhere to his task of explaining the Torah according to its direct *pshat*.

The Ari saw how depressed the Alshich was and blessed him with success in his monumental commentary on the *Tanach*, telling him that this would win him immortality for all generations to come.[6]

Yet, the Alshich was still not resigned to his fate. He still yearned to warm himself by the heat of the Ari's fire in *Kabbalah*. R' Moshe was the master in the revealed Torah of the Ari's most prominent disciple, R' Chaim Vital. And he asked R' Chaim to teach him what he had learned from the Ari. But R' Chaim put him off. It is told that eighteen years after the Arizal passed away, when the Alshich was sitting in the *beis midrash* before his students, the cleaning woman entered. She saw R' Moshe looking very sad and asked, "What is troubling you, Rabbenu?"

"Why should I not be sad," he replied, "if my own *talmid*, R' Chaim Vital, refuses to teach me *Kabbalah*?"

The woman was surprised and said, "And is your disciple then greater than you, Rebbe?"

The Alshich told her his history: how the Ari had refused to teach him, telling him to study from his disciple, R' Chaim. "And when I asked if he was really so great," the Alshich explained, "he said, 'My whole purpose in life was to reveal my teachings to this man.' I asked the Ari how I could become his student, if I was his teacher. He replied, 'If our Sages had not said that a person is capable of being jealous of anyone — except his own student — I, myself would envy him the heights that he will attain. They are immeasurable.'" R' Moshe sighed sadly. "But he evades me and will not teach me. Is that not cause for sadness?"[7]

His desire to learn *Kabbalah* was so strong that he did acquire much of the Ari's teachings and considered the Ari as his master.

R' Yitzchak Luria lived in Tsefas for less than three years, from 5330 (1570) until 5332 (1572). His reputation spread far beyond Tsefas.

The Ari spent his time speaking on *Kabbalah* but was also involved in his duties as one of the ten *memunim* — the communal inspectors. He continued to serve in this capacity even after he became weak from pain and suffering, just before his death.

It is told that one year the promiment men of Tsefas decided to omit some of the *kinos* of *Tisha B'Av* which describe the lowly state of the Jewish people in its exile. They also deleted the paragraph, "How has the light of the moon become dark, and the secret of Torah — is there anyone to draw it to the light? And who is the one who protects his generation?" — because of the greatness of the Ari, who *did* draw out the secrets of the Torah and who *did* protect the people of his city. After his death, they included these verses once again in their *Tisha B'Av* prayers.[8]

1. "Shem Hagedolim" on the Arizal
2. "Shivchei HaAri" p.37
3. Ibid, p. 38
4. From a Jerusalem 'maggid'
5. "Shivchei HaAri"; "Maaseh Nisim" chapter 10
6. "Divrei Yosef' p. 226
7. "Shivchei R' Chaim Vital" (Jerusalem, the year of TeShUVaH, 5713) p. 6
8. "Shaar Hagilgulim" part I, p. 5

CHAPTER ELEVEN
FACE READING AND PALMISTRY

"**I**f I were to attempt to write of the extent of his greatness and the vastness of his wisdom and extraordinary intellect... But believe me, this man's soul had absolutely nothing in common with those of the present generations. He was sent directly by *Hakadosh baruch Hu* to benefit this generation and illuminate the eyes of the world with the true light of the wisdom and understanding to be found in the *Zohar*. But because of our sins, he lived in *Eretz Yisrael* for only a short while and imparted of his wisdom for a mere two years...

Had we been worthy that he live in our midst for five years, he would have restored the entire world to its perfect state through *teshuvah* and would have brought the Redemption. The wicked and the evildoers feared him. For they heard that he was able to tell a man what he had done in times gone by, what he did in his innermost chambers or even what he thought in his heart. He could tell how one had sinned in a previous *gilgul* (existence) and why he had been sent down to earth. Evil men fled from him as if from a lion; they feared to let him look into their faces. Those who wished to repent came before him and, falling at his feet, would plead that he tell them how they had sinned and how to mend their ways. The Ari told them of their sins and reminded them where they had sinned, who had been present at the time and similar details until they confessed all. Then he gave them certain prescriptions by which they might gain forgiveness — each one according to his particular sin — and helped them mend the flaw in their souls. He cured them and no trace of their sins remained.

And not only this. He knew of the lost souls which moved from misery to misery with no eternal rest, souls which were too black with sin to be admitted into *gehinnom*. He would tell his disciples how these lost souls came to him in the thousands and tens of thousands whenever he went out to the fields. The trees were filled with them and the rivers swept them along in multitudes. He would ask them all about the heavenly spheres and they would tell him how highly he was revered there. They would beg him to help them for they knew he had the power to do so. And he would reply: If *Hashem* so decrees — I can rehabilitate you and the entire world."
(*Shivchei HaArizal* p. 31; *Maaseh Nisim* chapter 4)

In short, the Ari was blessed with a special power; he need only look at person to see all of the evil deeds he had done in his lifetime. Select *tzaddikim* in each generation, men of sublime qualities and supreme holiness are able to do this.

The *Zohar* explains the portion dealing with Yisro along these lines: "And you shall seek out from the entire nation men of valor, who fear G-d..." (*Shemos* 18:21). Moshe was told to use his powers in reading the face and thus seek out men who are G-d fearing. Even Moshe Rabbenu was only able to use this power after the *Shechinah* had endowed him with it.[1]

The Arizal bequeathed this wisdom to his disciples. R' Eliyahu de Vidash testifies:

"We have seen here in Tsefas in the Upper Galilee wise men upon whom the blessing 'Who gave of His wisdom to those who fear Him' can be said; we have also seen wise men who are expert in the art of face reading and who are able to tell everything that a person did, whether good or bad. They could only have acquired such a marvelous power, which is close to divine intuition, through their good deeds and piety."

Reishis Chochmah (Shaar Ha'ahauah, Chapter 6)

Kindness to Creatures

There was a worthy, G-d fearing man in the city who spent all of his days repenting. One time he came before the Ari and asked him to reveal any sins which he had overlooked and to tell him how to atone for them.

R' Yitzchak looked at his forehead and said, "You are a perfect *tzaddik*. You are blameless. But there is one thing in your home which needs attention. I see on your forehead a vague hint of *tzaar baalei chaim*, unkindness to animals, which you must repair."

The man was deeply grieved to hear this. He tried to remember what he had done to animals but nothing came to mind. He went home and inquired about the deeds of his family. He finally discovered that his maid didn't feed the chickens; they had to go foraging for food in the courtyards of neighbors.

The good man told his wife to scatter food each day not only for their chickens but also for those of their neighbors. When he returned to the Ari and asked him to look at his forehead, the latter happily informed him that the sign had vanished; the sin had been erased.[2]

The Interchanged Letters

One of the Ramak's disciples once ate at the Ari's table. In the course of the meal, the Ari suddenly noticed that his guest had difficulty in moving; he sat stiffly. "What is the matter?" the Ari asked. "Are you in pain?"

The man nodded. "I have been suffering from shoulder pains for quite some time now and I can't imagine why. I did not receive any blow there nor am I ill. But it pains me terribly."

The Ari looked into his face and immediately understood the reason. "I see that you are not careful enough in washing *mayim acharonim*. You do not say *bircas hamazon* immediately afterwards."

The guest nodded, explaining, "That is true, but I have a reason. Our Sages said: If three people eat at a table and do not say *divrei Torah*, it is as if they have eaten from the sacrifices of idolators.' I, therefore, made it a practice to study a *perek mishnayos* before *bircas hamazon*."

"Nevertheless," said the Ari, "the pains in your shoulder are a result of that practice. Our Sages tell us to say the blessings immediately (*Techef*) after washing. Since you take that word lightly, you are being punished in your shoulder (*Catef*)."[3]

Saved From Sin

In the Galilee the earth is lush and fertile. The fields around Tsefas in those days produced a bounty of fruits and vegetables of all sorts. The greengrocers in the city were G-d fearing people who knew the laws pertaining to the land. When they brought back the produce from the various farms, they did not put it up for sale until they had set aside the necessary *terumos umaasros* (tithes) and they were careful not to buy fruits which grew in the prohibited years (*orla*).

The residents of Tsefas relied on them so implicitly in these matters that they stopped asking each time if the fruits were permissible. But over the years new storekeepers, who were not as knowledgeable, set up their stands in the Tsefas markets. People who bought from them did not realize that they were buying forbidden produce and they sinned, time and again.

The rabbis warned the people not to patronize those dealers, but their warnings fell upon deaf ears. People continued to buy produce from which *maaser* had not been set aside. Heaven finally stepped in to save the Jews of Tsefas.

There was a wine-maker in Tsefas who, though G-d fearing, was ignorant. Each harvest, he would go among the villages and buy up grapes to make his excellent wine. It graced the *Shabbos* and *Yom tov* tables of many Tsefas families and was used at other times when wine was needed for a *mitzvah* or an occasion of joy. People knew how sincere and pious the man was and did not bother to question him. Only the scholars of Tsefas, who did not rely on anyone's word, always set aside *maaser* themselves, just to be on the safe side.

The wine-maker once visited the Ari. When that holy man looked at his forehead, he gave a start and said angrily, "Shame on you! I see that you are guilty of the sin of *tevel*; you have not set aside *terumos* and *maasros*. You cause the people who buy your wine to sin without realizing it!"

The wine-maker was shaken and frightened. He admitted his guilt and begged for atonement, explaining that his sin stemmed from ignorance.

When it became known that the wine-maker, whom everyone had trusted so implicitly, had, out of ignorance, misled all of his customers into using wine from which *maaser* had not been set aside, people were horrified. They finally realized that even the most sincere of people could not be relied on unless he knew the laws thoroughly. From that day on, people learned to heed the warnings of their rabbis and were exceptionally scrupulous in observing the laws dealing with the fruits of the land.[4]

The Sinner Who Tested the Ari

The Ari's skill in reading faces captured people's imagination and his fame spread quickly. One wealthy man from Constantinople, who came to Tsefas to celebrate *Pesach*, visited the various *batei knesses*. He attended *shiurim* and met with those who attended them. Thus, he learned that the Ari could look at a person's face and see his past and his future, his innermost thoughts and his most private deeds; a person's life lay like an open book before him. When the visitor heard this, he was astounded and upon his return to Constantinople, he could not stop talking about what he had heard.

One of the people in his congregation was a bully who disdained everything holy. People suspected that he had violated all of the commandments of the Torah. He caused many people to suffer, but no one dared stand up to him for fear of his strong arm. And so, people bore his outrages in silence.

When this roughneck heard the rich man praise the Ari, he mocked him. "How naive can you get!" he laughed derisively. "You believe everything that you hear. Do you really mean to say that this R' Yitzchak can reveal a person's sins just by looking at his face? What a fool you are!"

"I am ready to swear to it," said the traveler heatedly.

"Do you know what?" said the bully. "I'll go to Tsefas myself and put your rabbi to the test. I would like to see what he can read in my face..."

It was no idle boast. The braggart packed and left for Tsefas. The trip was a long one with frequent stops at wayside inns. He never inquired about the *kashrus* of the food but ate and drank indiscriminately to his heart's content. He would change his weary horses for fresh ones and then continue on his way, whistling lightheartedly, a wastrel who had nothing to do in life. At one inn, when he was feasting himself, a flask of red wine before him, he suddenly felt in high spirits. He lifted up the goblet in a toast and exclaimed, "To you, *Chacham* R' Yitzchak, and to our meeting!"

At that very moment the Ari was sitting among his *talmidim* when suddenly, he smiled. The men looked at one another: there was nothing in the content of their study which warranted this good humor. Were they, perhaps, at fault? Each man began examining his own deeds and thoughts to see if he was the cause of the Ari's smile.

"My dear *talmidim*," said the Ari, "at this very moment, a wicked wastrel from Constantinople is on his way to Tsefas to test me. I can see him now, sitting at a table with a goblet of wine in his hand, half drunk. He thinks that he can best me, but we will see who has the last word. He will soon be here." The Ari gave the exact moment when he expected him to arrive. "I'll be waiting for him. As soon as he comes, make sure to fetch him and bring him before me at once."

R' Yitzchak described the man exactly so that the disciples would recognize him without difficulty. Then he added that this braggart was really the *gilgul* of an exalted soul which sought help through a *tikkun*. He would do his best to save him by making him repent.

The *talmidim* listened attentively and looked forward to the event.

At the designated hour, the man appeared at the gates of Tsefas, a dusty traveler astride a weary horse, a small knapsack over his shoulder. A look of derision was etched upon his face, weary as it was, and the lines around his mouth bespoke an arrogant character and evil heart. As soon as he asked for the home of R' Yitzchak Ashkenazi, people looked at him and saw that he fit the Ari's description perfectly. This must be the man for whom they were waiting.

The townspeople directed him towards the *beis midrash*. The stranger dismounted and strode confidently towards the door. But as soon as he stood on the threshold, his arrogance began to melt away. He could not explain what suddenly came over him. Doubts and questions assailed him... By the time he stood before R' Yitzchak, he was a different person from the coarse, brazen lout who had left Constantinople.

The Ari pretended that he did not know him and asked him what he wanted.

"I have come from Constantinople," he said, "to verify what I heard about you. They say wonderful things about your miraculous powers, especially in reading faces. I have come to test you and see if the rumors are true. I wonder whether, simply by looking at me, you can tell all of the wicked deeds I have committed in my lifetime. If so, I will know that you are a truly godly person and I will abandon my evil ways."

The man was silent. He waited for the Ari to reply. The Ari told everyone to leave the room since the commandment of rebuking a fellow man was modified by the phrase, "...and you shall not bear sin because of him." One must take care not to embarrass or shame anyone in public when rebuking him.

When all had left, the Ari began to give him a detailed account of all his past sins, from the grave ones to the ones that a person commits out of carelessness. He did not omit a single wrong. The man stood before the Ari for a long time, listening with a bowed head. His shoulders drooped and he bent over more and more with each passing moment; his haughty brow was furrowed with pain and guilt. The Ari's words penetrated deep into his heart and he felt genuine remorse.

When R' Yitzchak had enumerated all the sins he had committed from the day he had begun to reason, the man fell at the *tzaddik*'s feet and with tears coursing down his cheeks, begged the Ari to tell him how to repent, to save his soul through a *tikkun*. "I am prepared to do whatever you tell me!" he said in a tear-choked voice, "even until death. If you decree that I die by any of the four deaths imposed by *beis din*: stoning, burning, sword or strangulation, I shall willingly accept my fate, as long as it guarantees my atonement."

R' Yitzchak raised him up from the ground and comforted him, "If you do exactly as I say, then I promise you that your sins will be wiped clean and your evil deeds forgiven." He then prescribed a program of atonement involving many physical hardships — fasting, wearing sackcloth and immersions in water. He also directed him to study ten pages of *Zohar* each day.

The Jew from Constantinople accepted this with joy. When he left the *beis midrash*, all of the disciples stared at him, wondering what had happened, for he was a changed being, a different man from the one who had entered. Gone were the mocking lines at the corners of his eyes, the arrogant brow, the sneer upon his mouth, the brazan stance. He had been transformed. Now he walked bowed and humbled, with a pleasant look on his face. The master had truly succeeded.

The penitent stranger returned to Constantinople. The news of his complete change of character spread like fire through the entire congregation. He had repented of his evil ways. People marveled at his new practices. "See how he mortifies himself with fasting and other *sigufim* (torments)?" one said to to another. "And do you know that he has begun approaching all of the people whom he has wronged in the past, asking their forgiveness?"

The man lived out his life following his new path and died a true and perfect *tzaddik*.[5]

A Rebuke for R' Chaim

The people who came to R' Yitzchak seeking programs for *teshuvah* were not only the sinners, but people who wished to improve themselves. Even the most exalted *tzaddikim* wished to purify themselves and attain even greater heights of holiness. They did not want the slightest stain upon their souls, even through an unconscious sin.

R' Chaim Vital, the Ari's loyal attendant, also received his master's rebuke for a sin he committed unintentionally.

Once, one of his relatives celebrated a son's wedding. R' Chaim participated in the *simchah* and, when it was over, went to his master's home carrying a basket full of cakes and sweets from the *seudas mitzvah* which the father of the *chasan* had sent along for the family.

R' Chaim sat down before his master. The latter turned to him and said, "I see, my dear student, that today you have transgressed a commandment. You have accidently eaten an insect, which the Torah forbids."

R' Chaim was alarmed. He racked his brain to remember what he had eaten that day, but the Ari interrupted his thoughts, "Why must you try so hard to remember when the second half of the insect is right there in your basket!" R' Chaim emptied the basket onto the table. R' Yitzchak selected one of the cakes and crumbled it up and there, in the middle, were the remains of an insect...[6]

R' Yitzchak rebuked his disciple upon another occasion. The Ari's disciples knew, from their master, that all the letters of the *alef-beis* could be found upon the folds and wrinkles in a person's body, upon the dimples and impressions in his flesh, and upon his hair. One time the Ari said to R' Chaim, "I see the letters on your forehead glowing as usual, except for the letter *gimmel* which is upside-down."

The *talmid* understood that he must have committed some sin. He pondered over his deeds until the Ari said to him, "You know, my dear R' Chaim, that *Hashem* takes the righteous to task for even minor sins. You, who honor your father as best you can, should show him even greater kindness, *gemilus chesed*, which begins with the letter *gimmel*."[7]

Palmistry

The Ari was not familiar with the reading of faces only, but was also able to read palms. By looking at the lines and folds which ran across a person's hand, he was able to reveal the past and predict the future. The Ari's disciples yearned to acquire this art but he refused to teach it to them. He even rebuffed R' Chaim, his favorite student, saying, "Why do you need this foreign skill? *Kabbalah* can impart to you all the knowledge you need."

R' Chaim Vital's desire to learn palm reading persisted. He sought the right moment to ask the Ari to teach him. But each time he was about to make his request the Ari evaded the issue and put him off. When R' Chaim finally realized that the direct approach would not work, he decided to employ different, more sophisticated tactics.

It was the season of Purim. R' Chaim sent for a widow who collected alms in order to sustain herself and her only daughter.

R' Chaim told her that on the next day, when all of

Tsefas sat down to their Purim feasts, she and her daughter were to go to the Ari and ask for *matanos la'evyonim* gifts for Purim. "He will want to give you money," he said, "but tell him that you want a different *matanah*, that you are very concerned for your only daughter and want him to read her palm favorably. As a reward for your efforts, I am giving you this sum of money with which to celebrate Purim."

R' Chaim intended to stand by his master's side when he read the daughter's palm. Hopefully, he would learn something of the art.

The next day was Purim. The *megillah* was read; people sent portions of food to one another and gave generously to the poor. The Ari's disciples gathered in the *beis midrash* to study, for even on Purim they did not neglect the Torah. They heard marvelous secrets pertaining to the day and felt a joyous exaltation. When they had finished learning, they sat down to celebrate the festive meal in their master's house.

In the midst of the merrymaking, there was a hesitant knock at the door. It was the destitute widow and her daughter. With eyes modestly lowered, she asked the Ari for *demei Purim* (Purim money). R' Yitzchak turned to a servant and said, "Bring my purse and give this woman enough money for her to make a lavish feast."

"No, no," she interrupted, "I do not want any money this time. I have come here with my daughter because I am so concerned. I want you to tell me what the future has in store for her. Would you read her palm?"

A smile crinkled up the corners of the Ari's twinkling eyes and he said good-naturedly, "As you wish. It is Purim today, after all, and one must satisfy all those who hold out their hand. But don't think that you can trick me. I know very well that my disciple, R' Chaim, is behind this. He was hoping that he would learn indirectly what I refused to teach him directly. Very well. Tell your daughter to stretch out her palm. But she must stand four cubits away from me, there, by the wall. That is fine..."

The Ari looked at the palm from across the room and began telling the girl all that had happened to her since she was born and up to the present. Then he continued on into the future until the day of her death. R' Chaim, who had been waiting impatiently for this moment, was frustrated, he was unable to learn anything. All he saw was an outstretched palm at the distance of four cubits; he could not see the pattern of lines. But he did see that nothing was to be concealed from the Ari. That was R' Chaim's last attempt to learn palmistry from his master.[8]

1. "Maaseh Nisim" Chapter 1
2. "Divrei Yosef", p. 206
3. "Kav Hayashar" by R' Tzvi Hirsh of Kodinov
4. "Charedim" (Published in Jerusalem, 5741) p. 213
5. "Divrei Yosef", p. 205
6. Ibid p. 216
7. "Kav Hayashar" Chapter 22; "Divrei Yosef" p. 215
8. "Divrei Yosef" p. 202

CHAPTER TWELVE

DIVINE VISION AND DIVINE POWERS

R' Chaim Vital, in his introduction to *Shaar Hahakdamos*, writes of the Ari: "He was able to tell every deed a person had done and would do. He knew a person's thoughts and could tell you what a person was about to do even before he did it."

The Suffering of the Baby Chicks

The Ari once had to travel away on business. There he was invited to stay at the home of a pious, upright man, who did not spare any effort in making his stay comfortable in every possible way. R' Yitzchak was very touched by his host's devotion. When he was about to leave, the Ari said to him, "How can I thank you for all your trouble, for all the care you lavished upon me? Ask of me what you wish, and I will bless you!"

The man gave a slight sigh and replied in a broken voice, "What shall I say, Rebbe? I have everything I need, thank G-d. I am blessed with riches and health. There is only one thing I lack to complete my happiness. My wife has borne me several sons but has stopped bearing, for no apparent reason. The doctors are at a loss to explain it. Perhaps you can bless us so that she will continue to have children?"

"I can see the reason for it," the distinguished visitor replied. "Kindness and sympathy is one of the outstanding traits of all the descendants of Avraham Avinu. A person must be on his guard at all times, lest he cause any person or creature distress. You have a chicken coop in your yard which used to have a ladder. The little chicks used to hop up and down the ladder to get their food from the grain and water troughs on the ground. But when your wife saw the mess that they were making, she told the maid to put the food and water trays inside the coop and take away the ladder. Since then, the chicks have been pining away, imprisoned in the dark. They no longer get any exercise and they miss the enjoyment of hopping up and down the ladder. They cheep with disappointment and frustration and these sounds of complaint have gone all the way up to Heaven. This is counted against your wife; it is causing her to be infertile so that she cannot bear more children."

The man listened to the Ari, openmouthed, and immediately went out to the yard to find the ladder. With his own hands he put it back against the chicken coop. All the little chicks tumbled out, squeaking with joy. Not long afterwards, the man's wife became pregnant and once again bore him children.[1]

The Punishment of One Who Shamed

Tsefas attracted many Marranos who, upon discovering their Jewish origins, fled from Spain and came to *Eretz Yisrael*. These people had a deep innate love for *Hashem* but were ignorant of *halachah*. They followed practices of their own making with simple sincerity.

One *Shabbos Shuvah* eve, a rabbi was sitting in the *beis knesses* preparing his sermon for the following day. A man entered with two fresh, fragrant *challos* and a bottle of choice red wine. The rabbi watched with amazement as the man went over to the *aron kodesh*, opened it and put them alongside the scrolls. The man muttered a few words under his breath and then closed the *aron kodesh*.

The rabbi called the Marrano over to him and asked him, "What did you just do?"

The man replied in all innocence, "I am a day laborer. I work very hard to earn my living but I happily scrimp together a few pennies each day in order to be able to bring this sacrifice to *Hashem*. Every Friday night I come here with my offering. I put it in the holiest spot in the *beis knesses*, the *aron kodesh*, and pray that it pleases *Hashem*."

When the rabbi heard these naive words, he did not know whether to laugh or to be angry at him for desecrating a holy place. In the end he compromised and rebuked him, "Do you really think that *Hashem* is like a mortal of flesh and blood, that He actually eats and drinks your sacrifices? Why, each day we affirm that He has no body and no form. He does not need to eat or to drink! He has no use for your *challos* or your wine!"

"I am a simple person, Rebbe," the man replied with a trembling voice. "I have never had the opportunity to study Torah or *halachah*. I thought that He appreciated my offering, that He ate it. You see, I have been doing this for a long time, every Friday night. And in the morning the *challos* and the wine are always gone. I was sure that He accepted my gift which I gave with all my heart."

The rabbi was angry at the simplicity of the man's thinking. "Fool! Idiot!" he shouted impatiently. "Don't you know that it must be the *shammash* who takes your gifts? He must be the one who found out what you were doing and was happy with the extra food for his family. That is the only explanation!"

The Marrano left the *beis knesses*, his face burning with embarrassment, bitterly disappointed that *Hashem* had no need for his offerings and that the *shammash* had been taking his hard-earned gifts. He felt terribly ashamed of his ignorance.

The Ari knew of all this. He summoned the rabbi to him and said sternly, "Go home to your family and tell them your last wishes for you must die. The Heavenly court has decreed your death for the way you shamed the poor Marrano."

The rabbi burst into tears and said, "But I was right! One must not think of *Hashem* as having a body or limbs! He cannot eat or drink! He is not mortal with human appetites! I merely tried to explain this to the ignorant man because he was making a terrible mistake. But he foolishly and stubbornly insisted that G-d accepted his offering each time. I had to show him how mistaken he was!"

"That is true. But, ever since the *Beis Hamikdash* has been destroyed there have been no sacrifices. *Hashem* has missed the *avodah*. When the Marrano brought his offering and presented it with all his heart, *Hashem* was pleased once again, for it is the good will in a person's heart that He seeks. And now you have prevented this. He will never again bring the wine and the *challos* which so pleased *Hashem*. And since you are the cause, you must pay with your life. Your fate is sealed."

The rabbi bowed his head and returned home. And the next day, he died.[2]

The Song of R' Yisrael Nag'ara

R' Yisrael Nag'ara was one of the saintliest figures of Tsefas. He often burst into spontaneous song, pouring out his overflowing love for the *Shechinah*. The Arizal said that R' Yisrael's soul was an offshoot of the soul of King David, the sweet singer of Israel. His hundreds of compositions, all based upon deep Kabbalistic concepts, became known through his book, *Zemiros Yisrael* which was printed in Tsefas in 5347 (1537). R' Yehudah Aryeh de Modena wrote of him, "There has not risen in Yisrael like Yisrael!"

In one of his poems he bitterly mourns the passing of a childhood comrade, R' Bezalel Ashkenazi, author of *Shitah Mekubetzes*. Many of his poems are sung to this very day by the Sefardim in the *Shiras Habakashos* said each *Shabbos* at dawn, among them: *"Yomar na Yisrael shirah l'K-el ayom"* and *"Yemosai kalu"* among many others.

And who does not sing one of his most famous songs, *"K-ah ribon olam"* on Friday nights? The first letters of each stanza spell out the author's name: R' Yisrael Nag'ara."

R' Yisrael would spend hours at his *Shabbos* table

singing *zemiros* — songs and praises to the Creator, with a heart filled with love and *devekus*. His songs caused a great commotion in heaven as the angels would descend to listen to those beautiful songs pouring forth from such a pure soul. In the summer, he would put his table outside. His singing would draw flocks of white doves who hovered above him or hopped about his feet. They listened enraptured to his marvelous singing.

One fine summer *Shabbos* day, R' Yisrael sat singing at his table with flocks of doves filling the air all around him. It was hot and R' Yisrael removed his hat and slipped out of his outer garment to relieve himself from the stifling heat. He was continuing his meal, when he noticed that one of the doves was flapping its wings frantically and chirping loudly. Soon, all the other doves were imitating it — and then, with a loud shriek, they all flew away; not one remained. R' Yisrael was puzzled by their strange behavior and decided to ask the Ari to explain the meaning of this incident.

At that very moment, R' Yitzchak Luria was also sitting at his *Shabbos* table, together with his family and close *talmidim*. They were singing and listening to the Ari expound upon the weekly *sidrah*. Suddenly, the Ari paused and said, "Did you know that R' Yisrael Nag'ara's song is especially favored in Heaven? It pleases the Heavenly hosts as much as did the songs of the *leviim* in the *Beis Hamikdash*. When he sits at his table, the angels flock to hear his song. But, just a short while ago, when R' Yisrael removed his hat and robe, he sang his holy songs with his forearms exposed. One of the angels descended to drive all of the others away, for this is no way to sit before the King." The Ari turned to two of his disciples and said, "Go to R' Yisrael and tell him to don

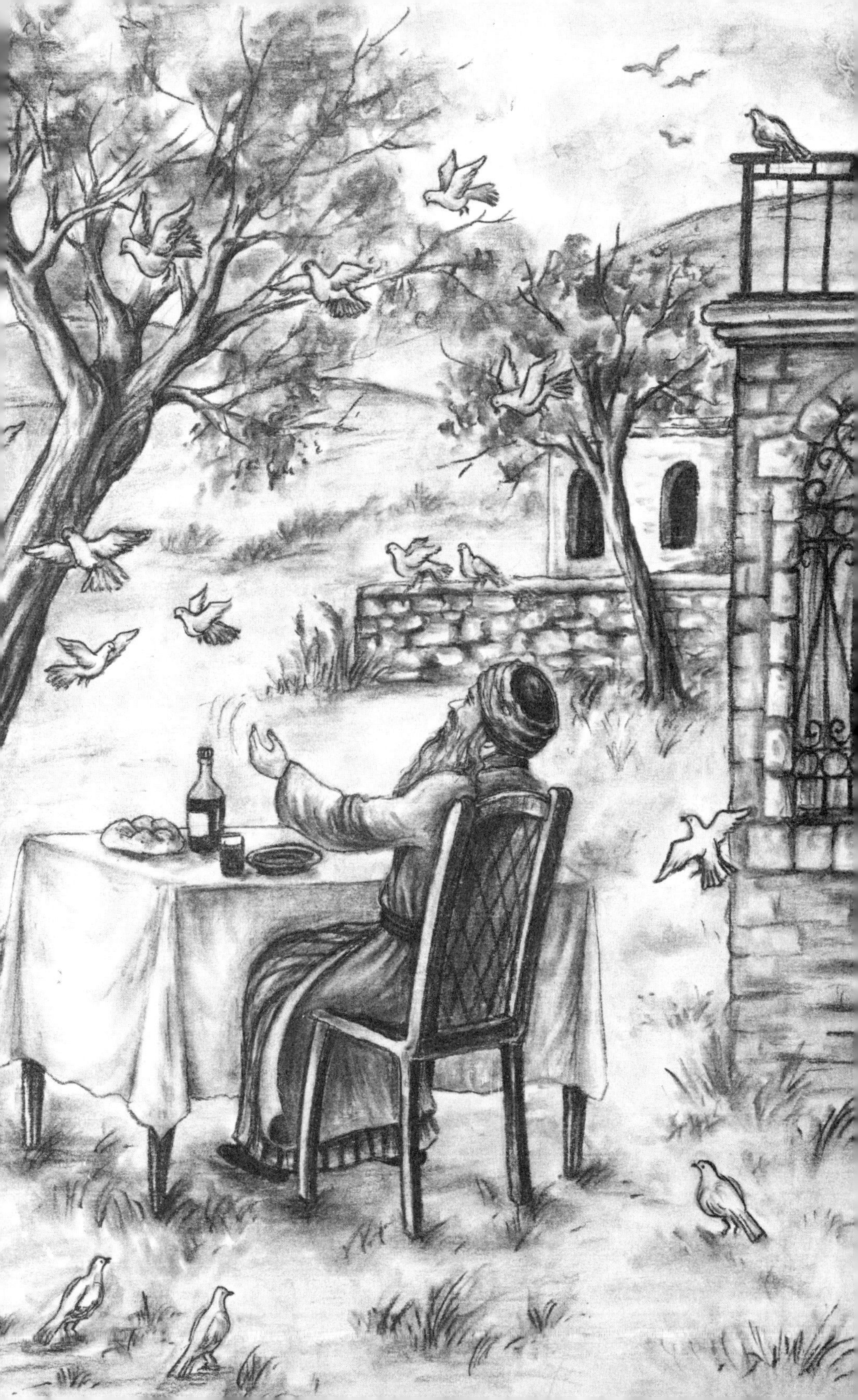

his hat and robe again so that the angels might return to his holy table."

When R' Yisrael received the message, he was overwhelmed with wonder at the Ari's divine intuition and aghast at what he had unwittingly done. With shaky knees he rose to his feet and told the two men what had just happened with the flocks of doves and how he had been about to go to the Ari to ask for an explanation. "Can another such man be found who possesses the spirit of G-d," he said.

R' Yisrael quickly put on his robe and hat and sat down again to resume his singing. After just a few notes, he heard the fluttering of many wings — the white doves had returned to hear his singing. This time, they remained until he finished.[3]

The Seven Shepherds are Called to the Torah

One *Shabbos* morning the Ari turned to his disciples, saying, "If you promise not to utter a syllable from the beginning of the service until the very end, or even to smile at what you see, I promise to show you something so marvelous the like of which no human eye has yet beheld." The disciples eagerly promised not to disturb the prayers in any way. "Fine. Then I will lead the *shacharis*. During the reading of the Torah, I will call up the Seven Shepherds: Avraham, Yitzchak and Yaakov, Moshe, Aharon, Yosef and David for an *aliyah* to the Torah. If you keep your promise, you will see them, as if in the flesh, going up to recite the blessing over the Torah. However, if I see that you do not keep your word, then one of us will have to suffer for the rest..."

R' Yitzchak began the *Shabbos* prayers. After *shacharis*, the Ari took out a *sefer Torah* and declared aloud, "*Shema Yisrael...*" Everyone thundered in reply, "*Shema Yisrael...*" announcing their total devotion to *Hashem*.

The Ari carried the scroll to the *bimah*, laid it down on the reading table and intoned the familiar words, "All give praise to our G-d and give honor to the Torah. Let the *kohen* approach. *Yaamod Aharon Hakohen!*" All hearts skipped a beat as an elderly man strode up to the platform, short of stature but venerable, his silken beard flowing down his chest. He approached the scroll and said the blessing in a resonant voice, "...Who has chosen us from all the nations... Blessed... the Giver of the Torah." He read his portion and concluded with the appropriate blessing after the reading.

The congregation was still reeling from the impact of the event when the Ari announced the second *aliyah*: "*Yaamod... Moshe Halevi*" Now Moshe Rabbenu entered, a tall figure striding forward with poise and authority, his face alight with a heavenly aura. He went up to the Torah, recited the blessing and read. The next to follow were Avraham, Yitzchak and Yaakov. Yosef Hatzaddik, an elderly man, dazzling in his handsomeness, was called up for the sixth *aliyah*. Now the Ari called out, "Yaamod David ben Yishai, King of Israel!" All eyes turned towards the entrance as King David made his appearance. He was dressed in cloth and was singing and dancing exuberantly, rejoicing with all his might in honor of the Torah.

The *talmidim* were overcome by what they had just witnessed: the Seven Shepherds in the flesh. But now, when King David cavorted merrily up the aisle, one of them was unable to contain himself; the corners of his mouth turned up in a faint smile, just as the Ari had fearfully predicted. Within that same year this young man was punished. He died in his prime.[4]

Let Him Repent — and He Will Be Healed

R' Chaim Vital suffered from pain in his eyes. He bore his pain in silence for a long time, telling no one of his great agony. But his master, the Ari, found out and took him aside one time. "Do you know why you suffer so?" he asked R' Chaim. "It is because you stare at me during the blessing of the *kohanim*. During this time I concentrate so deeply that the very *Shechinah* descends and stands before me. Your eyes are unable to bear the holiness of such a sight."

When R' Chaim heard this, he resolved never to gaze upon the Ari during *bircas kohanim*. And sure enough, his eyes were healed and he no longer suffered any pain.[5]

The Poor Man's Revenge

The spirits of certain people are permitted to descend after death to harm others. They enter a person's body as a *dybbuk* and cause this host to become severely ill as a Heavenly punishment for sins. Whenever a person became possessed by an evil spirit, he would be taken to a *tzaddik* who, in his divine intuition, was able to see the problem and heal the soul. He would offer up prayers for the lost soul and appease it until it agreed to leave and the afflicted person was cured.

The Ari was especially famous for his ability to exorcise evil spirits. *Mekubalim* (those who studied the *Kabbalah*) would often bring people suffering from evil spirits to the Ari to be treated. In the course of time, the Ari revealed the secret of exorcism to his *talmidim*.

Once, a young boy from a noted Tsefas family became ill. He writhed in pain for a long time. The doctors were baffled by his strange disease, which grew worse and worse. His parents were beside themselves with grief and despair when they saw that the most renowned doctors were helpless. They gave great sums to charity, but this did not help either. Nor were the holy men of Tsefas able to help with their *kameyos*, charms and prayers.

The rabbis finally sent the stricken father to the Ari who asked that the patient be brought to him. He felt the boy's pulse and said that an evil spirit had taken possession of the boy's body. The Ari then had the spirit speak up and tell its story.

A strange voice issued from the boy's throat, saying, "I am the spirit of so and so who lived many years ago. In that lifetime, the person whose body I am inhabiting was a treasurer in charge of dispensing funds to the poor people of the city. I, myself, was destitute and starving. I was once very, very hungry, not having eaten for several days, and I came before the treasurer, begging for alms to buy some bread. He turned me away emptyhanded — and I starved to death. When I came before the Heavenly court, I blamed my death upon the hard-hearted treasurer. The court accepted my charge and permitted me to inflict revenge. And here I am, now, invading this boy's body with full justification. Nor will I leave until he dies."

The voice ceased. All eyes turned to the Ari. R' Yitzchak raised his voice authoritatively, "You have no right to inflict punishment for a sin committed in a different lifetime, for this is a different body which does not owe you a thing! You had better leave of your own free will, for if you refuse, I will have to exorcise you!"

The spirit was frightened and agreed to leave, but on one condition: "This boy must not gaze upon the face of a woman for an entire week. If during the coming week he even glimpses a female face, I will claim my due and he will die!"

R' Yitzchak turned to the parents. "Do you think that you can abide by this condition?" he asked. "If so, I will evict the spirit but if not, I will leave the boy be, for his life will be in danger." The parents nodded in agreement and the Ari ordered the boy returned to his home.

As soon as the boy reached home, he began to improve. He opened his eyes and looked around him, then asked for some water. His family leaped to fill his request. The news of his speedy recovery spread throughout the city.

The parents were beside themselves with joy and decided that as soon as the week was over, they would hold a thanksgiving banquet. On the seventh day, the house was all abustle. The family was busy with the preparations for the feast and the boy was left, for a while, alone in the house, asleep in bed.

Just at this time, one of the boy's relatives was on her way to Tsefas from Sidon. She had learned about the boy's miraculous recovery and rejoiced. But she had not heard of the exact details of his recovery and did not know about the condition which the spirit had imposed. As soon as she arrived in the city she went directly to his home to greet him and rejoice with his parents.

She knocked on the door but there was no answer; no one was home. Impatiently, she opened the door and walked in. She saw that the house was empty, but there, in the bedroom, lay the boy, resting peacefully, his cheeks a healthy pink. She cried out with joy. The boy awoke and opened his eyes. As soon as he beheld the woman, he began shrieking violently; a few minutes later he was dead. The spirit had kept its promise.[6]

The Punishment

A widow of Tsefas was once possessed by an evil spirit which afflicted her severely. Her cries of pain could be heard from afar and they aroused the sympathy of all her neighbors. They went to many holy men in Tsefas, seeking help, but to no avail. As soon as a *tzaddik* would approach her, the spirit would begin shouting, describing all of the evil things it had done in its past life. The holy men would flee in embarrassment.

A disciple of the Ari, R' Yosef Arzin, was asked to help. When he came, the spirit addressed him with warmth and respect, "*Shalom*! Peace unto you, master!" R' Yosef asked the spirit to reveal who it was.

"I am so and so, your own disciple from Egypt," said the spirit. "Don't you remember how you used to rebuke me for my evil ways when I sat before you? But I ignored your wise words and turned away from the right path. I sinned and was punished. Now that I am dead, I am denied peace in the World of Truth."

After hearing this sad tale, R' Yosef went to the Ari for advice. R' Yitzchak was ill, at the time, and could not help the widow. But he summoned R' Chaim Vital and taught him how to exorcise an evil spirit, then sent him along with R' Yosef to the widow's home.

As soon as the two men entered the cottage, the widow turned her face in hiding. R' Chaim cried out to the spirit, "Sinner! Why do you turn your face to the wall?"

"I cannot bear to look at such holy faces for I have sinned so greatly during my life."

"I demand that you turn around to look at us!" R' Chaim ordered. The widow turned to face him.

"And now, tell your tale!" he demanded.

"I have been dead for twenty-five years now," the spirit said weeping. "When I came before the Heavenly court, all of my wicked deeds were reviewed. They were so numerous that even *gehinnom* could not purge them and I was sentenced to wander restlessly throughout the world, accompanied by three avenging angels until I found the proper *tikkun* (corrective) for my miserable soul. I have wandered for the last twenty-five years, beaten by the three accompanying angels. They strike me and shout, 'Thus shall be done to the one who has multiplied sins in Israel!' If I can cleanse the stains on my soul, I will still have to go to *gehinnom* for an additional twelve months. There the remaining stains will be rubbed away and my soul will be cleansed anew."

"When did you die? And where?" R' Chaim asked when the voice fell silent. "Did you confess before you died?"

"I was drowned. We were sailing from Alexandria to Cairo when our ship crashed against some rocks and sank. All of the passengers drowned. I struggled in the water for a while and had no opportunity to think of *vidui* (confession). My body was washed ashore and found by some Jews who gave me a proper Jewish burial. Since then, my soul has wandered about, finding no peace and I came to the body of this widow."

"How long must you still wander about before you find atonement?" R' Chaim asked. "And why have you chosen this poor woman as your victim? Why must she suffer for your sins?"

"I must be made to suffer as long as the wickedness which I did still has an effect in this world. I cannot rest until that evil is no more. As for your second question — why I chose this helpless widow as my host — I will tell you. When I came to Tsefas, I visited many homes and found all the people to be fine and upright. I could not get a foothold into their bodies. But one night I came to this cottage. In the morning, the widow went to her stove to cook some breakfast. She tried to light the fire but the flame flickered and failed, time after time. She became so angry that she flung the pot to the floor and began cursing. At that moment I was given permission to possess her body."

R' Chaim was surprised. "How can it be," he said. "that a person is made to suffer so horribly because of a few curse words uttered in anger?"

"That is not her only sin. This woman's faith is weak. She denies the miracles which *Hashem* performed for His people, especially the miracles of the exodus from Egypt. On Passover eve, when all Jewish families sit around their *seder* tables recounting the wonderful miracles related in the *Haggadah*, she sits and mocks, denying that any miracle ever happened."

R' Chaim now addressed the widow herself. "Tell me honestly, do you believe that *Hashem* created heaven and earth, that He is the A-mighty King over the entire world and that He guides it in His Providence? Do you believe that it is in His power to do whatever He so wishes?"

"I truly believe!" she cried out, her body wracked with sobs. "I declare that G-d is the Guiding Force of the world! His is the power and the might! I promise that from this day on I will firmly believe in all of the miracles which He performed for His people, that He took them out of Egypt and split the sea for them!"

R' Chaim then made use of what his master had taught him. He said the prayers and incantations which would drive the evil spirit from the widow's body. As soon as he spoke, the widow's big toe swelled up. Shortly afterwards it returned to its normal size and everyone could see that the spirit was gone.

Nevertheless, from time to time, the spirit would return to plague the widow and frighten her. Her neighbors returned to the Ari to seek his help once more. This time the Ari told R' Chaim to go to the widow's house and examine the *mezuzah* on her doorpost. R' Chaim found the *mezuzah* to be improper and changed it. From that time on, the woman was free of the evil spirit.

The soul of the wayward *talmid* was forced out of the widow's body, but it still could find no permanant rest, for it had not as yet completed its atonement. It sought revenge against R' Chaim Vital. The Ari, aware of this, told his devoted disciple not to go out at night through the streets and markets of Tsefas, since he would then be easy prey for this and other evil spirits. R' Chaim was not afraid, but out of deference to his master, refrained from going out at night.

Once, while R' Chaim was studying with the Ari, they became so absorbed in the subject that they did not realize that night had already fallen. When R' Chaim prepared to leave for home, the Ari offered him a place to sleep. But R' Chaim said that he had to be home that

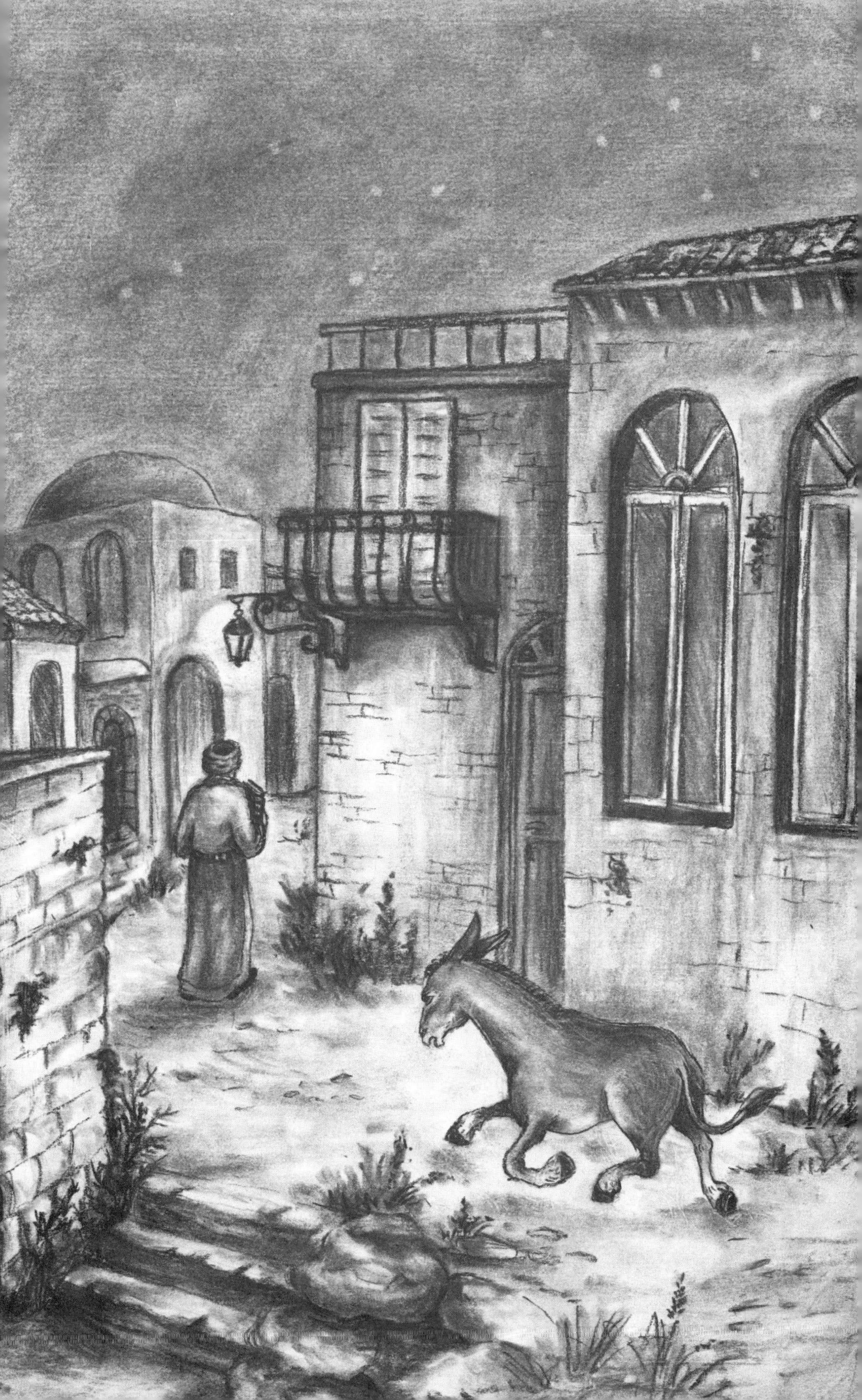

night. The Ari accompanied him to the gate and sent him off, but with a foreboding heart.

R' Chaim walked through the narrow lanes of Tsefas when, suddenly, he heard the sound of hoofbeats. Turning around, he saw a large, fearsome donkey running after him. There was no place for him to flee; the houses penned him in from both sides. The berserk donkey would be upon him in minutes. R' Chaim recalled his master's warnings and, petrified with fear, he fell to the ground. The mad beast hurtled on and trampled him.

Wounded and bleeding, he lay there in the lonely alley, unable to move. The donkey had disappeared down the narrow road. Moaning and groaning with pain, R' Chaim finally picked himself up. He dragged his way painfully homeward. He tried to support himself on the stone fences which ran the length of the lane and discovered that his right hand was badly hurt. The donkey had stamped on it with its full weight and the bones seemed to have been crushed. His pain increased as he inched his way along, on the verge of collapse.

Early the next morning, a messenger tapped upon R' Chaim's door. The Ari had sent him to find out if R' Chaim had arrived home safely. R' Chaim raised his eyes to heaven in thanksgiving, "Praised be *Hashem*, I am still alive!" he exclaimed, and told the messenger the entire story.

He remained bedridden for the next few days, his body racked with pain. When he had somewhat recovered, he hastened to visit his master. The Ari greeted him with concern in his voice, "I feared for you that night. I knew that the powers of evil were strong enough to do you harm. I even stood by my gate, looking after you for a long time, even after you had long passed from sight, praying for your welfare. I am sorry that you did not listen to me when I told you not to go out at night. You should have slept over."

R' Chaim bowed his head, humbly acknowledging that his master had been right. He promised not to venture out after dark again. And indeed, from then on, if he chanced to remain at the Ari after sunset, he stayed there for the night.

R' Chaim held up his hand for the Ari to see. "My right hand still pains me excruciatingly, I cannot use it." R' Yitzchak laid his palm upon his *talmid*'s wounded arm and behold! All the pain disappeared and the hand was whole once more. R' Chaim flexed his wrist and fingers and they moved to his will, as if nothing had ever happened![7]

---

1. "Kav Hayashar" Chapter 7, as quoted from "Charedim"
2. "Taamei Haminhagim", excerpts, Siman 88, quoted from "Mishnas Chachamim"
3. "Maasim Tovim", Baghdad 5650, Siman 20
4. "Maaseh Nisim" Chapter 7
5. "Divrei Yosef" p. 215
6. Ibid, p. 216
7. "Shivchei HaAri"; "Kav Hayashar" Chapter 7; "Divrei Yosef" p. 220; "Nishmas Chaim" Essay 4, Chapter 20, Amsterdam (5412) p. 103

CHAPTER THIRTEEN
GILGULIM

Knowledge of *gilgulim*, the rebirth of souls, is one of the branches of *Kabbalah*. The heavenly court gives a person after death the opportunity to straighten the crooked paths of his life. His soul descends to earth and is reborn in a new body. During its new life, this soul tries to repair the damage and correct the faults of its previous life.

The Arizal expounded upon the verse, "*Hashem*'s Torah is perfect; it restores the spirit" as follows: The Torah is truly perfect and whole; whoever fulfills it in its entirety attains perfection himself. But if he does not achieve perfection, the Torah causes his spirit to descend; it is 'restored', that is, returned, so that it might complete what it did not accomplish in its first lifetime.[1]

Souls are recycled into a new life and a new shape, sometimes a strange one, in order to repair the particular flaw which they acquired. Writings of the Jewish Sages say that people who in their lifetime, sinned through idolatry are reborn as animals, since idolators are compared to beasts. Those who, in their lifetime were not careful about what they ate and consumed, *treife*, are reborn as dogs, since the Torah says that we should throw our *treife* meat to the dogs (*Shemos* 22:30). Gossipers and slanderers also, at times, take on the form of dogs in their next *gilgul*, as our Sages taught: "Whoever speaks *lashon hara* deserves to be thrown to the dogs."[2]

The Ari used to say that *tzaddikim* return to this world in the shape of fish and are eaten in honor of *Shabbos*, thus achieving their *tikkun*.[2] He revealed that some souls even return in vegetable or inanimate form. Those who sin with their tongues return as rocks; those who caused Jews to sin by eating forbidden food, return as leaves on a tree which are blown away by the wind.[4]

Mekubalim, expert in this matter of rebirth of the souls, explained that there is a difference between souls which return to the world as humans and souls that return as stones, plants or animals. When a person is reborn, he does not remember anything about his former life, nor does he realize that he is a *gilgul*. But if he returns to earth in the shape of an animal, a plant or an inanimate object, he is very much aware of his former existence. Throughout his second 'lifetime' he suffers acutely by constantly remembering why he is on earth. He waits and yearns for the moment when he will achieve fulfillment or perfection in this world.

The Ari was a giant in this branch of *Kabbalah*. Not only was he able to discover the secret of the previous life of a person or an object — he also knew what to do in order to help wayward souls achieve perfection.[5]

A Stone Cries Out From the Wall

R' Yitzchak Luria once took his disciples to Tveryah to pray by the tombs of the holy men buried there.

The ancient *batei knesses* dating back to the times of the *tanaim* and *amoraim* who had resided in Tveryah were still intact and there were many graves of Jewish Sages from ancient times up to the Ari's own era. They prayed at the various tombs and then walked through the lanes of Tveryah. Suddenly, the Ari stopped by one of the houses, pointed to a stone embedded in a wall, and said, "Surely, you recall what the *midrash* says about the stones that Yaakov Avinu placed under his head at night. While he slept, they quarreled among themselves, each arguing that the *tzaddik* rest his holy head upon it. *Hashem* performed a miracle, uniting the stones into one. Stones have a language of their own, as it says, 'A stone cries out from the wall.' Well, that very stone just told me that it is the rebirth of a soul which needs a *tikkun*. It begs us to pray for it."[6]

Black Ravens

The Ari and his *talmidim*, together with several of the scholars of Tsefas, once left the city in the direction of Kfar Ein Zeisim to pray at the tomb of the saintly *tana*, R' Yehudah bar Ilai for the needs of the people. Before they reached the tomb, they stopped to rest under some olive trees to prepare themselves for prayer at such a holy site.

As they sat there, a black raven flew up to the Ari and cawed hoarsely, "Krraaa, krraaa! Krraaa, krraaa!" and flew off. A few minutes later it returned and again cawed raucously and flew away. It repeated this several times.

The disciples looked towards their master for an explanation. The Ari turned to one of the group, R' Moshe Galanti, who was familiar with Tsefas and its inhabitants, and asked, "Do you recall the late Shabsai, the tax collector?"

"Of course," he replied at once. "Who can forget him? He terrorized us all. What a cruel, evil man he was! Shabsai did not hesitate to oppress even the poorest of us who did not even have a crust. He extorted the last coins from many impoverished people. Oh, I could tell you of many people whom he actually beat to death!"

R' Moshe waxed indignant. He raised his voice in angry reminiscence and it echoed back to him from the surrounding mountains long after he had fallen silent. The Ari turned to the raven and rebuked it, "Evil, wicked sinner! Leave me be! I refuse to mend your soul after you persecuted your brethren so brutally!"

The raven flew off and did not return.

Upon another occasion, when R' Yitzchak and his disciples were sitting under a thick tree, they noticed a pair of pitch black ravens sitting upon a branch. The Ari was so engrossed that he did not notice them until a feather fell out and floated before his eyes. He looked up and saw them. Then he fixed his gaze upon them.

After a few moments of studied silence, he called up to them, "Sinners! While you were on earth you did your best to uproot the Jewish people from under G-d's heaven and now, that you are sentenced to the fire of *gehinnom*, you come to me to repair your souls?! Indeed, I will not do so! I am not at liberty to do so, nor do I wish to overlook what you did to my people! Begone, Balak and Bilam, you wicked ones!"[7]

The Punishment of an Informer

"Do you remember so and so from Tsefas?" the Ari once asked his disciples.

"Yes," several of the older ones nodded. "We knew that *rasha*, may his memory rot. He used to inform upon the Jews of Tsefas before the authorities, causing much harm. Many people rejoiced at his death and sighed in relief."

"Then it would interest you to know that that evil man was reborn as a mouse. He seeks my help to restore his soul. Quick, bring me a mouse trap and I will show him to you."

Someone fetched a mousetrap and laid it on the floor in the middle of the room. Within a minute, there was a click and a thud; something was caught in the trap. It was a grey mouse struggling to get out.

"*Rasha!*" the Ari raised his voice angrily. "When you were alive and informed upon your fellow Jews to the authorities, did you really think that you would escape judgement and not be brought before the Heavenly court?"

"Please, O master," the tiny voice squeaked pitifully, "have mercy and pray for me. Pray that I be sent to *gehinnom* where my soul can be purged and cleansed, for in this form I suffer far more than do those who burn in hell!"

"You don't deserve it!" R' Yitzchak said sternly. "Go back to your hole until your time comes. Meanwhile, you must suffer. Go!" He released the mouse and it scurried quickly into its hole.[8]

Beware of the Dog!

R' Avraham ben Puah was one of the most distinguished residents of Tsefas. He was wealthy but, also, pious and most generous. R' Avraham never turned anyone away; he always had a ready ear for the hardships of his unfortunate brothers. He would listen patiently, comfort his visitors with cheering words and send them away with a generous sum. R' Avraham had a golden reputation and was revered by everyone in the city.

He had a neighbor who was also a wealthy man. They often did business with one another. The neighbor became ill and his condition grew worse and worse. Despite the ministrations of the best doctors which the family could find, he died soon after.

The family moved away and a different family moved into the house. Soon the deceased was all but forgotten. Years passed and R' Avraham was beset by a disturbing nuisance; one of the stray dogs in the city took up residence in his courtyard, refusing to budge. Black, ugly and belligerent, the dog drove off all visitors. The servants tried to chase it away with shouts and clubs, but it frightened them away with its frightful howling and menacing snapping. After many unsuccessful attempts to drive off the stubborn dog, the family capitulated and let it remain in their yard.

The dog was not satisfied with this. It began following R' Avraham wherever he went. From early morning, when R' Avraham went to the *beis knesses*, it was already at his heels, snapping ill-temperedly. R' Avraham would chase it away with his cane and hurry into the *beis knesses*. The beast would crouch by the door, waiting for him to emerge and continue to follow in his footsteps.

R' Avraham sought the advice of the wise men of Tsefas. But they could not help him. The dog continued to haunt R' Avraham relentlessly.

One wintry morning, R' Avraham left his home for the *beis knesses* and forgot to lock the door. There was no one home except his wife, who was still in bed. To R' Avraham's surprise, the dog did not follow him to the *beis knesses*. However, as soon as R' Avraham had turned the nearby corner, it rushed into the house. It ran into the bedroom, pounced upon the sleeping woman and sank its teeth into her flesh. She awoke in terror and began screaming hysterically, but the dog would not leave off. It bit her again and again until she was a mass of bloody gashes. Only then, did it stop and dash out of the house.

The neighbors had come running to see what was the cause of the cries. They were appalled by the sight that met their eyes. Some of them began dressing the woman's wounds; others rushed off to fetch her husband from the *beis knesses*; still others went to fetch a doctor. R' Avraham did not go home at once. He ran to the Ari first and told him what had happened, tearfully begging that the Ari save his wife.

The Ari, in his divine intuition, knew what had happened and why it had happened. "Do you recall your neighbor of many years ago who died from a painful illness?" he asked R' Avraham. "Yes," said R' Avraham, "poor man. He suffered very much."

"Your wife persuaded this man to enter into a partnership in a shady business deal which promised great profits. He was punished soon after by dying from a painful illness and returning to earth in the form of a dog until he found his proper *tikkun* (corrective)."

R' Avraham turned pale but listened intently. "This, as you must have guessed, is the dog which has taken up residence in your yard. It has come to avenge the wrong which your wife wheedled him into doing. If your wife confesses to the truth, she will die in a state of wholehearted repentance and her sin will be forgiven. The dog will also thereby find its redress."

Shaking from this revelation, the rich man returned home and told his wife what R' Yitzchak had said. She confessed her sin and told him everything that had happened many years before. When she had finished her *vidui,* she closed her eyes and died.

This unnerving tale quickly spread all over Tsefas. The people marveled more than ever at the saintliness of the Ari. He was a prophet who lived in their midst.[9]

Six Months and Six Hundred Gold Coins

One of the sages of Tsefas once had to travel on some urgent matter. Before leaving, he went to the Ari for a blessing and for advice, but he had to wait until the Ari could give him his attention. When the Ari was free, the visitor was about to speak about his forthcoming journey, but saw that it was unnecessary. The Ari already knew all about his plans, for he said, "I know that you have come to part with me before setting out on your voyage."

The sage was amazed by the Ari's divine intuition and nodded. "Sit down for a moment," the Ari said, "and let me tell you what will happen to you." The scholar opened his eyes wide in eager expectation, overcome by curiosity.

"When you reach a certain city (he mentioned a name) you will be very successful. You will gain an excellent reputation among the Jews there and people will suggest many fine matches for you. In the end, you will decide to marry a virtuous woman who has all the traits a good woman should have, besides which she will be wealthy. You will live a life of ease in the home of your new father-in-law.

But your days of comfort will not last long. After six months your wife will pass away, leaving you the sum of six hundred gold coins, a considerable figure, but no more."

The scholar listened to the Ari with openmouthed wonder. Finally, he burst out saying, "What do the six months and the six hundred coins symbolize? Surely such exact figures have special significance?"

The Ari nodded. "Your question was apt and there is a reason for those numbers. In your previous *gilgul* you were partners with a man for six months during which your business thrived. But your colleague complained incessantly and tried to remove you from the partnership. In the end, he trumped up charges and brought you to a gentile court, which is forbidden by the Torah. He was able to 'prove' through false witnesses that you had embezzled a large sum. The court found you guilty to the sum of six hundred gold coins. After the partner died and his soul came before the Heavenly Judge, he was sentenced to descend to this world in the form of a woman and you — in your present form. His *tikkun* will come through being married to you for six months. You will be rewarded with six months of comfort and ease, after which you will inherit the six hundred gold coins which is your due."

The scholar went his way. He returned to Tsefas after a long time. Everything that the Ari had predicted had come true, down to the smallest detail![10]

Several of the neighbors who shared a courtyard with the Ari sought excuses to start up with him. They did their best to make his life miserable."

The Ari was, by nature, a merciful, tender person who bore a deep love for all of *Hashem*'s creatures. His pupil, R' Chaim, has testified that his master took special care never to kill an insect, even an annoying one like a mosquito or fly![12] And yet, he stood up against his bitter neighbors with full vigor. Once, when these same neighbors mocked his practices and teachings, the Ari rebuked them angrily and said, "Do you intend to continue your wicked ways? Know that it is in my power to have the earth swallow you up alive!"

When his *talmidim* heard this, they were frightened. Such behavior was so out of character for their master who was generally so calm and peace-loving, so resigned to any suffering that fell to his lot. How sharp these words were! They felt compelled to ask for an explanation.

"These neighbors are a *gilgul* of Dasan and Aviram. They have been sent back to earth to repair the evil they did in defying Moshe Rabbenu. Their only hope is in obeying and honoring me, since my soul stems from that of Moshe Rabbenu. But they refuse to repent and I was forced to remind them of the punishment which they have already experienced in the desert."[13]

1. "Choshev Machashavos" quoting the Arizal as brought in "Taamei Haminhagim" p. 431, Last Essay, Os 5
2. "Charedim" Chapter 33
3. "Taamei Haminhagim", Last Essay, p. 144
4. "Nishmas Chaim", Essay 4, Chapter 13, p. 99
5. "Kav Hayashar" Chapter 5, p. 6
6. "Shivchei HaAri" p. 29; "Maaseh Nisim" Chapter 4
7. "Divrei Yosef" p. 211-212
8. Ibid, p. 214
9. "Kav Hayashar" p. 50, Chapter 34
10. "Divrei Yosef" p. 208
11. "Divrei Yosef" p. 215
12. "Shaar Hamitzvos" Parashas Noach, quoted in "Psora D'Abba" vol. II, Siman 9
13. Ibid

CHAPTER FOURTEEN
RELIEF AND DELIVERANCE FOR THE JEWS

A group of disciples sat on the grass near the tomb of Hoshea Hanavi, surrounding their master. The Ari, his eyes blazing with a holy light, was speaking when, suddenly, he fell silent and his face clouded over. Then he said anxiously, "I hear a great noise in Heaven. The Heavenly court has decreed that Tsefas be afflicted by a plague of locusts which will spread throughout our borders, devouring everything edible — every fruit on a tree, every blade of grass. Nothing will be left. For one of the good people of Tsefas has cried out to Heaven that he and his family are starving to death." The Ari turned to his disciples and asked, "Surely you know R' Yaakov Alteretz, the erudite and pious scholar. He is down to his last crust of bread. His neighbors know about his poverty but shrug it off. They are not concerned. His cry has ascended directly to Heaven and now we are being threatened with the plague of locusts which will bring famine to all of us."

The Ari was thoughtful for a moment, then continued, "Let us gather a sum of money among ourselves and give it to R' Yaakov so that he can buy food for his starving family. We will be saving all those people from death and, hopefully, we can avert the evil decree which has been passed in Heaven."

The disciples quickly gave what they could and sent the sum with R' Yitzchak Cohen, to the Alteretz home.

The messenger went and found the poor scholar sitting in tears with his head between his knees. R' Yitzchak spoke to him gently, asking why he was weeping. R' Yaakov told him about his poverty, how the few pennies he managed to scrape together did not even provide his children with a scant portion of bread. Besides, he had to pay something to the water carrier. "Today," he said, "one of my children bumped into one of the earthenware pitchers which he uses. It broke and the water spilled to the ground. Now I must buy him a new pitcher but I don't even have money to pay for the water which was spilled. Here I sit, overwhelmed by my bitter fate. What shall become of me? What shall I do? I poured out my heart to *Hashem* just now, saying, 'Master of the world! Why must I be so poor? Am I in any way at fault that I must suffer so terribly? Am I so wicked? Are You not a benevolent King? Where, then, is Your mercy?' These are the words that escaped my mouth as I sat here, just now. I can't help feeling thus; I am so miserable!" And he wept bitterly.

R' Yitzchak Hakohen gave him the money which his comrades had collected, saying, "See how far-seeing is our master, R' Yitzchak Luria, who knew of your plight. Here, take this. It should be enough to buy the water-carrier a new pitcher, to pay for the spilt water and to buy plenty of food for your family. But my master warns you to be careful in the future and not complain, since your prayers almost brought calamity down upon all of Tsefas!"

R' Yaakov's eyes lit up at the sight of the money. He wiped away his tears and thanked his kind Father in Heaven for having come to his rescue through his worthy messengers — R' Yitzchak Luria and his *talmidim*.

R' Yitzchak Hakohen returned to the group still sitting near the tomb of Hoshea ben Be'eri and told them what he had seen and heard. The Ari now reassured them that the danger had been averted. "We have successfully hushed up the voice of the prosecution against us. The decree of locusts has been cancelled by the Heavenly court. We are saved."

They resumed their study. Soon they were so deeply involved that they forgot all about the world around them. Suddenly, a thick black cloud blocked out the sun. They looked up in confusion to see a gigantic swarm of locusts rising from the south and flying overhead. Soon it would spread all over Tsefas and the surrounding mountains. It could destroy every inch of vegetation, leaving nothing for the people to eat! They trembled in fear. Only the Ari remained calm and serene. He smiled reassuringly and said, "Didn't I already tell you that there is nothing to fear? The decree has been cancelled. Nothing will happen to the fields of the Galilee.'

Just as the swarm was about to reach the city, a heavy wind arose. It swept the entire cloud of locusts right into the sea. The people of Tsefas were saved.

The story of this miracle spread throughout the city. And from that day on, his neighbors helped R' Yaakov. Some time later, R' Yaakov Alteretz was offered the rabbinate in Tripoli in Syria. He accepted and the *kehillah* there supported him lavishly and he never hungered again.[1]

The Ruler's Own Signature

A Jewish community far from Tsefas once found itself in dire danger. It had always suffered under the hands of a despotic, anti-Semitic ruler but now he issued a decree throughout his kingdom demanding that the Jews pay a huge sum of money within three months or suffer banishment.

The Jews were devastated. What were they to do? How could they possibly raise such an astronomical sum? "Even if we were to sell all our possessions we could not gather such a sum!" they said to one another in despair. The ruler was hard-hearted and would not agree to compromise at all. From whence would come their help?

Following centuries-old tradition, they all gathered in the *batei knesses* — men, women and children — to pray. They blew *shofaros*, said *selichos* and wept in the hope that *Hashem* would see their plight and have mercy upon them. They sent messengers to all the Jewish communities world-wide to urge them to pray as well. The messengers traveled day and night without rest, knowing full well the danger that faced them and their people.

Late one Friday afternoon they reached Tsefas, weary, dusty and travel-worn. Before they made any arrangements for the coming *Shabbos*, they rushed to the home of the Ari and told him of the impending calamity threatening their community. For R' Yitzchak was famed as a holy man and miracle worker — and they knew that he was the person to whom to turn.

When they reached his home, they found him dressed for *Shabbos* in a flowing white robe. He looked like a heavenly angel. His *talmidim* had already gathered about him, prepared to go out to the fields, as usual, to greet the Sabbath Queen. But a glance at the dusty, nervous travelers showed that they were there on pressing matters. The Ari sat them down and gave them his undivided attention.

Weeping and breathless, they gasped out their tale of woe. The Ari reassured them, saying, "Do not fear. *Hashem*'s salvation comes in the blink of an eye. You will be my guests this *Shabbos*. Go now, and prepare yourselves; forget your worries and get ready to greet the *Shabbos* Queen, for it is already late. Do not be sad. *Shabbos* is not the time for anxious prayer. Relax and put your trust in *Hashem* for you will see, when *Shabbos* is over, your salvation will already be at hand!"

The messengers quickly readied themselves for the holy day. They spent the *Shabbos* by the Ari and came to realize that all they had heard about this holy man was true. Never in their lives had they experienced such an exalted, wonderful holy day of rest.

After *havdalah*, the Ari turned to his guests and invited them to come along with him. He told his disciples to bring some strong ropes and come as well. The Ari went first. The way was dimly lit by the flickering stars. No one knew where they were going but they followed confidently behind their master. The group proceeded thus for a long time, not uttering a syllable, until the Ari came to a halt. The Ari pointed to a spot in front of him. By squinting, the men could make out a deep pit.

"Unwind the ropes and lower them into the pit," the Ari commanded. The *talmidim* did as he said. When only the ends remained in their hands, the Ari ordered them to pull. They began hauling the ropes back up, but felt, at once, that the ropes had been caught onto something. They heaved and pulled while the Ari stood over them, urging them on. They tugged with all their might. Slowly, the weight at the end of the rope rose. Finally the object came into view. They had drawn up a magnificent four-poster canopied mahogany bed. And in it lay a figure, still fast asleep. His clothing and his appearance told them that he was a man accustomed to ruling others.

The Ari approached the bed and began shaking the sleeping figure violently, waking him. The man looked all around him, perturbed. The Ari addressed him angrily, "Are you still stubbornly determined to banish the Jews of your country?" The man looked back at him arrogantly and said, "Yes!" The messengers recognized him to be their king.

"Very well," said the Ari, "then you must draw up all the water in this pit with this before morning. And he handed him a pail which lacked a bottom.

The king looked at the pail and shuddered. "How can I do that?" he asked. "Were I to live one thousand years, I would not be able to draw up even a single drop of water with that!" R' Yitzchak ignored him. "Get to work, or else..." The king was terrified and begged for mercy.

"How do you expect me to show pity when you yourself are heartless? The decree you passed against the Jews of your land is just as impossible as this task. They do not have the means to raise such a preposterous sum of money! If you do not agree to abolish your decree, this

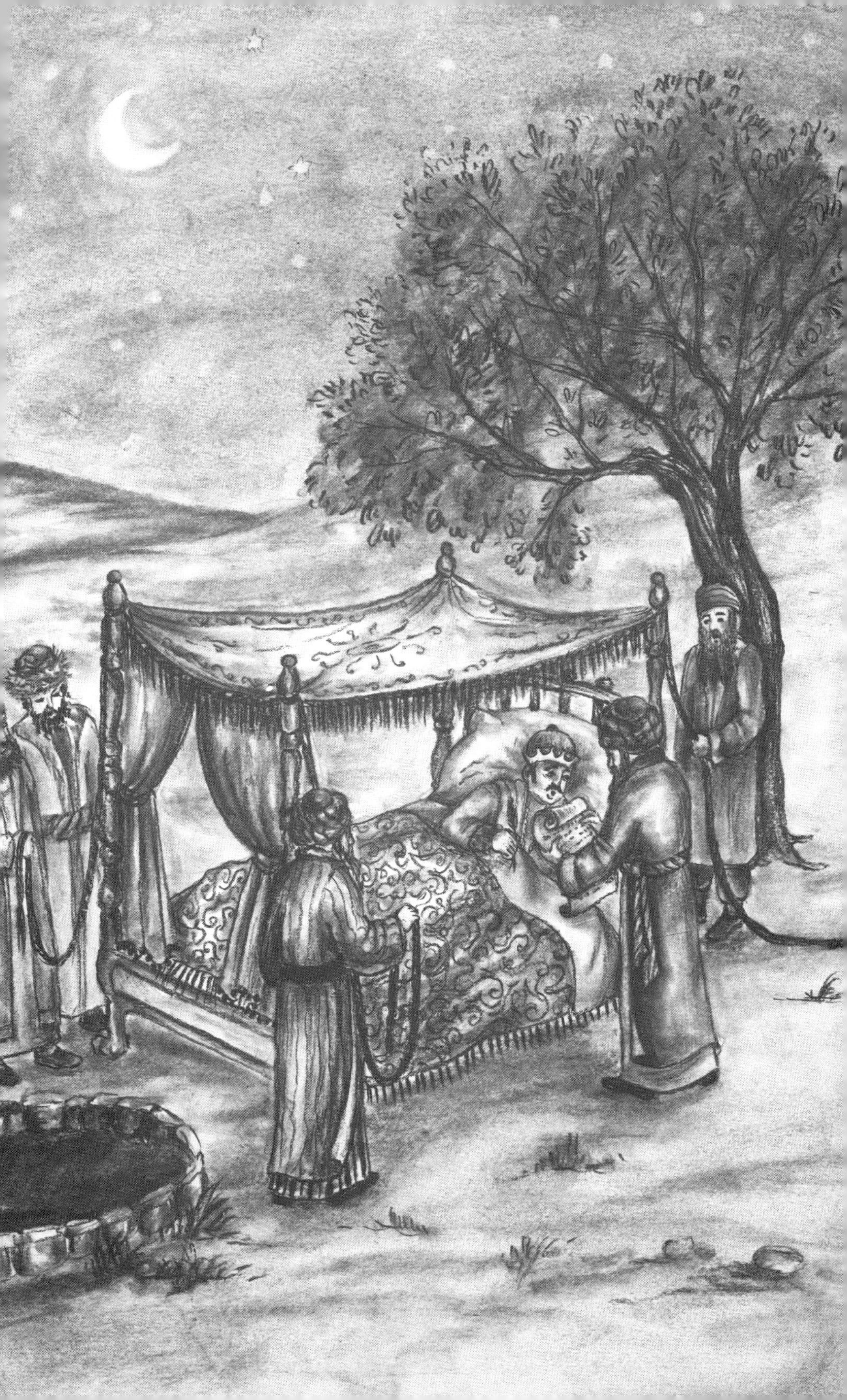

very pit will be your grave!" the Ari thundered at him.

The king trembled uncontrollably. His teeth chattered with fear; he stammered a promise to nullify the decree against the Jews of his land. The Ari then drew out a document, already written out, and read it aloud: "I hereby affirm by my own hand, that I have received the sum imposed upon the Jews of my country and that said sum has been deposited into the royal treasury. Thus, the decree is hereby null and void." The king nodded and with a shaking hand, signed his name at the bottom of the document and handed it back to the Ari. The Ari rolled it up and gave it to the messengers who stood there, hardly believing their eyes. The Ari now turned to his disciples and told them to lower the bed back down into the pit.

The next morning when the king awoke, he found himself in his own bed, in his own bedchamber in the palace. His head ached and his limbs felt heavy. "What a strange dream I had last night," he murmured. "What curious figures peopled my dream. I must have overexerted myself yesterday for I feel as if I have come from afar. And, oh, how my head whirls!"

The king forgot about his strange dream. The three months ultimatum drew to a close and he gleefully began making plans for spending the money or getting rid of the hated Jews. He would gain much wealth whether they paid the fine or not. For if they were banished, he would confiscate all of their property. He congratulated himself upon his brilliant plan.

On the designated day, he sat in his palace, impatiently awaiting the arrival of the Jewish representatives. He waited, but, in vain; they did not appear. Vexed, he sent his soldiers to the heads of the Jewish community, demanding that they appear before sundown, or he would banish them all from his borders.

The messengers who had been sent to Tsefas went to the king, bowed before him and said, "Your Majesty, may your kingdom flourish, we have already paid up the sum. Here is the document which you, yourself, signed. We do not owe you anything. The decree is null and void." They unfurled the scroll bearing the king's signature and showed it to him.

The king looked at the document and, suddenly, a veil lifted from his memory. He relived the events of that terror-filled night. So! It had not been only a nightmare, after all! Who knows what else that mighty rabbi intended to do to him. If the Jew had been powerful enough to transport him in his bed in the middle of the night, he was completely at his mercy!

With trembling lips, the king acknowledged that he had, indeed, received the full sum and that the edict was no longer in effect. And from that time on, he was very wary of his Jewish subjects. In fact, he issued a new decree proclaiming that the Jewish people were his protected subjects and whoever harmed them in any way would be severly punished.

It is said that after the king learned the identity of the holy rabbi who had whisked him away in the middle of the night, he always begged the Jews in his land to mention him to the Ari and ask him for a blessing. And in uttering his name, he would shake his head incredulously and murmur, "He cannot be mortal. Surely he is a living angel!"[2]

Abolishing the House of Evil

There was a well known house of idolatry in Damascus called *Beis Rimon*. The powers of evil ran rampant there. Sorcerers bewitched the place so that whoever passed by the building suddenly felt an uncontrollable urge to enter and offer up a sacrifice to the idols. The magic was so potent that it even worked on the dead; whenever a funeral procession passed by, the dead man would suddenly arise and run into the temple.

This house of infamy was situated in the heart of the city, on a main thoroughfare. Whoever wished to go from one neighborhood to another had to pass by that abominable place. The Jews of Damascus always gave it a wide berth, to their great inconvenience and annoyance.

The Ari learned that the time had come to rid the city of this abomination. He immediately sent R' Chaim Vital to Damascus, instructing him how to abolish that temple and he promised that he would pray for his success and welfare.

R' Chaim set out at once. He reached the capital of Syria and was given a royal welcome by the Jewish community. All the scholars, rabbis and notables of the city came to pay him their respects and drink thirstily of his wisdom. The common folk also flocked to receive his holy blessing and to bask in his presence. R' Chaim, on his part, had a single request. He asked to be informed of the next death in Damascus as soon as possible, for he wished to attend the funeral.

A few days after his arrival, the rabbis of the city sent a messenger to R' Chaim to tell him of a funeral which was to take place that day. R' Chaim went at once. During the funeral procession, the communal leaders told him that they were forced to make a long detour to the cemetery because of the bewitched temple. R' Chaim informed them that he had come to Damascus specifically to destroy that temple and dispell its evil forces. "With the help of *Hashem* I intend to fight this sorcery until it has vanished from the face of the earth," he declared.

R' Chaim directed the procession towards the temple. As soon as they approached the building, the pall bearers, suddenly, felt that their burden had become feather-light. They pulled back the *tallis* which had been spread over the body and discovered to their horror that the body of the dead man had disappeared! A frightful wailing arose from the mourners, who begged R' Chaim to do something at once.

"Cease your weeping!" he said, "and pray for me because I am going in." Everyone moved aside as he strode quickly into the den of sorcery. They stood there, transfixed, their lips murmuring a heartfelt prayer for his safety and success.

R' Chaim remained inside the building for a long time. All were tense and anxious. Finally, he emerged and there was an audible sigh of relief.

He pointed to the pall bearers. "Divide yourselves into four groups; each group will proceed in a different direction of the compass. I will instruct you which special *yichudim* ('unities') to say. But you must not be frightened by anything you are about to see." He quickly told them the required incantations.

Just then, the door of the temple burst open and a pack of wild, howling dogs burst out. Snarling ferociously, they attacked the Jews, their mouths foaming, their pointed white fangs gleaming and their black flanks heaving with the thrill of the hunt. They looked as if they were about to tear their prey limb from limb. The Jews were terrified but remembered R' Chaim's promise that they would come to no harm. They concentrated on their prayers and continued in the direction in which they had been sent.

They had gone some way, when they came upon the discarded body of the deceased. They took it up and brought it back to the stretcher. As soon as they touched the body, the dogs drew back in fear, hissed and slowly sank to the ground, dead.

The Jews of Damascus who had witnessed the entire scene, were dumbstruck. R' Chaim, then, approached the bier and recited *kaddish*. The people came to their senses and thundered the appropriate replies.

"Let us now continue with the funeral," said R' Chaim.

They went on to the cemetery and laid the body to rest. Afterwards, R' Chaim announced that his mission had been successful. With the help of *Hashem*, he had overcome the powers of evil in *Beis Rimon*. "The dogs which you saw drop dead were agents of the sorcerers whom I killed inside the temple. They have now been wiped out. From this day on you have no cause to fear the bewitched temple, for it can no longer do any harm."

R' Chaim Vital returned to Tsefas, but for years afterwards his name was still mentioned by the Jews of Damascus with awe and reverence, as they lovingly recounted the story of his bravery.

R' Chaim eventually settled in Damascus, long after the death of his master, the Ari, and remained there until he passed away. The rabbis of the community dug his grave directly opposite that very temple of infamy, so that the memory of his deeds be forever fresh in their hearts. Thus, whenever the Jews of Damascus went to pray by his tomb, they would recall the kindness he had done to them in saving them from that terrible menace.

With time, other rabbis of Damascus also requested to be buried there, so that the place eventually became an official cemetery for the great rabbis of the city.[3]

1. "Shivchei HaArizal" (Aram Tzova 5634) p. 13; "Maaseh Nisim" end of Chapter 8
2. "Maaseh Nisim" by Shlomo Bachur Chutzin, Siman 13
3. "Shivchei Rabbenu Chaim Vital" (Jerusalem 5613, the Year of Teshuvah — taf, shin, vav, beis, hey), as brought by "Shaar Yerushalayim

CHAPTER FIFTEEN
THE ROSH YESHIVAH

The Ari generally taught in the fields, in the mountains or in the valleys surrounding the city.[1] Each Friday at sunset he and his disciples would go together outside the city to greet the Sabbath Queen with special intense prayers based upon mystic secrets.

From time to time, the Ari and his 'cubs' would visit the holy sites around Tsefas to pray for the salvation of the Jewish people by concentrating upon the holy Names and thoughts which the Ari taught them. These would elevate them to exalted, sublime spiritual heights and open their minds and hearts to be able to absorb even more of the holy secrets of the Torah.

Their School of Study

Each morning after prayers, the *talmidim* would gather to study *halachah* from the Ari. He would show them seven different approaches to the understanding of the *halachah*, six according to *pshat*, the direct interpretations; the seventh was the mystic interpretation. These seven ways represented the seven days of the week; the six corresponded to the six days of human endeavor and the seventh, to the Sabbath, upon which *Hashem* 'rested' or recharged His spirit, as it were (*'vayinafash — nefesh'*). On this day the spirit receives inspiration; it is elevated and its capacity to understand the secrets of the Torah is enhanced.

The Ari took great pains with his teaching. All of his 248 limbs and 365 sinews were involved in Torah study. He exerted himself to such a degree that he would drip with sweat and his disciples, seeing him thus, were afraid that he overtax himself and became ill. They tried to restrain him, but he would thrust them aside, saying, that when a person invested all of his powers in study, he subdued those forces which try to interfere with his success.[2]

He taught the secrets of the *Zohar* by heart, without a text in front of him.[3] He also taught his disciples special *yichudim* and *kavanos*. But he did not transmit all of his knowledge to his *talmidim* directly. He would first give them only the introductory remarks. R' Chaim alone would receive the full explanations and expand on his master's words for the benefit of others.[4]

He Could Not Write

His *talmidim* begged R' Yitzchak Luria to write down his teachings, so that they might study them more closely and so that future generations would also be able to benefit from them. But the Ari felt that it was best for

R' Chaim to record his lessons as the words fell from his mouth.

R' Chaim was the faithful scribe and the only one whom the Ari trusted for this difficult task; he relied on his keen understanding, knowing that R' Chaim was best equipped to absorb and convey what he wished to say.[5]

It is told that R' Moshe Mashlim, another of the Ari's disciples, also used to write down his master's lectures, much to the Ari's disapproval. Once, during the week of *Parashas Vayelech*, the Ari gave his usual lecture, after which his disciples rose to kiss his hand, as was their custom. R' Moshe stood in line, waiting for his turn, but R' Yitzchak turned to him and scolded him for disobeying him.

R' Moshe was disconcerted. He wished to appease his angry master and for the sake of preserving peace he lied and denied the accusation. "Don't lie!" the Ari warned him. "The week's portion says: 'And Moshe wrote this Torah': Besides, I know exactly where you hide your notebooks," and he began enumerating which lectures R' Moshe had committed to writing and where he kept them.

R' Moshe saw that it was no use hiding anything from his master and stopped writing down his lectures.[6]

The Souls of Tzaddikim Attend the Lectures

Sometimes the Ari requested his students to prepare themselves for the coming lecture by studying the subject in advance. He once told them to review a certain passage in the *Zohar*, warning them in advance that the subject was complex and required intense effort.

The *talmidim* approached the passage with trepidation, but, when they faced it, they found no difficulty at all. They studied it over and over again, trying to find complexities, but everything seemed crystal clear. They discussed it among themselves and were unanimous in seeing it as direct and forthright. "But it cannot be," they reminded one another, "because our master warned us that it would be difficult." They all sat down to study the matter together once more, but it was as clear as daylight. They eagerly awaited the next day to see how the Ari would deal with the matter.

The next day, as they were seated in the shade of some trees, the Ari asked how they had found the topic. "We had no difficulty in understanding it," they confessed, "unless our copy is different than the Rebbe's."

"The texts are identical," the Ari assured them. "But if you understood it so easily, let one of you stand up and explain it to us."

They chose one man to explain the subject as they had studied it the previous day. As he was talking, swarms of birds began flocking to the trees under which they were sitting. They perched upon the branches and began chirping loudly, as if in protest. There were so many of them that their sound drowned out the student's voice and he was forced to stop.

The Ari smiled at his *talmidim* and said, "These birds are the souls of departed *tzaddikim* who are studying in the *yeshivah shel maalah*, the Heavenly academy of Torah. They have come here to tell you that your explanation to the passage in the *Zohar* is incorrect."

The Ari now showed them where their error lay and explained the passage correctly. The students were awed by the depths of his understanding and had to admit that they had been mistaken. The Ari then explained the same words in a different way, revealing to them even greater secrets implied in the very same words of the *Zohar*. When he finished, he rose to leave, as he always did.

His *talmidim* were suddenly overwhelmed by a deep love for their master. They fell at his feet and begged the Ari not to leave them but to remain and teach them more and more of the wonderful secrets of the Torah.[7]

The Ari held his *yeshivah* for some time in the Sefardi *beis knesses* in Tsefas, and he supported the disciples who had dedicated their entire lives to Torah study. The Ari was a wealthy man who owned much property and gave charity generously, especially during the Ten Days of Penitence. On the meal preceding *Yom Kippur*, he used to gather all the poor scholars of the city to his table so that it would serve as an altar of atonement, so to speak.[8]

The Ari was not the only source of support for the *yeshivah*. There were others, among them, R' Yosef Bagilar, who will receive further mention later on.

Feats of His Intellect

Through constant contact with the Ari, his disciples came to realize that what they saw was only the tip of the iceberg of his greatness. R' Chaim Vital, the closest to him, wrote of the Ari as follows in the introduction to his work *Etz Chaim* which contains his master's teachings:

> "...were it not for this, I would relate something of his ways and his wonders which only my eyes witnessed, awesome things which no one has seen in the entire land since the time of the *tanaim* like Rashbi (R' Shimon bar Yochai) and his companions.

From Rashbi until Raavid (R' Avraham ben David, one of the great Ashkenazi kabbalists) this knowledge was transmitted by word of mouth. Eliyahu revealed himself to select scholars until the Ramban. From the Ramban until my master there was no one who could grasp this knowledge properly. The Ari knew *mishnah, Talmud, aggados* and *midrashim* in the various different approaches of *pardes*, including the mystic one, *maaseh bereishis* (the workings of the universe) and *maaseh merkavah* (mystic speculations on the Divine Chariot), the language of the birds, trees and grasses, and even of inanimate things such as stones, of flames and of angels. He conversed with spirits of the past who had been reborn, both good and evil. He knew where people's souls had come from. He was also able to divine secrets by the smell of garments. He was capable of addressing the spirit of a *dybbuk*, speaking with it and then exorcising it from the host body. He could see souls leaving the body, in a cemetery, or going to Gan Eden every Friday afternoon.

He was able to speak to the souls of departed *tzaddikim* residing in the World of Truth; they confided secrets of their world to him. He was able to read faces and palms and could interpret dreams. By looking at a person's forehead, he was able to divine his thoughts and dreams. He also knew which verse the soul read when it went to Gan Eden each night. He taught the meaning of the origins of souls and could read upon a person's forehead all of his merits and sins. He was able to find the specific *tikkun* for each individual in accordance with his nature and the origin of his soul.

He knew where mistakes had crept into holy works.

He was able to cause temporary blindness. He knew exactly what his friends had been studying.

He was filled with piety, courtesy, modesty, fear of G-d, love for G-d, fear of sin; he possessed all the good traits and deeds.

He was capable of all the above at any given time; these powers were at his fingertips, as I am witness. He acquired these powers through his great piety and abstinence after long study of ancient and later works dealing with those branches of knowledge. Then he increased his piety, purity and saintliness and these brought him to *ruach hakodesh*. Eliyahu Hanavi appeared to him constantly. I know this to be true..."

R' Chaim Vital was not the only one to leave us written testimony of his master's immeasurable greatness. The Ari's other disciples also told and wrote marvelous things about him:

"He knew which *yichudim* to say upon the tombs of *tzaddikim*. He would prostrate his full length upon a grave and summon the spirit of a particular *tzaddik* and speak to him. And the spirit would reveal to him esoteric secrets which had been studied in the *mesivtah d'rakiya* (the Heavenly academy), and then his face would glow like the sun, so that no one could bear to gaze upon him. He was never bothered by a fly at his table and the fragrance of Gan Eden rose from his bed...

He used to hear the Heavenly decrees being announced about future events on earth. At *neilah* (the closing prayer) on *Yom Kippur* he was able to say who would live and who would die during the coming year. He knew many such things but would not reveal them in deference to his peers.

The Ari himself said that in the verse, "You ascended to Heaven and captured prisoners — *SheVI* - the *shin, beis, yud* — of *SheVI* referred to R' Shimon Bar Yochai (*shin, beis, yud*). However, the letters of the same word can apply to him: Yitzchak Ben Shlomo, in reverse.

1. "Shivchei HaArizal" p. 10
2. "Divrei Yosef" p. 200
3. "Maaseh Nisim" chapter 3
4. In the introduction to "Mekor Chaim" by R' Chaim Hakohen (a talmid of R' Chaim Vital), Petrikov 5632
5. "Divrei Yosef" ibid; "Shivchei HaArizal" pp. 6-7; "Maaseh Nisim" Chapter 2
6. "Divrei Yosef" ibid
7. "Divrei Yosef" p. 201
8. A tradition among mekubalim
9. "Divrei Yosef" p. 197

CHAPTER SIXTEEN

AT THE GRAVES OF TZADDIKIM

One of the most prominent practices to which the Ari accustomed his disciples was prayer upon the tombs of *tzaddikim*. He regarded this as vital in achieving one's highest aspirations in the worship of G-d and Torah knowledge. This practice became entrenched, not only among those of his inner circle, but also, among the rest of the community of Tsefas, and from there it spread and became accepted by many other circles to this very day.

R' Shlomo Shlumil, in his letters of 5367 (1607), writes of this custom as practiced by the people of Tsefas:

> "Every *erev Rosh Chodesh* was treated like *erev Yom Kippur* until midday; no work was done. The entire community would gather at one large *beis knesses* or go to the grave of the prophet Hoshea ben Be'eri above which a large impressive dome has been built. They congregated here, or inside the cave of the saintly *tana*, Abba Shaul, in Kfar Biriya nearby, or by the

grave of R' Yehudah bar Ilai, all of whom are buried near Tsefas. They prayed there intensely until midday or sometimes spent the entire day there in prayer and *drashos*."[1]

R' Chaim Vital offers a reason for this practice: When a person prostrates himself on the tomb of a *tzaddik*, his soul clings to the spirit of the man buried there and the spiritual quality of the deceased spreads through his body. The visitor is given the opportunity to make requests of the *tzaddik*. If the visitor is a humble, G-d fearing person, he is rewarded with revelation of hidden things and special assistance in the study of Torah and the observance of *mitzvos*.[2]

Only men of great sanctity are able to achieve heights in this manner, through intense concentration. The disciples of the Ari were successful during the lifetime of their master, but after his death, except for R' Chaim Vital, they desisted, out of fear that they were not sufficiently exalted, for then it is dangerous for a person's soul. The special *yichudim* ('unities') which the Arizal taught them to help them concentrate when praying upon a *tzaddik*'s tomb are mentioned in the writings of R' Chaim.

We have a vivid description:[3]

"Once our master went to pray by the grave of Shemayah and Avtalyon in Gush Chalav, some four miles from Tsefas, to ask them to reveal a certain secret of the Torah. This was a common practice of his. Whenever he found it necessary to speak to a *tana* or prophet, he would visit his tomb, prostrate himself and concentrate on the unity of *Hashem* to raise the spirit of that great man. He would speak to him as any person converses with a friend. All these *yichudim* are recorded in my writings for the Ari taught them to his *talmidim*, who used them to raise spirits and speak to *tzaddikim* long deceased, to ask them questions and hear their replies..."

In Meron

The *mekubalim* of Tsefas often visited the tomb of R' Shimon bar Yochai and his son R' Elazar in Meron and those of other holy men buried in the vicinity — Hillel and Shammai, R' Yochanan HaSandlar, among them. Then they would gather near R' Shimon bar Yochai's tomb and study *Zohar*. They remained there for ten days and ten nights, far removed from all worldly affairs and isolated from contact with other people aside from the four armed gentile guards and a cook who saw to their physical needs.

They did this twice a year: ten days before *Shavuos* and ten days before *Rosh Hashanah*. During these periods each of the disciples was given his turn to expound upon the *Zohar* before the others.

The tomb was visited by thousands of Jews from all walks of life. On *Lag BaOmer*, especially, which is the anniversary of his death, they came to Meron to sing and dance around his grave. It was customary to bring small children of three there for their first haircut, the *chalakah* ceremony, to fulfill the commandment of not shearing off the *peyos*, and to be blessed in the name of R' Shimon.

Even though he lived in Egypt at the time, the Ari traveled to Meron with his family for the *chalakah* of his three-year-old son. He was not put off by the difficulties and expenses of the trip, for he felt that this custom was very significant. And when he finally settled in Tsefas, he would celebrate *Lag BaOmer* as if it were a *Yom Tov* with joy and exultation. He even composed special prayers and *divrei Torah* to be said each time upon that occasion.

Who Was the Dancing Sage?

One *Lag BaOmer* the Ari and his disciples were dancing enthusiastically together with the multitudes who had gathered to celebrate the special day. Circles upon circles of dancers filled the courtyard. Here were the *mekubalim* of Tsefas, dancing with other-worldly enthusiasm. Their souls seemed to depart from their bodies. There, a group of visitors from Damascus, in their distinguished attire, joined hands with Jews from Egypt and energetically stamped their feet. But in the middle of one circle danced an old man who stood out from all the rest by his remarkable stature and features. Taller by a head than all, wearing a white robe, he danced with an ethereal ecstacy — eyes tightly shut, feet barely touching the ground. His thoughts seemed to be roaming in the upper realms. All eyes were drawn to the distinctive figure and soon many encircled him, clapping their hands and singing while he danced alone. "Who was he?" people wondered. "Surely, he must be a most saintly person."

The Ari, who was totally absorbed in dance and joy, raised his eyes briefly. His gaze fell directly upon this singular figure and he became very excited. R' Yitzchak left the circle of his disciples and cut a path through the merrymakers until he reached the old man. Extending both hands to him, he began dancing with the stranger. The Ari's disciples quickly followed him and joined the circle of spectators. The stranger stopped for a moment to seek out the *shammash* of the Tsefas *beis midrash* to include him in their dance. The three men twirled and whirled around in rapture for a long time and when the stranger pulled away, the remaining two continued to dance, grasping one another's shoulders. The *talmidim* looked on and wondered, "What was the master doing, dancing so long with the simple *shammash*, R' Elazar Azcari, in such devotion?"

At the end of the day, when they were on the road leading back to Tsefas, one of the disciples turned to his master. With a note of displeasure, he asked, "Please do not take offence, my master, if I ask you a question. Could you explain that strange dance with the mysterious stranger and the *shammash*? The first one lent an impression of being a great man in Torah and piety. But was it altogether fitting for you, our great master, to dance with R' Elazar the *shammash*? Was this showing proper respect for the Torah?"

The Ari smiled and said, "Perhaps you can tell me what I should have done. The saintly *tana* R' Shimon bar Yochai himself drew him into our dance? Should I, the younger, have protested?!"

The listeners were overwhelemed by this revelation. They had been wondering who the venerable stranger was. He had been R' Shimon bar Yochai himself, come to join the celebration at Meron. Now they regarded the 'simple' *shammash* in an entirely different light. "Can you imagine how great R' Elazar must be... and we thought him to be a common person," they remarked to one another.

From that day on the Ari's disciples were particularly respectful towards R' Elazar Azkari, the reticent *shammash* of their *beis midrash* who later became famous as the author of *Charedim*.[4]

Sparks from the Souls of the Inner Circle

The Ari was a more frequent visitor of the Rashbi's tomb than most of the holy men. He often went there with his *talmidim* to study *Zohar* at the burial place of its author, explaining to them that this was the very site where R' Shimon originally taught it to his own *talmidim* and traces of their aura still remained there and illuminated the eyes of those who sought to understand those teachings properly.

Once, when the group was gathered in Meron to study *Zohar*, the Ari described the seating arrangement of the *chevraya kadisha*, the holy circle of R' Shimon and his disciples. "Here is where R' Shimon sat," — he pointed to one spot, "and there is where R' Elazar, his son, sat," — he indicated a different spot, "here R' Abba and there R' Yehudah." He continued pointing out the seat of each *tana*. Then he confided further, "I want you to know, my dear *talmidim*, that you are the sparks of those very Sages." He then showed each of them where to sit. He took R' Shimon's seat while indicating to R' Chaim Vital to sit where R' Elazar had sat. His disciple, R' Yonasan was to sit where R' Abba of the *Zohar* had sat and R' Gedalyah was to fill the place of R' Yehudah. R' Yosef Maaravi was given the seat of the *tana*, R' Yossi, while R' Yitzchak Hakohen Ashkenazi was placed where R' Yitzchak had once sat. He continued thus, assigning the different seats to his disciples according to the origins of their particular souls. Then they began their study.

When they were deeply immersed in study, the Ari revealed further that they were now surrounded by an intense spiritual light which was not sensed by the human eye. This was because Rashbi and his *talmidim* and all the Sages of the *Zohar*, together with the souls of all the Sages who had studied *Kabbalah* throughout the ages, the *tanaim, amoraim* and others, had come that day to hear the living Torah issuing from their mouths. "Would that you could see those souls... But only I have been permitted to have a glimpse."

When they were finished studying, the group went to pray at the grave and to thank *Hashem* for having enabled them to reach such an exalted level of holiness that day.[5]

Identifying Graves

The Ari revealed to his disciples that the soul of a deceased person always hovers over his grave.[6] Since he was expert in the secrets of souls, the Ari was able to identify the sites of ancient graves which had been forgotten over the ages.

They tell in Tsefas that when the Ari walked through the local cemetery, he would say, "So and so is buried here," or "That *tzaddik* is buried there," even though the stone markers had long disappeared. His disciples would remember his remarks and ask the old men of Tsefas if they knew of such a thing. They always found corroborations for their master's statements!

Once he said to them, "I see a great light in this spot. The soul of a great man must rest here but I don't know who it is. Yet the light emanating from this grave is very, very bright. It must belong to one of the *tanaim*, though the grave itself is fresh, only one generation old, which is very surprising!"

The *talmidim* approached the oldest men of Tsefas, to try to solve the mystery of the *tzaddik* buried there. They went from one old man to another, but no one could enlighten them. Finally, one of the most ancient answered this question and said, "When I was very young there was a holy man who was considered the greatest of all the pious sages at the time. He is dead now some thirty years. In his will, he forbade anyone to eulogize him or even inform the people in Tsefas of his death. Only a few came to his funeral, but I know, for a fact, that he was buried upon the site that your master indicated. He was so reticent that only a few people knew the measure of his greatness and over the years, his memory has faded altogether."[7]

The Ari made a list of all the tombs of great Jewish figures throughout the ages whose location had not been generally known. He also arranged prayers that were to be said and material that was to be studied at each one of these graves for the elevation of the souls of the people buried there.[8] He transmitted this list to his *shammash*, R' Yaakov Gevizo. R' Shmuel Vital, son of R' Chaim, copied it over and printed it at the end of *Shaar Hagilgulim* with the following introduction:

> "Shmuel said: I have seen fit to agree to append a listing of all the grave sites, some of which are well known and some of which are hidden. Some of those mentioned are known to all. I shall now write down the locations of the graves of *tzaddikim* as I received them from my master, who was capable of divining the souls of the *tzaddikim* at any time and anywhere,

and, most certainly, when he stood at their graves, for that is where the souls hover, as it is known. But he could also do this from afar. He was able to determine the resting place of every holy sage and would converse or study with them. I have often tried to verify his statements through careful investigation and have always found his words to be true. But it is not proper to dwell upon this since such things are exalted and sublime and cannot be contained in a mere book.[9]"

In his list we find departures from what was traditionally accepted concerning certain holy sites. For example, the Ari claimed that what was thought to be the grave of Hoshea ben Be'eri, the prophet, was actually the burial place of the *tana* R' Yehoshua. The list includes tombs in and around Tsefas and Tveryah and notes the graves of Biblical figures like Nachum HaElkoshi; Benayahu ben Yehoyada; Adino HaEzni; Shmuel Hanavi and his father, Elkanah, as well as *tanaim* and *amoraim* mentioned in the Talmud and *Zohar*; also rabbinical figures from the period of *rishonim* like R' Maimon, father of the Rambam and others.

The Ari also expressed an opinion about the holy sites in Jerusalem, though he refused to enter the city gates, for reasons which he did not reveal. And yet, he was able to accurately describe the city within and to refer to a certain spot and say, for example, "There lies buried Zecharyah Hanavi" or "There is the tomb of Chuldah Haneviah" and so on.[10]

"Baruch Haba!"

"I want you to go to Kfar Avnis," the Ari said to R' Chaim on *erev Rosh Chodesh Elul* of 5331 (1561), "to pray at the graves of Abaye and Rava." He taught him the special *yichudim* ('Unities') which were necessary, what he was to learn and the prayers he was to say so that his soul would become bound up with theirs, thus enabling him to understand the secrets of Torah which the *amoraim* were then discussing in the Heavenly *yeshivah*.

R' Chaim went to Kfar Avnis. The sun beat down upon his head and he stopped to rest on a mound of stones. While sitting there, he reviewed all the things his master had taught him so that they would flow smoothly when the time would come to prostrate himself on the grave.

When he arrived, he fulfilled his master's instructions. He prayed, prostrated himself and concentrated upon all the esoteric words which the Ari had prepared for him. And he suddenly felt his heart open up within him and deep secrets were revealed which he would never have understood by his own efforts.

R' Chaim returned to Tsefas in excellent spirits and went at once to tell his master what he had succeeded in learning since last seeing him. He knocked upon the Ari's door and entered to find him surrounded by the group of people who always attended his lectures. The Ari looked up at R' Chaim standing in the doorway and rose in his honor, exclaiming aloud, *"Baruch haba!* Welcome!" He made a place for R' Chaim at his very side. R' Chaim realized that this betokened something, for his master had never shown him such deference before.

When the listeners had gone, R' Chaim could no longer contain himself and asked, "What have I done to deserve this unusual show of respect and welcome?"

"My dear disciple," R' Yitzchak replied, "The deference I showed you was in respect for Benayahu ben Yehoyada who accompanied you when you entered."

The *talmid* was surprised and asked, "But I only visited the tombs of Abaye and Rava. Their spirits should have escorted me. How did Benayahu's spirit become entwined with mine?"

The Ari explained, "The souls of these two *amoraim* are sparks of the soul of Benayahu and the order of study and prayer which I told you to go through at their grave is fitting for his soul also. Now did you, somewhere on your way to Kfar Avnis, stop to review what I had taught you?"

R' Chaim nodded his head. "Then," said the Ari, "the spot where you stopped off must be the precise location of the tomb of Benayahau ben Yohoyada. That is how his soul came to be bound up with yours!"

Some time later the Ari and his disciples visited many tombs. Along the way, between Kfar Biriya and Kfar Avnis, R' Chaim saw the mound of stones where he had rested on his previous trip. As the group passed this spot, the Ari stopped and said to his *talmidim*, "See, this is the grave of Benayahu ben Yehoyada. Let us pray here for we will then merit the revelation of profound things from him."

Only then, did R' Chaim fully understand what his master had told him on that *erev Rosh Chodesh Elul*.[11]

Beware, Lest You Speak

The Ari once called R' Yitzchak Hakohen to him and taught him several holy prayers and words to recite upon the grave of R' Yehudah bar Ilai which lies in Ein Zeisim, south of Tsefas.

"While you are there, doing what I have instructed, your soul will become bound up with his and he will reveal to you the meaning of a certain difficult passage in *Zohar*," the Ari promised. "But this will only happen, if you do not talk to anyone along the way. Do not even reply to a simple greeting."

The disciple purified himself in preparation and went there. To his dismay, the spirit of that *tana* did not come to him and the difficult passage in *Zohar* remained as obscure and closed to him as before.

Disappointed and depressed, he returned to Tsefas. Morbid thoughts ate away at him. "I must have sinned. I must have been found wanting and unfit to hear the secrets of the Torah. Perhaps I am so wicked that a terrible punishment awaits me in the World-to-Come!" R' Yitzchak returned to his master in a gloomy mood. "I did everything that you instructed," he confessed shamefully, "but the passage remained as obscure to me as before. I must have sinned and all my prayers and *yichudim* were in vain."

"I know that your mission was unsuccessful," the Ari chided him. "That is not due to your shortcomings or sins for you are a pure *tzaddik*. That is why I singled you out in particular from all your peers. But you are to blame for having disobeyed my warning. I told you not to say anything to anyone along the way but you greeted the wife of one of your acquaintances. You are all the more at fault, for you spoke first, not she!"

Suddenly, R' Yitzchak Hakohen recalled that brief episode and was overcome with remorse. Why had he not been more careful! He had foolishly forfeited a golden opportunity of meriting a Heavenly revelation from R' Yehudah. He was grief-stricken, but he found some measure of consolation, however, in the fact that he was still considered a *tzaddik* and that it had not been his sins which had prevented the revelation.[12]

The Ari's Extraordinary Shammash

The Ari had a *shammash* to attend to various matters of practical detail. He was R' Yaakov Gevizo.

R' Yaakov came from an illustrious family, many of whose members became famous in Tsefas. R' Yaakov himself was pure and saintly, wise and devout. He served all of the villages around Tsefas as *mohel* and would exhort the women to behave modestly. He also taught the villagers and guided them in Jewish law and practice.[13] He earned a meager living as a water carrier and was barely able to provide enough bread for his family.

One can catch a glimpse of his greatness through the following testimonial:

> "The pious R' Yaakov Gevizo was a noted miracle worker. Like Yaakov Avinu, he was perfect, wholesome, upright, G-d fearing, and avoided sin. He spared no effort in going from place to place to do good works and visit the sick. He went to distant villages all alone, late at night, to perform a *bris* the next morning.

The Arab villagers used to seek his blessings for they knew that he was a holy man. And if thieves crossed his path when he was out on the road at night, they would kiss his hands and say, 'Yaakov Avinu, bless us!" And he would say, "May you be blessed from Heaven on condition that you don't harm any Jew, ever, either his person or his property. If you find a Jew in trouble, help him, or if he has lost his way, accompany him to his destination." And they would keep their promises.

In their times of trouble they would make pledges to the G-d of Yaakov and bring these to R' Yaakov to distribute. They brought him part of their loot, too. Whenever they met up with Jewish merchants, they would say to them, "You are being spared in the merit of our father Yaakov."

After he died, they burned a candle at his grave every Friday, and still do so to this very day, may his soul be bound up in the bond of life.[14]

The ruler of the Galilee once ordered his soldiers to bring R' Yaakov to him. He was determined to execute him, probably because of his connections with the thieves. R' Yaakov evaded his pursuers by using practical *Kabbalah*. He flew up into the air and remained suspended for three days and three nights until the ruler abolished the arrest warrant and the danger had passed.

The Ari gave the list of tombs of great Jewish men to this remarkable man. All knowledge of their burial places had been forgotten over the years. The Ari, in his divine intuition, rediscovered them, and entrusted this list to R' Yaakov because he held him in such high esteem. He directed him to bequeath the list to his sons and they to their sons as a sacred trust, from generation to generation. The author of *Yedei Moshe* tells us that in his own time, some two hundred years after the passing of the Ari, these lists were still preserved in the hands of R' Yaakov Gevizo's descendants. Whoever wished to pray upon the graves of great men of the past, went to them and hired them as guides.

1. "Shivchei HaAri" p. 18
2. Footnotes on "Shivchei HaAri"
3. "Shivchei HaAri" p. 8
4. "Taamei Haminhagim" p. 260 concerning the Lag BaOmer celebrations at Meron, footnote 28, as quoted from "Masaos Yerushalayim"
5. "Divrei Yosef" p. 209; "Shivchei HaAri" 26
6. "Taamei Haminhagim" 1070 p. 474
7. "Shivchei HaAri" p. 28; "Maaseh Nisim" Chapter 4
8. "Yedei Moshe" (in Yiddish), travels to the holy sites in Eretz Yisrael in 5559
9. End of "Shaar Hagilgulim", Jerusalem 5672, p. 73
10. "Chibas Yerushalayim" essay called "Mevaseres Zion" Chapter 19
11. "Divrei Yosef" p. 210
12. Ibid
13. "Yedei Moshe" p. 10
14. "Divrei Yosef" p. 228

CHAPTER SEVENTEEN
THE LAST YEARS OF HIS LIFE

The Ari died in the prime of life; he was only thirty-eight years old. In the three short years in which he lived in Tsefas he became known throughout the Jewish world. He became the *urim vetumim* — the final voice of decision in Tsefas. Its sages came to him whenever they encountered difficulties and he would enlighten their eyes in every aspect with clarity and wisdom.

Despite his relative youth, the Ari was very weak during his last year of life. He had already expended all of his energy in intensive Torah study and worship of G-d. Teaching had also weakened him. His health became so fragile that his elderly mother forbade him to immerse himself in a *mikveh*, and he bowed to her wish. During the six winter months he did not purify himself in a *mikveh* even though throughout his life he had been very careful to immerse himself daily, insisting that this was a vital preparation for reaching spiritual heights in *avodas Hashem*.

His pain and suffering were pitiful; many facts indicate that he knew that his end was near; he is said to have revealed this to his *talmidim*.

The Death of His Son

R' Yitzchak Luria's devotion to all his disciples was unsurpassed. He was prepared to teach them under any circumstances and at any price. And what price could be dearer than the life of one's beloved son?

The Ari once sat among his disciples, teaching them *Zohar* on the chapter, of the Jewish bondage in Egypt. In the course of his lecture he happened to mention that there was one animal which can only give birth through its own death. When the time to give birth comes, *Hashem* sends a snake to bite it and it dies in its birthpangs. "This matter," he said, "contains many deep secrets which cannot even be uttered. Neither R' Shimon or even Moshe Rabbenu taught these mystic secrets for the person who reveals them endangers his own life."

The *talmidim*, thirsty for knowledge, repeatedly begged their master to reveal the secrets implied in this chapter but he refused and they eventually desisted. R' Chaim Vital, however, was unable to ignore his powerful urge to understand those very secrets. He implored and pleaded so much that the Ari finally gave in. He remembered that Eliyahu Hanavi had told him to settle in Tsefas, so that this very student, R' Chaim Vital, could absorb all that he had to teach and later disseminate it. And so, he sat him down and taught him all that he knew on the subject. When he had finished, he burst into bitter weeping. With his hands supporting his head and his eyes streaming with tears, he brokenly groaned, "*Baruch dayan emes* — praised be the True Judge."

The *talmidim* were aghast. A deathly silence filled the room, broken only by the master's heart-rending tears. "I see that I have been punished for having revealed these esoteric secrets. My beloved son, Moshe, will die within the week."

The men gathered there wept along with their master. Their heads bent with agony, they escorted the Ari home and then each went his own way. Only R' Chaim remained with his master to sustain him in his grief.

"How are my children?" he asked his wife when he entered the house. Instead of hearing her usual reply that all was well, thank G-d, she said, "I don't know what's the matter but Moshe came home a few hours ago complaining about a fierce headache. I put him to bed but he is writhing with pain."

The two men went over to the bed, felt the child's forehead and saw that he was burning with fever.

The Ari remained by his son's bedside for the next few days. R' Chaim gathered all of the disciples to pray for the child's recovery. When the other scholars in Tsefas heard that the child was critically ill they, too, met in the *batei knesses* and *batei midrash* to pray. They publicly declared that whoever was aware of his sins should repent and they hoped that *Hashem* would have mercy and retract the harsh decree.

But the edict was not rescinded. Moshe gave his soul back to its Creator. The Ari tore his garments and sat in mourning for his beloved son for the seven days.

When the mourning period was over he sent a message to his disciples: "Do not be disheartened and do not fear that I will stop teaching you the secrets of the Torah.

Even though my son has already died and even though I may be the next to leave the world, I will not withhold my knowledge from you. I will continue to teach you so that you can improve your souls and illuminate the entire world."

The *talmidim* could not help but be overwhelmed by their master's devotion and noble spirit. With trembling and awe, they kissed his hands and blessed him, 'May Rabbenu live a long life, he and his sons forever!'"[1]

The Master Sacrifices His Own Life

A short time later, the Ari sat with R' Chaim studying the *parashah Metzora* according to the *Zohar*. They reached a difficult passage which R' Chaim could not understand.

"My dear R' Chaim," said the Ari, to the latter's surprise, "leave me be. Don't ask me to explain this to you. Believe me, it is for your good as well as for mine." Noticing his disciple's look of astonishment, he added, "There is a deep mystical secret in this matter which Heaven forbids me to reveal."

R' Chaim shut his *sefer* with a deep sigh, saying, "I am perplexed. I think I had better stop. Perhaps, when I return tomorrow, I will be able to understand it better."

The Ari saw R' Chaim's distress and said kindly, "My dear R' Chaim, if I do reveal the deep secrets, I know that you will regret it. On the other hand, I am duty bound to teach you what I know. And so, I advise you to return home and continue to labor over the *Zohar*, even if you make no progress."

R' Chaim went his way. All that night he toiled to understand the sealed passage. When he returned to the Ari the next morning, he admitted that he had not slept that night. And he said, "I still yearn to understand this matter, no matter what the price."

"If you really insist, in spite of my warning, I will explain it to you, but I am cautioning you again — the risk is great."

R' Chaim stood there, unable to make his decision. On the one hand, he felt a driving compulsion to dispel the darkness of his ignorance. And yet, his master's warning echoed in his ears. He stood there vacillating for a long time. Finally, the balance tipped in favor of wisdom.

The Ari obligingly explained the passage in all of its aspects. He answered all of R' Chaim's questions and solved all of his problems. The *talmid's* eyes glowed with the joy of knowledge. But then, like a thunderbolt, this joy was dispelled with the Ari's next words:

"And now, my dear *talmid*, that I have revealed this secret to you, Heaven has decreed that I must die within the year. Had you not pleaded so insistently, I would have been able to continue teaching you for many years. But you disregarded my warning and brought calamity upon yourself with your own hands. Don't think that I feel sorry for myself. Not in the least," he said, laying his hand tenderly upon R' Chaim's shoulder. "Nor do I mourn for my family. I grieve for you, because you still need me..."

When the disciple heard these terrible tidings, his eyes overflowed with tears. "Forgive me, Rebbe!" he wept. "Forgive me!"

R' Chaim did not reveal what had happened to his companions; he did not teach them what he had learned then either. And for the rest of his life, he never forgave himself for having demanded such a sacrifice from the Ari.[2]

The Lost Opportunity

It was *erev Shabbos* at sunset. As usual, the Ari and his disciples went out to the fields to greet the descending Queen. The psalms flowed from their lips and the sound of their song reverberated from the mountains all around.

Suddenly, the Rebbe turned to his disciples and asked, "Would you like me to use my powers of practical *Kabbalah* to transport us all to Jerusalem to spend *Shabbos* there?"

The disciples looked at one another in confusion. "We are ready to go with you to Jerusalem, master, even by foot, but we must first take leave of our families and let them know where we are going," they said, somewhat hesitantly.

The Ari shuddered at these words. Clapping his hands together in dismay, he moaned aloud, "Alas! Alas, that we just missed our chance to be redeemed! Had you greeted my offer with unanimous joy, had you shown yourselves ready to follow me this very instant, then all of Jewry would have been redeemed! This was the right moment in time. But you hesitated. And now our chance for *geulah* is gone. Who knows how long the *galus* will last now!"[3]

Dispirited, the group returned to the city. Their hearts ached for the lost opportunity. They thought about their master's words, trying to understand what he had meant. Only R' Chaim Vital knew clearly, that the Ari was none other than a spark of the soul of *mashiach ben Yosef*. Had the generation been worthy, he would have been the forerunner of the Redeemer. R' Chaim based his assumption upon many hints. He recalled what his master had once told him, that two signs indicated the identity of the Redeemer: he was a "man of suffering and studied in illness." This characterized the Ari very well: the master was always in pain, he always ached for the suffering of his people, besides which, he had a chronic physical illness.[4]

Six months after the death of his son, Moshe, the Ari went with his disciples to pray at the graves of *tzaddikim*, among them, Shemayah and Avtalyon in Gush Chalav. He wanted these two great spirits to reveal a certain mystic secret to him. He prayed upon their graves with special Names and *yichudim* until he succeeded in raising them. He spoke to them, then turned to his *talmidim* and said, "My dear disciples, Shemayah and Avtalyon told me to ask you to pray that *Mashiach ben Yosef* live out his years and not die in your lifetime."[5]

R' Chaim described this event at length:

> "On the day that we visited the graves of Shemayah and Avtalyon, my master emphasized the importance of our concentrating upon the words 'and the throne of Your servant David'. He repeated himself, adding that in every prayer that made mention of 'Your servant David' we were to concentrate powerfully upon the phrase that *Mashiach ben Yosef* live and not die, for he is also referred to as the 'throne of David'... We did not understand his words but *Hashem* knows hidden things. Now, our hindsight explains the significance of that episode; our master passed away, because of our many sins."[6]

The Imminent Plague

Some four months before the Arizal's death, he and his disciples were sitting in the fields, studying Torah. It was a torrid day; the summer sun beat down with blinding brilliance. Heat rose from the baked earth as if from a kiln. Every living creature sought shelter from the harsh blaze. Only the Ari and his *talmidim* were oblivious to their surroundings as they sat under the protective shade of a leafy tree.

Suddenly, the heavens turned dark. A thick, grey cloud spread above Tsefas and hid the sun. The *talmidim* raised their eyes in fright and remembered a similar incident in the previous year. Then it had foreboded evil; it had been sent by Satan and his evil forces who were about to unleash disaster and calamity upon the city. Had it not been for their master, who had urged them to pray then and there, Tsefas would have been destroyed.

The Ari interrupted his lecture and began praying fervently. His expression of fear deepened. This impending danger must be even more frightful than the previous one. The Ari turned to his disciples and said, "The cloud has told me that Tsefas is doomed to total destruction, may *Hashem* preserve us. Last year we succeeded in averting the danger, but this time there is a serious charge against us. One of the men prominent in the city's public affairs is wicked. He extorts money from the poor and treats them despicably, but no one dares to protest or attempts to champion the cause of the persecuted, for all dread his mighty arm. But the cry of the oppressed has risen to Heaven and come before the A-mighty's Throne. The Heavenly court has weighed the merits of our city against its faults and, because no protest was made against that wicked man, the faults were the heavier. We must continue to study with greater intensity. Perhaps this will abolish the evil edict. Our Sages said that "even though a sharp sword rests on a person's throat, he should not despair of Heaven's mercy."

The group resumed its study with enthusiasm but in vain. Tsefas became gripped by plague.[7]

In the Company of Friends

The homes of Tsefas were sealed off; doors were locked and shutters closed. The markets were deserted; none dared venture forth.

The Ari knew that his end was near. He gathered together his closer disciples and assigned a room within the compound of his courtyard to each one and his family. Here they were isolated from all contact with the outside world. They organized classes for the children, set up a communal oven for baking bread and did everything within the confines of this courtyard.

They were convinced that only Torah study would protect them from the sword of the Angel of Death who roamed the alleys of Tsefas. They immersed themselves in their study. The *shiurim* which the Ari gave then were more profound and comprehensive than ever. And it was then that he revealed to this inner circle certain secrets which he had never divulged before. He emphasized the need for brotherly love. For he said that when people live in harmony, Satan was rendered powerless; that when *Hashem* sees unity and brotherhood between Jews, He sends his good angels to protect them from evil.[8]

This theme is emphasized in his writings:

"Before a person goes to offer up prayers in the *beis haknesses...* he should accept upon himself the obligations of *'ve'ahavta lereacha kamocha* — loving his fellow Jew as he does himself. This will enable his prayer to rise up, entwined with the other prayers of Jewry. Most significant is the love between one another among those who study Torah together. Each member of the group should consider himself like a limb of a whole body. He should be aware of his comrades' souls. If any one member is in trouble, all the others should join in his pain — whether he suffers from sickness or his children suffer, G-d forbid, and pray for him."[9]

Satan at Work

The *talmidim* and their families lived in the Ari's courtyard in peace and harmony. The fear of the plague hovered above them, yet they studied diligently; the Avenging Angel was powerless against them. But after four months, they became complacent and felt that they were immune to all harm. This very complacency was the source of their downfall. For as soon as they were off their guard, Satan found a breach and forced his way into their fortress of Torah and brotherhood. It all came about in this way:

Life inside the compound was so harmonious that this very lack of friction caused the people to become restless. One day, some of the children began quarreling over some small matter. Their mothers in their boredom joined the fray. The argument grew louder and more violent as other families became embroiled. Soon, all the women were divided into two warring factions. Satan had found a foothold and succeeded in involving the husbands as well. The Ari was unable to reestablish peace. He was heartbroken over his helplessness, for he realized that the quarrel might lead to disaster. The forces of evil might very well make their way into the camp. His *chaburah kedoshah* (saintly company) was no longer immune; their Torah had not been strong enough.

The Ari was devastated by the knowledge. Of what purpose was life altogether, if they did not fulfill their task and serve the Creator completely?

One Friday, the quarrel reached its peak. The shouting and railing could be heard from afar. The Ari looked on helplessly, his heart bleeding within him. Even the disciples understood that this terrible situation could not continue much longer. They, too, began to fear heavenly retribution.

That Friday evening, they went out to the fields with their master, to receive the *Shabbos* but they did not feel the usual joy and spiritual uplift. They said *Tehillim* in a spirit of gloom. They could sense the Ari's air of melancholy. He sighed and moaned during the *maariv* (evening prayer). The *talmidim* were frightened.

As they returned to the courtyard, R' Chaim asked his master for the reason for the sighing. The Ari replied with restrained anger, "Throughout your stay with me, I warned you, time and again, to live in harmony and brotherhood, but you ignored me and followed your evil inclinations. And once you became embroiled in the petty argument, you gave Satan a foothold. This very evening I saw an angel with a thousand eyes holding a scroll bearing the verse, 'Both you and your king shall die'

(*Shmuel* I 12:25). I understood this to mean that my days here are numbered. Soon I will be leaving you for the world of souls, because the Angel of Death has been given power over me. Nor am I the only one who will suffer. Several of you will also perish in this terrible epidemic."

In that week the Ari departed from this world along with a great number of his *talmidim* — exactly as he had foretold.

The Sun Sets at Noon

On the fifth day of *Av*, 5332 (1572), when he was only thirty-eight years old, the soul of R' Yitzchak Luria Ashkenazi went up to heaven. It was a Tuesday. Two days before, on the Sunday of that week, the Ari was still involved in his business matters. After he had finished going over his records and accounts, he announced to his family and close friends and business associates that his end was near. "If you ever cheated me, I forgive you," he said, "and if I ever shortchanged you, tell me and I will make up the difference."[10]

On that day, he also took his closest disciple, R' Chaim, aside and spoke to him about the others of the group. He revealed to him the nature of their souls, instructed him to continue teaching after he died and told him to be selective about choosing his students. The Ari expressed an opinion on each and every disciple and told R' Chaim to whom he should draw close and whom he should keep at a distance. Finally, he blessed him that he be strong so that he might be able to withstand the jealousy and dissension which might arise when he rejected certain students.[11]

By Tuesday, he was already so weak that he had to remain in bed. His loyal *talmidim* surrounded him, trying to do everything in their power to ease his suffering, while not missing a precious syllable which fell from his mouth. Only R' Chaim was absent.

The master blessed each of his students with a pertinent blessing in keeping with his particular soul needs. "Where is R' Chaim?" he asked.

"He is busy gathering the Jews of Tsefas to pray for the master's recovery," they explained.

"Hasten and fetch him," urged the Ari. "His efforts are all in vain, for the decree has already been signed and sealed. No one can repeal it!"

The disciples rushed out to find R' Chaim and brought him to his master's deathbed. The Ari grasped R' Chaim's hands in his own and, embracing him, blessed him that he succeed in all his endeavors. "I weep for you, my son Chaim," he said, "that we must be separated, but I cannot alter the decree. And now, sit down and ask what you wish of me before I leave you. Do not hesitate to ask what your heart desires, for, if you do not, you will surely regret not having done so, afterwards. Use this opportunity to clarify whatever is not fully clear to you."

He then turned to the others and spoke his final words, "Always take care to honor one another. Be especially strict in maintaining peace among yourselves. Forget your quarrels; cast aside your petty differences. I beg of you, be most respectful to R' Chaim Vital; for there is a living Torah within him which he will spread throughout all of Israel, for he is my trusted servant."

When he had expressed his last wishes, he began revealing deep secrets to them for a long time while they listened avidly. "My house is filled with the souls of past *tzaddikim*," he said to those around him, "for the Heavenly academy has descended to hear the words of Torah which I am expounding to you. Afterwards, they will accompany me to my place in the World-to-Come. Now, this is what I would like you to do after my death. I want no man to touch my bier unless he has purified himself in a *mikveh*; nor shall any woman touch my bier. I do not want the regular members of the *chevra kadisha* to occupy themselves with my burial; only you, my beloved disciples. You are to carry me to the *mikveh* before burial. Do not immerse me, however. Leave that to me. And now, hurry to purify yourselves so that you will be ready to care for me."[12]

The disciples rushed out to do his bidding. Only R' Yitzchak Hakohen remained with him. As a *kohen*, he was forbidden to participate in the burial. The Ari told him that he had warned R' Chaim not to reveal his teachings to others. "The sole purpose of my descending to this world was to refine the soul of R' Chaim. And if he reveals my teachings to others, he will be harmed, for others are not yet ready to be exposed to such profound knowledge."[13]

The Ari was silent for a moment. Then he sighed deeply and continued, "Had this generation been worthy, it would have been redeemed this very year, for such a ripe opportunity has not presented itself since the times of R' Shimon bar Yochai." After a brief pause, he quoted the verse, "And she gave birth again to a son and she called his name Shelah. And he was in Keziv when she bore him" (*Bereishis* 38:5), without explaining himself. But R' Yitzchak could imagine what he was hinting at; he was probably referring to what he had taught them at the tombs of Shemayah and Avtalyon in Gush Chalav (when he had spoken of *mashiach*).

R' Yitzchak Hakohen burst into tears and said that he still had hope that the Ari would live to a ripe old age, but the master silenced him sternly. "If one of my *talmidim* were worthy, I would be granted longer life. And now, tell me," he said suddenly, "where has R' Chaim gone now? I would like to tell him something in secrecy."

"He left upon the master's behest," said R' Yitzchak, "to immerse himself in a *mikveh*." R' Yitzchak tried to pick up the loose ends of their talk and asked painfully, "But what are we to do after the master leaves us?"

"Tell all of your friends in my name that, from now on, they are to cease studying my teachings, since they have not understood them sufficiently and they will come to harm — all, except for R' Chaim. If you improve yourselves and become worthy enough to understand my teachings, I myself will come to you and teach you. And now, my son, please do not ask how I will appear, if in a dream or a wakeful vision, for that is none of your affair right now."[14]

Just as he had finished speaking, the others began to return. They entered the room where the Ari lay. He raised his head from the pillow and announced aloud, "R' Yitzchak Kohen — leave the room now! The Angel of Death is already present. Take care lest you become impure, for you are a *kohen*."

R' Yitzchak hurried out of the house. Now the Ari's head fell back to the pillow and he began reciting the deathbed *vidui* (confession). He then exclaimed with extraordinary devotion, "*Shema Yisrael Hashem Elokeinu Hashem echad!*" His face was afire and alight with an unearthly glow. His disciples could see that his lips still murmured something. They bent close and heard him saying in Ladino (Judaeo-Spanish), "Preserve me from pride!"[15] He then shut his eyes and his soul flowed out of his body in a painless death, a kiss of G-d, so to speak, and rose up to heaven, accompanied by the souls of all the visiting *tzaddikim*.

A wailing arose from the Arizal's house. The family and the *talmidim* wept bitterly over their master who had left them. So many tears were shed then that it was said that had they been gathered up, they would have sufficed to bathe their beloved master's body. And R' Chaim wept most profusely of all, refusing to be comforted. He cried, "Father! Father! The chariot of Israel and its riders! Who shall console me?"

The Funeral

The news of the Ari's death flew through the city like an arrow shot from a bow. Throngs upon throngs flocked to the *mikveh* where the *talmidim* had brought his body to to be immersed before burial. They lifted the body and brought it close to the *mikveh* pool. Then they turned to the dead master and said, "We have carried out your instructions. You have ordered us not to immerse you for you wish to do so yourself." At once, the body rose up like a living person, entered the water, immersed completely and returned to its place.

The disciples dressed the body in linen shrouds and prepared it for the final journey. Meanwhile, the rabbis of Tsefas issued a proclamation that *kohanim* would be permitted to participate in the funeral of this holy saint. The entire city then gathered by the *mikveh* and accompanied the bier to the *beis knesses* where the Ari was eulogized. The sounds of mourning were deafening.

From there, the funeral continued on to the cemetery. The *talmidim*, bearing their master's bier, were at the head of the procession. They walked barefoot, their garments rent and their heads strewn with ashes, just as on *Tisha B'Av*. Tears flowed from their eyes as they cried out plaintively, "O holy Torah! Mourn over the passing of this angel who knew your innermost secrets!"

They were followed by the mourning populace of Tsefas. Even the gentiles — Arabs and others — came to pay their respects to the Jewish sage, whom they also recognized as being holy and saintly.

R' Chaim Vital almost went mad with grief. He walked before his master's bier, beating his head with both hands. His world had crumbled about him.

The funeral took a long time. The Arizal's grave was dug next to the Ramak's. When the body was lowered into place, R' Chaim leapt into the pit, embraced his master's body and shrieked, "Alas for these feet which hurried to do their Creator's will! How were they ensnared, for my sins? How can I restrain myself now that the ark of G-d is being buried and removed from me?" The others lifted him up from the pit with great difficulty. Then they filled it with earth.

The one in charge of the burial stepped forward to beg the Ari's forgiveness, lest they had not treated him respectfully enough. Then he added, "Our master has gone to his eternal rest, leaving us bereft and mourning. May it be the Divine will that his merit protect us and all of Jewry, spare us from suffering and trouble and redeem us speedily, for His Name's sake. *Amen,* may this truly be the Divine will."

The mourners dispersed in agony and pain and returned to their homes. The grief was greatest amongst the inner circle of *talmidim* which had just prematurely lost its leader and teacher.

1. "Divrei Yosef", p. 220
2. "Shivchei HaAri", p. 33
3. "Shivchei HaAri", p. 9
4. "Toras Chacham" by R' Chaim Kohen (Talmid of R' Chaim Vital), Venice, 5414, p. 17
5. "Divrei Yosef" p. 221
6. "Pri Etz chaim" Shaar HaAmidah, Chapter 19, with the footnotes of R' Nasan Shapira, Karetz Press 5542
7. "Divrei Yosef" p. 222
8. Ibid, p. 223
9. "Psora D'Abba" I parag. 2
10. Said by R' Yedidyah Galanti who heard it from R' Yaakov Abulafya, a friend of the Ari
11. "Shivchei R' Chaim Vital" p. 55
12. "Divrei Yosef" p. 221
13. "Shivchei R' Chaim Vital" p. 23
14. Ibid, p. 48
15. "Taamei Haminhagim" as quoted from "Notzer Chesed" by the Admor of Komarna

CHAPTER EIGHTEEN
THE BOOK OF WISDOM IS BURIED

After the death of their master, his disciples continued to study in his *yeshivah* under the guidance of R' Chaim Vital. Shortly after the Ari's death, another five of his disciples fell victim to the plague, just as the Ari had predicted, but a few new faces were added.

The new patron and supporter of the *yeshivah* was R' Yosef Bagiliar. He maintained it out of his own pocket for ten years after the Ari's passing. This R' Yosef, a pure and saintly man, drew close to the *talmidim* of the Ari and they brought him into their inner circle.

R' Chaim served as the new *rosh yeshivah*, while R' Yosef ibn Tabul replaced him during those times that he was away on various affairs. He was held to be the greatest among them, R' Chaim aside.

The Fountains of Wisdom are Sealed Off

The parting words of his master echoed and reechoed in R' Chaim's ears: the disciples would not be able to continue studying *Kabbalah* after his death for they were unworthy. Moreover, as he expressed it: "And I, the least significant, was told that I would be tested severely to see if my love for my master was truly strong. I intended to drive away the entire group from me and allow only three or four trusted friends to remain by my side."[1]

R' Chaim did not disband the group of students but he did gather up all of the notebooks in which they had written down their lessons, against their master's express wish. He buried all of these, refusing to publish them, even though the *talmidim* begged that he do so. R' Chaim claimed that after the death of the Ari, all of the fountains and sources of *Kabbalah* which had flowed down to them from Heaven had been sealed off. For the next fifteen years, R' Chaim worked at classifying his master's teachings according to topics; this the Ari had never done.[2] At the end of this period, the writings of the Arizal were finally brought to light, compiled and arranged by his closest disciple, R' Chaim.

Not only were the writings stored away from foreign eyes, even his oral teachings were to be kept secret. R' Chaim forbade his students to spread these as well, for fear that those who would study them might not be worthy. They took extreme care that the Ari's teachings should not leave the borders of *Eretz Yisrael*. The sages of Tsefas went so far as to issue a *cherem* (ban) against any person who dared to do so.[3]

R' Chaim was the most cautious of all. He did not reveal even a trace of his master's teachings to outsiders.

He could not overlook the bitter fact that even though his master had been given permission to reveal the Torah's secrets to his disciples, he had nevertheless died very young. "As for me," he said fearfully, "I have not received permission from Heaven to transmit the Ari's teachings to others." Many years later, when he was already old and almost blind, R' Chaim acknowledged that he had finally been permitted to transmit the Arizal's teachings to others.

R' Chaim had yet another reason for refusing, for many years, to teach what he had learned from the Ari — it had been the Ari's express wish. The Ari had appeared to him in a dream during the week of *shivah*, on the third day after his death. When R' Chaim had asked him why he had died so prematurely and suddenly, the Ari had replied, "Because I did not find even one person who was perfect in my eyes." R' Chaim asked in wonder, "But, many times when I sat before you in study, you repeatedly said that your only purpose in descending to this world was to transmit your knowledge to me so that I might make it known. I now fear that what the master had said might be wrong..." "Do not fear," the Ari reassured him. "When the proper time comes, I myself will come and guide you. I will tell you what to teach and how you are to do it."

R' Chaim testified that his master revealed himself to him nearly every night for twenty years. The Ari would comfort him, encourage him and teach him his Torah. After this period of twenty years R' Chaim would dream of the Ari once a month and, with the passage of time, the Ari would appear even less frequently, once in three months.[4]

THE BOOK OF WISDOM IS BURIED / 235

The Loyalty Pact

The frightful impression of the quarrels and dissension which led to the death of their master was still fresh in the minds of the *talmidim*. The Ari's dying words about the need for close friendship, for brotherhood and harmony were engraved upon their hearts. They decided to unite under the leadership of R' Chaim Vital, as their master had instructed them.

The disciples, especially those who had been close to R' Chaim in the Ari's lifetime, assembled and unanimously accepted him as their head. They subjected themselves totally to his authority and vowed not to reveal the slightest hint of what they learned from him. Drawing up a list of their resolutions, they each approved and signed it. This 'Loyalty Pact' stated as follows:

> "We, the undersigned, have resolved to form a society to serve *Hashem* and to learn His Torah day and night, in every way that our master, the wise, perfect and godly R' Chaim Vital requires of us. We will undertake the study of truth (*Kabbalah*) and be trustworthy. We will not divulge anything of what we learn. We will not trouble him by urging him to explain things which he refuses to reveal nor will we breathe a word of what he will teach us, or taught us in the past, or even what he taught us in the lifetime of Moreinu R' Yitzchak Luria Ashkenazi — without his permission... This resolution is tantamount to a strict vow in the Name of *Hashem*, with the knowledge of our master, R' Chaim, as of today and henceforth, for the ten years to come.
>
> On this day, the 25th of *Menachem Av* 5335 (1575),

here, Tsefas. Everything is valid and attested to. Signed: R' Yosef Arzin, R' Yehoshua bin Nun, R' Yonasan Sagish, R' Gedalyah Halevi, R' Shmuel de Ozida, R' Yitchak Katz, R' Yaakov Masoud, R' Yaakov Shneur, R' Yehudah Mishan, R' Yosef Bagiliar, R' Yosef Latin, R' Shem Tov.[5]

(Not long ago, a *genizah* (repository) of torn and discarded holy writings was unearthed in Stolin, Lithuania, containing this document, most probably a copy of the original, and this may be why some of the names of the signators are missing and some others are mispelled by the copyist. Only the first six signatures appear plus that of R' Eliyahu Flachol or Falcon. The others are omitted.)

The participants limited their commitment to a ten year period, until 5345 (1585), but in 5338 (1578) we already find R' Chaim living in Jerusalem. This seems to indicate that the group had dissolved.

Jewish sages yearned to cling to the spirit of the Ari Hakadosh. Many tried to gain possession of some religious article that had belonged to him. It is told that his *tefillin* were secretly sold for the astronomical sum of twenty-five gold coins to a distinguished Jew from Egypt. The Ari's biographers claim that had they been publicly auctioned, they would have fetched double that amount, if not more.

Many tried in particular to obtain the Ari's writings. But R' Chaim kept his firm decision and guarded them vigilantly lest they slip out of his possession.

Revelation Anew

The *talmidim* learned of the promise that the Arizal had made to R' Yitzchak Hakohen right before his death — that he would return to them, that he would reveal himself once again and would teach them. They waited expectantly and hopefully for many years. Thirty-five years after the Ari's death, R' Gedalyah, one of his disciples, tells how they still awaited the appearance of a wise man whose soul would be a *gilgul* (rebirth) of their master's.[6]

They yearned for this new revelation. They wished to be close to a *tzaddik* and to receive secrets of the mystic Torah. But there was another reason, too.

Shortly before his death, the Ari had warned his *talmid*, R' Yonasan Sagis, not to pursue the study of *Kabbalah* with his comrades for they might misunderstand and be led astray. But he did promise that, if the generation was worthy, he would come himself to teach them this branch of Torah in its entirety. They all eagerly awaited for this promise to be realized.

When R' Yonasan Sagis had heard the words of his master, he understood them to mean that the Ari would return in some different form. "But if that is true," he had said, "we must wait for the soul to be reborn into the body of an infant. If we must wait until he matures, we will all be old men and our master will be tender of years!" The Ari had said that he would return to them while they slept, in a dream, or while they were awake and that he need not involve himself in such mysteries.

Many years passed and the Ari's writings were discovered and became known to Torah scholars. The Sages of the generations studied them in depth, but even though they were written by R' Chaim Vital, they were like a sealed book, words without explanation or commentary. The *mekubalim* who tried to study the Ari's teachings used the commentaries which the other *talmidim* recorded as having heard from their master.

The scholars of the mystic gathered in groups and even established special *yeshivos* to labor over the Ari's teachings. One of the most successful was that of R' Gedalyah Chayun, who gathered the *gedolim* of his generation and, in 5497 (1737), founded the famous *Beis El Yeshivah* which studied *Kabbalah* according to the Ari's approach.

And then R' Shalom Mizrachi arrived from Sharaab, Yemen, to study *Kabbalah* in Jerusalem. He was modest and reticent. He seemed to be a simple *shammash*. But the day came when his greatness was acknowledged by all. Thanks to his sanctity and intellectual brilliance, he succeeded in explaining the words of the Ari to the students of *Beis El*. The Rashash, as he became known (R' SHalam SHaraabi), wrote down his explanations. These became the key to the Ari's teachings. It is written of him: "Whoever studies *Etz Chaim* (by R' Chaim Vital) without the commentary of Sar Shalom, can be said to be going through the motions of study. He can only expect to become hopelessly confused, since that work is a massive difficulty from beginning to end, and he will wander about like a drunkard at sea who does not know where to turn."[7]

After his death, people again quoted the verse — this time in reference to him: "You rose to heaven and captured *SheVI*"(Shin-Beis-Yod). It had been previously used to refer to R' Shimon Bar Yochai and the Ari — R' Yitzchak Ben Shlomo (the first letters of his names are in reverse order). Now it referred to SHalom Ben Yitzchak — R' Shalom Sharaabi.

R' Chaim Palagi, in his *Tochachas Chaim, Parashas Tetzaveh*, writes as follows:

> "R' Sar Shalom Sharaabi was a giant in Torah and piety and famous in *Kabbalah*. The Ari's promise to his disciples to return, if they were worthy, was said to have been fulfilled through the rebirth of the Ari's soul in Rabbenu Shalom Sharaabi."

The Rashash's *talmid*, R' Aharon Moshe Firira, in his work *Efer Yitzchak* wrote:

> "Rabbenu the Rashash revealed (his knowledge to us) generously. Of such was it said, 'The generous of eye shall be blessed for he gave of his bread to the poor.' Whoever was able to appreciate his marvelous wisdom will admit that what the Arizal said to his *talmidim* before his death, that if they were worthy, he would return, was most probably realized in the Rashash who revealed all that we lacked. If we study the introductions to his works *Nehar Shalom* and *Rechovos Hanahar* we see that he embraced both heaven and earth."[8]

1. "Shivchei R' Chaim Vital" p. 55
2. "Shivchei HaAri" p. 35
3. Ibid p. 24
4. "Shivchei R' Chaim Vital" p. 35
5. "Bircas HaAretz" by R' Baruch David Kahane of Tsefas (Jerusalem 5668) p. 61, Siman 324
6. "Shivchei HaAri" p. 38
7. The approbation of R' Refael Yedidya Abulafya to "Etz Chaim", Jerusalem 5627
8. All that is said here about the Rashash is based on "Or Vashemesh" (Jerusalem 5730) by Y. S. Gefner

CHAPTER NINETEEN
THE LION CUBS

The epithet "Ari Hakadosh" which was conferred upon R' Yitzchak Luria Ashkenazi was not merely a combination of the letters *alef, resh, yod* — Ashkenazi R' Yitzchak, or of the phrases used by his adherents and admirers *Adoneinu R' Yitzchak* or of the *Amar R' Yitzchak* (R' Yitzchak said) which they used when writing down his Torah. Rather, *Ari*, lion, reflected his powerful personality. The Lion was king of the beasts and the Ari towered majestically over all the other great figures.

His closest followers who studied directly with him, were dubbed lion cubs or *gurei HaAri*, for their greatness. They were the potential leaders of the next generation who would mature into lions as well. The title 'Lion Cubs' clung to the disciples long after the passing of the master, even, up to the present day.

Not all of the *talmidim* were of equal stature. The first and foremost was R' Chaim Vital, who towered above the rest. He was the closest to the Ari and derived the most from his wisdom. Below him was a group of ten and below them, another class of ten of lesser stature. To these we may add numerous scholars who were not on the level to receive the Ari's teachings face to face. Nevertheless, they considered themselves his *talmidim*; they followed his practices and sought to absorb as much as they could from his teachings, if not directly, at least from those who were worthy to be in the immediate company of the Ari.

Those of the highest level were privileged to study the most sublime topics with their master — the true secrets of the Torah[1], which may be revealed to the very few who stand out by their sanctity and purity. They learned the rules governing the study of the *Zohar* and the introductions to the inner chambers of the Torah. R' Chaim would later expand and elaborate upon these concepts. The second level was not as privileged. The Ari only exposed them to *halachic* principles and laws according to *Kabbalah*.

R' Chaim Vital

The lives of the Ari and of his closest disciple, R' Chaim, were intertwined and inseparable. And yet, their joint period of study was actually very brief — only twenty-two months! But the impact of this period upon both their lives and upon the spiritual legacy of the Ari was immeasurable. The Ari esteemed him highly and revealed to him secrets which he disclosed to no other living soul. Eliyahu Hanavi had revealed to the Ari in Egypt that his chief purpose in descending to this world was to teach R' Chaim, for the latter would spread those teachings throughout the world. This revelation was the catalyst of the union between R' Chaim and the Ari. It was this that brought him to Tsefas.

R' Chaim became the first and foremost of the disciples. He recorded his master's teachings, compiled his writings and edited them. R' Chaim's works constitute the fundamental text and key to the Ari's school of thought in *Kabbalah*. Those who dedicate themselves to *Toras HaCheN* draw the Ari's teaching from this well of R' Chaim to this very day. Even during his master's lifetime, R' Chaim was already the acknowledged mentor of the others, for he always expanded upon and explained the succinct and abbreviated lessons of the master.

Before his death, the Ari instructed his disciples to crown R' Chaim as his successor and so they did.

Who was this R' Chaim, who merited such distinction, whose soul — the master testified, was a spark of the soul of R' Elazer ben R' Shimon bar Yochai?

The Tidings that were Realized

In the province of Calabria, in the southern tip of Italy, lived R' Yosef Vital and his virtuous wife. R' Yosef was hailed throughout his district for his piety and greatness and noted for his knowledge in *Kabbalah*. His true fame, however, rested on his talent in the art of writing *sifrei Torah*, *tefillin* and *mezuzos*. People came from far and wide to obtain *parashiyos* for their *tefillin* from his skilled and G-d fearing hands. R' Yosef Sambari writes as follows:

> "Fortunate is the man who possesses *tefillin* written by the above-mentioned rabbi, for they were an item of great value. There are some to be found here in

Egypt; they are called R' Calabri's *tefillin* and are sold very dearly."²

R' Yosef's house was a magnet for visiting Torah scholars. Everyone was invited to that house which was permeated with Torah and *yiras shamayim*. In 5301 (1541), one of the great leaders of the generation, R' Chaim Ashkenazi, was a guest there. He foretold that R' Yosef would eventually leave Calabria to settle in Tsefas and that two years afterwards, he would father a son.

"I request that you name this son Chaim, after me. This child is destined for a future of greatness," he prophesied. "He will surpass the greatest of his peers and will be the unparalleled leader of his generation."

Upon hearing these glad tidings, R' Yosef gathered up his belongings, left Calabria with his family and went to Tsefas. And just as R' Chaim Ashkenazi had foretold, two years later, in 5303 (1543), his son, Chaim, was born.³

The child grew up in Tsefas, rich in its giants of spirit and wisdom. He acquired his knowledge in the revealed Torah from R' Moshe Alshich. He filled himself with *shas* and *poskim* and became a brilliant scholar.

Even in his youth he had already made a name for himself. At the age of fourteen, he was already considered a shining light by the elite of Tsefas. It is told that in 5317 (1557), R' Yosef Karo urged the Alshich to devote his greatest efforts to teaching R' Chaim. He revealed that his *maggid* angel told him that R' Chaim Vital would someday inherit R' Moshe's own position. And furthermore, the world existed upon the merit of two *tzaddikim* alone, R' Yosef and his son, R' Chaim Vital!⁴

R' Chaim was ordained as *rav* and *dayan* by his master, R' Moshe Alshich, on the 20th of Elul, 5350 (1590).

R' Chaim and the Ari met for the first time in 5331 (1571). In the short period of one year and ten months he succeeded in acquiring the master's wealth of knowledge. The scholars of his time were astonished and regarded this as wondrous.[5]

R' Chaim's thirst for his master's wisdom was insatiable. Whenever the Ari finished studying with him, R' Chaim would beg him to continue. R' Chaim used his G-d-given talents to their fullest. He was blessed with a sublime soul, which by nature was fit for the study of *Chen*. But there was yet another factor which helped him to acquire an extraordinary grasp of the Ari's teachings in so short a time. R' Chaim describes this himself:

> "When I came to my master to study this branch of knowledge, he took me on the Kinneres in Tveryah in a small boat. When we were opposite the windows of the *beis knesses* he looked at me and said, 'Now you will be able to absorb this knowledge for you have drunk from the well of Miriam the Prophetess.' From that time on I was able to acquire this knowledge." (The *midrash* tells us that Miriam's well, which followed the Jews throughout their travels in the desert, came as far as the lake of Tveryah and sank into its midst. Tradition has it that whoever drinks from its waters is rewarded with a capacity for sublime achievements.)[6]

R' Chaim became the Ari's successor as the master had requested. He conducted the affairs of the *yeshivah* for the next five years, but in 5338 (1578) he left Tsefas and

THE LION CUBS / 245

settled in Jerusalem. There, he addressed the public every *Shabbos*.[7] He was numbered among the most prominent rabbis of Jerusalem, as we see from R' Shlomo Adani's introduction to *Meleches Shlomo* on the *mishnah*:

"I was brought to the holy city of Jerusalem, may it be speedily rebuilt. I always crouched at the feet of the sages, the pillars of the Diaspora and Jerusalem, such as that perfect, godly *mekubal*, R' Chaim Vital and Morenu R' Ashkenazi Bezalel."

The Secret of the Gichon

The sage of Tsefas settled in Jerusalem. There, he became renowned for his miracles and *segulos*. Even the Arabs held him in great esteem for his prodigious powers, though this became his undoing; eventually he was forced to leave Jerusalem unexpectedly and flee to Damascus. This story passed down through the generations and even two centuries later, was cause for amazement.

In ancient times a large river, the Gichon, flowed right outside Jerusalem. When Sancheriv and his army laid siege to the city, King Chizkiyahu diverted all of the fountains and streams outside the city and made them flow inside. The beleagured Jews of the City of David now had a supply of precious water and the enemy was denied access to it (*Divrei Hayamim* II, 32:3-4 and 30), but the Sages at the time were opposed to the king's action. Since then, the Gichon has been flowing underground.

When our story takes place, the majority of Jerusalem's residents were Moslem. Every Friday they would gather in numbers at the *Har Habayis* (Temple Mount) to offer their prayers upon the site of the destroyed Temple. The rest of the city would be empty of people, then; business would be at a standstill and the gates were closed to prevent robbers from entering. Anyone strolling by the Jaffa Gate near the Tower of David at these quiet moments could easily hear the rushing waters of the Gichon flowing beneath the houses.

At that time Abu Sayfin, a despotic brutal man, was appointed *pasha* (governor) of Jerusalem. After his arrival, he would walk through the streets and lanes of the city in order to become familiar with it and its people. One Friday he heard the muffled sound of water running beneath the Jaffa Gate. His curiosity aroused, he inquired and learned about the rerouting of the Gichon by King Chizkiyahu.

"Is there anyone today capable of releasing the water?" he asked.

"Yes," replied the members of his retinue, the local inhabitants. "There is a Jewish sage, a saintly man by the name of R' Chaim Vital, who undoubtedly would be able to do so."

Abu Sayfin demanded that R' Chaim be brought to him at once. When R' Chaim was before him he said, "You are well aware of the severe shortage of water existing in Jerusalem."

"Yes, Your Excellency," he replied.

The governor continued, "I know for a fact that it is in your power to release the waters of the river which your king once diverted. I am now going to the *Har Habayis* for my weekly prayers. If the river does not begin flowing by the time I return — you will pay with your life." He turned on his heel and left.

R' Chaim was in a quandary. He, finally, decided to flee

Jerusalem. Uttering certain Names which he knew through practical *Kabbalah*, he was wafted into the air and borne aloft to Damascus.

That night the Arizal appeared to him in a dream and spoke harshly, "You did a foolish thing! That ruler was none other than Sancheriv reborn, as his very name indicates — Abu Sayfin, Father of the Swords. And you, my disciple, are an offshoot of the soul of Chizkiyahu. You had the opportunity to repair the damage done by Chizkiyahu when he disobeyed the Sages of his time. Had you released the waters of the Gichon, you would have ushered in the beginning of the *geulah* (redemption) of Israel!"

R' Chaim cringed at his master's rebuke. He justified himself, saying, "But how could I have obeyed him — I would have had to use holy Names. I did not want to do that!"

"How, then, did you come to Damascus if not by the use of holy Names? It had been far better if you had used them for a worthwhile purpose, to release the river, for that would have been a great *kiddush Hashem*, a tremendous accomplishment!"

R' Chaim agonized over his error. "Then let me return to Jerusalem and make good my mistake."

"Certainly not!" said the Ari. "The moment of *geulah* has passed."[8]

R' Chaim lived in Damascus for a few years, until his death on the 30th of *Nisan*, 5380 (1620), and was buried there. In his will he requested that his sons and *talmidim* bury his *kabbalistic* writings — the teachings of the Arizal — together with his remains, which they did.

The Treetop and the Branches

One Friday, on the 24th of *Tammuz* 5332 (1572), just before dawn, R' Chaim Vital awoke. In a dreamy trance, he suddenly exclaimed aloud, "On that day the glory of Yaakov will be thinned and the fat of his flesh will be lean... Yet there shall remain gleanings as when the olive tree is picked, two or three olives at the treetop, four or five in the boughs of the fruitful tree" (Yeshayahu 17:4-6). Then he explained his words, "The glory of Yaakov refers to the master, R' Yitzchak Luria. The thinning of the flesh applies to the two classes of his disciples, which are called 'the remnant of Yaakov'." He continued, still half asleep, "Some of the members of the first class, which is called the top of the tree because it is most important, will die, though the number has not yet been determined. Perhaps all but two will die; perhaps five ('two' plus 'three'), or perhaps six ('two' times 'three') will survive."

"And *talmidim* from the second group, which is called its boughs, that is, the lower branches, will also die; four or five will survive."

As soon as he finished this prophetic statement, he awoke fully. His ears rang with what he had just uttered. His parents hurried to his side and repeated what they had heard him say.

On the following *Shabbos* the Ari was struck down, together with several of his students.

R' Chaim related this vision in the year 5370 (1610), forty-seven years after the Ari's death. He wrote: "Now, in the year 5370 (1610), only a few remain from the first group: I, R' Gedalyah, R' Avraham Gavriel, R' Yosef Tobol Hamugrabi and R' Yehudah Mishan; from the second group: R' Yom Tov Tzahalon, R' David Kohen; R' Yitzchak Krispin, R' Yaakov Alterez, R' Yisrael Uri and R' Yishmael HaLevi Ashkenazi."[9] He also notes there that during his lifetime, the Ari demoted R' Avraham Gavriel, R' Yosef ben Tobol and R' Yehudah Mishan from the first group.

R' Chaim related that three days before his master's death, the Ari reestablished the standing of his disciples. The first group was to consist of R' Eliyah Falcon, R' Yosef Arzin, R' Yanosan Sagis, R' Gedalya Halevi, R' Yitzchak Hakohen and R' Shmuel Ozeida. The three mentioned above and R' Shabsai Moshe, were to be demoted; their souls were not on par with the rest.

With the thinning of the ranks, others came to replace them. In the Loyalty Pact which was signed by the Gurei Ari in 5335 (1575), three years after the Ari's death, we find additional signatures: R' Yosef Latin, R' Yehoshua bin Nun, R' Yaakov Shneur, R' Yosef Bagiliar and R' Shem Tov.

R' Shmuel de Ozeida

R' Shmuel was one of the Ari's most distinguished disciples and one of those who signed the Loyalty Pact. His name appears upon the list of the Tsefas scholars to whom the Ari revealed the roots of their souls. He was one of the trustees of the city,[10] and is listed among the rabbis who gave their approval to the ruling which R' Yosef of Trani handed down in 5361.[11] R' Shmuel was the author of many commentaries, the most famous being *Lechem Dima*, *Midrash Shmuel* on *Avos* and *Iggeres Shmuel* on *Rus*.

He was especially noted for his righteousness and good works, one of which became especially well known, thanks to the discerning eye of his master, the Ari. One day, when R' Shmuel was still young, he entered his master's home to consult with him on some matter. To his great surprise, R' Yitzchak Luria stood up, placed him to his right and treated him as if he were the most distinguished of guests. R' Shmuel was somewhat disconcerted. Feeling ill at ease, he asked his question and upon receiving an answer, left at once.

R' Chaim Vital happened to be present and noticed the unusual act of esteem which his master had shown towards the young Shmuel and realized that there must be a specific reason for it. He asked the Ari who smiled at his dear student and said, "I did not rise for R' Shmuel's sake but in honor of the soul of the *tana*, R' Pinchas ben Yair, which hovered above his head. The soul of that great Sage accompanied him because of a certain good deed he did which was of the same nature as the good deeds which R' Pinchas used to do."

R' Chaim became jealous of his comrade's spiritual elevation. He, too, wished to be visited by the soul of the great *tana*, R' Pinchas ben Yair. He ran after R' Shmuel to learn what he had done. Perhaps he could do that, also.

He was out of breath when he finally overtook R' Shmuel and begged him to tell him what he had done that day. "Nothing unusual," said R' Shmuel innocently. "Early this morning I went to the *beis knesses* to pray with the daybreak *minyan*. On the way I suddenly heard the sound of weeping from one of the houses. It was a bitter, heart-rending sound. I entered that house to see if I could help in any way and found an entire family weeping broken-heartedly. Thieves had stolen into their

THE LION CUBS / 251

house at night and robbed them of every possession. They did not even have the necessary clothing to leave the house and go to work! I comforted them and returned home. I took off my clothing, put on my *Shabbos* garments and returned with my weekday clothing, so that the father could, at least, go out and face the world."

R' Chaim was deeply impressed. He kissed his friend on the forehead and rushed back to tell the Ari what he had just heard. "Didn't I tell you so?" the Ari asked. "This good deed drew the soul of R' Pinchas ben Yair to our R' Shmuel, for it was like the deeds that he performed during his lifetime. He devoted his life to *pidyon shevuyim* (ransoming captives) and helping the downtrodden."[12]

Aside from the two groups already mentioned, there also existed two other groups of scholars who, apparently, did not study directly under the Ari but practiced all of the customs of the Gurei Ari and were attached to them. At certain times they also joined the group. R' Chaim Vital describes them:

> "The first group is the inner circle comprised of the most brilliant minds. There is another group which is like 'clothing' to the first. A third group is called the 'outer garments'. This group consists of my own master, R' Moshe Alshich; R' Moshe Nag'ara; R' Yitzchak Archa; R' Shlomo Saban; R' Mordechai Gallico; R' Yaakov Masoud; R' Yosef Alton; R' Moshe Mintz; R' Moshe Yonah and R' Avraham Gevakil. There is yet a fourth group which is the fringe of the fringe; this corresponds to the second inner circle mentioned above. It consists of R' Avraham Halevi, R' Moshe Meshamesh and R' Yehuda Ramono etc."[13]

In other words, each 'inner' circle had its corresponding

'outer' circle, four in all. The rabbis of Tsefas and its most prominent scholars were included in the outer circles; their names are mentioned in the material dealing with the disciples of the Ari.

R' Mordechai Gallico and his Brother

R' Chaim Vital mentioned the name of R' Mordechai in his visions as part of the group of scholars parallel to his own group. R' Moshe's brother, R' Elisha Gallico, was a respected rabbi in Tsefas and a disciple of *Maran* R' Yosef Karo and the teacher of R' Shmuel de Ozeida.

The Gallico family was well known in Italy. There was a family tradition that they stemmed from a distinguished branch of Yehudah which had been exiled to Rome by the wicked Titus. There, the Gallico ancestors had established a *beis knesses* bearing their name, as well as a famous *yeshivah* known as the *Yeshivas Bnei Gallico* which existed in Firenza, Italy, until a century ago.[14]

In one of R' Chaim's stories we learn that the two brothers, R' Mordechai and R' Elisha Gallico, were two of the most esteemed scholars and leaders of Tsefas:

During the epidemic which claimed so many Jewish lives, one of the women of Tsefas — the sister of R' Chayati, — dreamt that she saw a magnificent *beis knesses* full to overflowing with Jews enveloped in *talleisim* and wearing *tefillin*, standing in prayer. Their faces were solemn and fearful. As they were praying, a Heavenly voice resounded, announcing: *"Tzedakah, tzedakah!* Charity saves from death!" Just then, two policemen entered and seized R' Yaakov Aboulafya. The heads of the community tried to dissuade the police from arresting him. They insisted that he could not possibly be guilty of any crime. R' Yaakov himself took advantage of the commotion and fled. The police in their anger seized one of the prominent Jews as hostage until R' Yaakov would give himself up to the authorities. R' Elisha Gallico and his brother, together with R' Moshe Cordovero again tried to convince the police that R' Yaakov must be innocent but they refused to listen.

The woman told her dream to the leaders of Tsefas. They interpreted it to mean that the epidemic would continue to rage and claim more victims. They, therefore, increased their prayers but apparently, the gates of prayer were sealed. Their bitter interpretation was realized all too soon.[15]

R' Avraham Beruchim

R' Avraham was distinguished in his piety and holiness. The great men of Tsefas praised him lavishly and pointed to his practices.[16] R' Chaim Vital tells us that he was greatly disturbed that his master had singled himself out from all the others — to draw him close and to teach him his Torah. All of Tsefas was bursting with scholars and scribes, men of piety and of good works whose stature — so he thought — surpassed his own tenfold. R' Chaim had only to think of Yosef Karo, the Radbaz and R' Avraham Halevi Beruchim.[17]

The *Kav Hayashar* tells of R' Avraham as follows:

> "...as we find with one pious man named R' Avraham, disciple of the Ari, who would walk through the markets and streets exhorting people to do *teshuvah*.

R' Avraham mourned and suffered over the *churban* (destruction of the Temple) and the bitter exile of his brethren. This was no great wonder, for the Ari revealed that he was a rebirth of the prophet Yirmiyahu. His grief and lament over the *churban* is described as follows:

"This is what the Ari said about the great Avraham Halevi, who composed *tikkunei Shabbos* and lived in Tsefas. Each midnight he would arise and encirle the Jewish quarter, weeping as he went, and saying, 'My brethren, the House of Israel, don't you realize that the very *Shechinah* is in exile, due to our own sins, and that our Temple has been burned? Jewry is in bitter exile and suffers harsh tortures. They are being slain in their multitudes, the best of them, men and women, young and old; they suffer all four forms of the death penalty; they are hanged and killed in all kinds of strange ways. Are you able to sleep in your beds serene and secure?! Rise and cry out to *Hashem*, Who is a merciful King; perhaps He will hearken to your prayers and take pity on the remnant of Jewry!' He would continue to cry out thus and not give the residents peace, until they also got up at one o'clock in the morning and gathered in the *batei midrash* to say the *tikkun chatzos*. They would study, each according to his level — *Kabbalah* and *Zohar*, *gemara* and *mishnayos* or *Tanach*. This would be followed by poetic prayers and *bakashos* until daybreak. He would rouse them to pity. The Ari praised his piety highly." (*Kav Hayashar*, p. 124, Chapter 92)

When the Ari was still new and unknown in Tsefas, R' Avraham Beruchim already recognized his greatness and befriended him. The *Lag BaOmer* festivities at Meron, in the Ari's first year in Tsefas, left an indelible impression on him, but brought great tragedy in their wake. R' Yitzchak Luria was carried away by his joy, while R' Avraham, unchangingly, mourned over the *churban.* Even that day, when he visited the tomb of the Rashbi, he added the *nachem* (Comfort O *Hashem*) — the addition which is customarily only said in the *minchah* of *Tisha B'Av* which he included on each weekday. When R' Avraham had stepped the three paces backwards at the end of the prayer, the Ari went over to him and said sternly, "During your prayer, I saw R' Shimon bar Yochai standing by his grave. He said to me: 'Tell that man, Avraham Halevi, that there is no call for saying *nachem* on this day of celebration. Why must he mourn today? Tell him that he will soon have reason to mourn and to be consoled." Within that same month, one of R' Avraham's sons died and he had to sit in mourning for him.[18]

One *Shabbos* afternoon, R' Avraham visited his master. The Ari made it a practice to sleep on *Shabbos* afternoons, claiming that this sleep was especially beneficial to the soul. R' Avraham Beruchim saw his master sleeping; his lips were murmuring. He could not restrain himself from bending over to hear what those holy lips were saying. The Ari awoke. He was startled to see his disciple leaning over him and demanded an explanation.

R' Avraham was embarrassed to have been caught in an unseemly act and trembled as he explained, "I saw the master whispering something in his sleep. Curiosity gripped me; I had to know what you were saying."

The Ari replied gently, "Whenever I sleep, my soul rises up to Heaven and wanders about the lanes of the *mesivta d'rakiya* (the Heavenly Academy). The angels come and lead my soul before the angel in charge of all the souls of Jewry and he asks me which *yeshivah* I want to visit. Wherever I choose to go, I am initiated into the wonderful, most hidden secrets of the Torah, which no human ear has ever heard before."

R' Avraham Halevi begged the Ari to reveal to him what he had learned just then. His master smiled and said, "Today (it was *parashas Balak*) I studied the chapter of Bilam and its deeper implications but I call upon heaven and earth to be my witnesses that, even if I had eighty years at my disposal, it would not be enough to tell you all that I learned today during my sleep!"[19]

The Ari, who could foretell the future through his divine intuition, already knew at *neilah* (the final prayer) on *Yom Kippur* which of his disciples would not live out the year. He rarely disclosed what he knew but once he made an exception. This was when he learned that R' Avraham Beruchim was destined to die, but that there was a way to avert this sentence.

The Ari summoned R' Avraham to him and told him the truth, "Your days are numbered. You are about to die. But there is still hope."

R' Avraham begged his master to show him how to arouse Heavenly mercy and abolish the decree.

"Your only hope," said the Ari, "is to go to Jerusalem, to the Western Wall. There, you are to pour out your heart before the A-mighty. If you are privileged to see the *Shechinah* before your very eyes, it will be a sign that the decree has been annulled."

R' Avraham hurried home to prepare for his trip. He first purified himself, for how could he possibly go the the Western Wall, the site from which the *Shechinah* has never moved, without becoming holier? He shut himself

THE LION CUBS / 257

up in a room for three days and nights, during which he fasted in sackcloth and ashes. After he felt sufficiently prepared, he left Tsefas and turned south, to the holy city and the holy site.

After a long and arduous journey, R' Avraham reached Jerusalem. He did not stop to rest at all. He immediately went to the remnant of the *Beis Hamikdash*. He clung to the holy stones and wet them with his tears. He offered up his most sincere prayers to the Giver of life, begging that He grant him added years. As he wept and prayed, the figure of a woman appeared before him. She was dressed all in black, like a widow in her grief. He understood that this must be the *Shechinah* mourning over the Destruction and the Exile. He was so moved that he began to shout and weep all the more. "Alas, that I must see you thus! Alas for my soul!" He was so carried away with grief that, all his energy spent, he collapsed on the ground and fell asleep.

He had a vision. He saw the holy *Shechinah*, this time magnificently dressed. She turned to him and said tenderly, "Be comforted, My son Avraham, for there is hope for your future. Sons shall return to their borders. I will restore the captives to their homeland and I will show them My compassion." With these words, his spirit returned to him and he woke up feeling refreshed and happy.

Upon his return to Tsefas, he went at once to the Ari to tell him what had happened. As soon as he entered, the Ari spoke first, and said, "I see that you were found worthy to have a vision of the *Shechinah*. You can rest assured that you will live for another twenty-two years."

And so it was. R' Avraham Beruchim, the pious of Tsefas, lived another twenty-two years, each of which was dedicated to holy service.[20]

R' Yehoshua bin Nun

R' Yehoshua did not study directly under the Ari but was drawn to the Ari's customs and teachings. As *av beis din* and head of all the *yeshivos* in Tsefas, he helped the disciples of the Ari maintain their *yeshivah*, even after the passing of the master. And they gathered him into their group. He was one of those who crowned R' Chaim Vital as the Ari's successor. We also find his signature upon the Loyalty Pact drawn up by the Ari's disciples.

R' Yehoshua was a treasurer and trustee of all monies coming in from Jews in the Diaspora. He was one of those who decided how to allocate the monies for the needs of the scholars of Tsefas and all of its orphans and widows. He had great personal wealth. But all of this was as nothing when he stood before R' Chaim Vital. He would kiss his hands and feet and beg him to teach him the secrets of the Torah. He gave him hundreds of gifts. He helped dress him, wash him and put on his shoes. He wished to be near him and hear the Ari's teachings.

Once when R' Chaim Vital left Jerusalem and went to Egypt, R' Yehoshua accompanied him.

He made a great effort to publish the works of the Arizal. But R' Chaim Vital, who possessed the writings, guarded them jealously and refused to allow access to them. He was adamantly determined not to have them published before he received explicit permission from the Ari. And so, R' Yehoshua was forced to wait and hope for mercy from Heaven.[21]

R' Yosef Bagiliar

After the death of the Arizal, R' Yosef Bagiliar assumed the financial burden of the *yeshivah* and he was one of those who signed the Loyalty Pact.

R' Yosef, eventually, settled in Egypt where he was held in great esteem. There, he led a group which pursued the study of *Kabbalah*. It was like the groups which had been formed in Tsefas, which followed the Ari's teachings and customs. When he was old and sated with years, he fell ill. All the prominent scholars and rabbis came to visit him in his sickness. While they were there R' Yosef told them, "My dear friends, on Friday, on this and this day of the month, I will be leaving you forever."

They listened to his words in amazement and noted them. On the specified date, R' Yosef gathered the members of the *chevra kadisha* (burial committee) and instructed them to prepare a grave for him, since he would die shortly. "I am fully prepared to go before my heavenly Father on the eve of this *Shabbos*."

They rushed to do his bidding. After midday, as the sun was beginning to dip westward, they sent the *shammash* to see how R' Yosef was feeling. "Is the grave ready?" the dying man asked. "Are the shrouds prepared?"

"Yes, master," the *shammash* nodded. "Everything is all in order."

"Then call all of my relatives and friends together," R' Yosef requested.

When they were all in his chamber, he summoned his waning strength and sat up in bed. He blessed his family, each as befitted him, and parted from them and from his comrades. He asked pardon from them all. Then he recited the *vidui* and said *shema Yisrael*. When he reached the final word, his soul departed in purity.

This scene left a deep impression upon the entire community. People were awed by this evidence of such holiness and greatness.[22]

The following was carved on his tombstone, "Ministers were a source of wonder in Jerusalem. And Yosef was in Egypt."[23]

R' Chaim Kapusi

R' Chaim was one of the noted rabbis of Egypt, a Torah sage who knew both the revealed and the secret Torah. He was especially close to R' Yosef Bagiliar. This close friendship with R' Yosef brought him into contact with the Gurei Ari, so that he is numbered among them.

R' Chaim Kapusi was dubbed the Wonder Worker because of a certain incident. He served as a *dayan* in Egypt. Once, his decision in a particular case caused people in the community to raise their eyebrows. They were convinced that he was in error and began talking evilly against him behind his back. "Surely R' Chaim must have accepted bribery," they said. Shortly afterwards R' Chaim became blind. This was sure proof of his guilt, they claimed, since the Torah itself says that "bribery blinds the eyes of the wise."

These wicked insinuations reached the ears of the blind R' Chaim. He prayed to *Hashem* with all his heart, begging Him to remove the shameful stigma from him, since he knew that he was innocent. One day, he declared in public, before the entire congregation, that people's suspicions were false and unfounded. "If it is true that I accepted bribery," he exclaimed, "then let me continue to be blind until the day I die. But if the allegations are false, let *Hashem* restore my sight!"

To the amazement of the entire *kehillah*, R' Chaim Kapusi's sight was suddenly and miraculously restored, then and there. The people hung their heads in shame at having suspected their worthy *dayan*. And from then on, many flocked to him to receive his blessing.

R' Chaim passed away on the twelfth of *Teves*, 5391 (1631), at the ripe age of ninety-one. He was buried in the Jewish cemetery of Cairo and his grave is considered a sacred site. The Chida wrote over a hundred years after his death that "to this day whoever swears falsely upon his grave is punished."[24] The anniversary of his death is a day of solemn celebration. People gather at his graveside to pray and light candles. The synagogue in Cairo where R' Chaim used to pray is called the *"Beis Knesses R' Chaim Baal Hanes"*. The Jews of Egypt mark the day of his death with elaborate public show in that *beis knesses*.

R' Yisrael Saruk

R' Yisrael did much to spread the study of the Ari's teachings among the sages of his generation who lived outside of *Eretz Yisrael*. His was a minority view. Most of his fellow disciples were opposed to having the Ari's Torah taught in the Diaspora. R' Yisrael spent some years in Italy where he was greatly honored as having been a *talmid* of the Ari. There, he stayed at the home of R' Aharon Berechyah of Modena, author of the well known *Maavar Yabok*. His host was deeply impressed by R'

Yisrael's ways and practices, in particular, his reciting of the *tikkun chatzos*, in the manner of the *mekubalim* of Tsefas.[25] The Rama (R' Menachem Azaryah) of Pano, one of the great Torah leaders in Italy, acquired his knowledge of *Kabbalah* according to the Ari from R' Yisrael Saruk. He passed it on to many others.

R' Yisrael visited Poland, too, in order to further spread the teachings of the Ari. It was through him that the Maharshal, author of *Chochmas Shlomo* and *Yam Shel Shlomo*, was introduced to the Ari's school of *Kabbalah*. Their meeting was unusual:

When the Maharshal learned that the Ari was teaching the mystic secrets of the Torah, he feared that the approach was unsound and that many might go astray. He, therefore, called together a meeting of scholars one Friday to discuss this matter. But the day was short and the rabbis decided to meet again some time the following week. They were all but convinced that the teachings of the Ari must be banned.

R' Yitzchak Luria learned of this through his divine vision. He greatly feared the censure of such great men as the Maharshal and his peers. He summoned R' Yisrael Saruk and told him to use practical *Kabbalah* to reach Poland that very day. There he was to present himself to the Maharshal and set things aright.

R' Yisrael did not hesitate and did as he was told. That same Friday he miraculously reached from Tsefas to the home of R' Shlomo Luria, the Maharshal, in Poland. There, they were busy with *Shabbos* preparations when he knocked on the door and begged to see the Maharshal. He said that he had something urgent to discuss with him.

The two sat and talked for a long time. R' Yisrael

proved through signs and wonders that the Ari's way was true and right. The Maharshal was won over; at the end of this meeting, the Maharashal became a sworn adherent to the Ari's school in *Kabbalah*. He sent a letter to him mentioning that they both were members of the same family, the Lurias.[26] The proposed ban was never imposed.

After his master passed away, R' Yisrael succeeded, after great effort, in acquiring the Ari's teachings as recorded by R' Chaim Vital. He paid a fortune for them — two hundred thaler![27] These writings were handed down to his daughter who married R' Shlomo Shlumil.

R' Shlomo Shlumil of Lutenberg reached Tsefas on *Succos* of 5363 (1603) in order to settle there and study the Torah of the Ari. He was determined to acquire this knowledge. When his first wife refused to accompany him to *Eretz Yisrael*, he divorced her and left his only daughter, a girl of thirteen, in her custody.

He knocked on the doors of all the great scholars of Tsefas for an entire year. He begged them to teach him *Kabbalah*, or, at least, lend him the writings of the Ari, so that he might study them on his own. He met with refusal, but he did not despair. He went from one to the other, again and again. From time to time, they would reveal a bit here or there but they would not open the gates of *Kabbalah* to him. They would say, "These things are told only to those in whom we trust, who are most worthy and deserve to behold the grace of *Hashem*; they are profound secrets which the Ancient of Days had stored away when the Rashbi died. The verse says, 'The glory of *Hashem* is in concealment.' This wisdom is not simply there for the taking."[28]

R' Shlomo Shlumil wandered aimlessly about for an

entire year, suffering, weeping and praying that his Creator enable him to see the light of life, the grace of *Hashem*. Finally, his prayers were answered. As he says, "*Hashem*, Who is truth, Who is the King of the Universe, saw my aching heart and my sincere intentions and opened up before me the gates of light. He raised my banner in the understanding of the writings of the Ari with greater power and greater might."[29]

R' Shlomo married the daughter of R' Yisrael Saruk and upon his father-in-law's death, acquired the writings of the Ari's teachings, more precious than gold, as they had been recorded by R' Chaim Vital. After tireless effort, he, too, was given the opportunity to drink his fill from the fountain of life-giving waters of knowledge.

1. "Shivchei HaAri" p. 26
2. "Divrei Yosef" p. 193
3. "Shivchei R' Chaim Vital", introduction
4. Ibid, and "Shem Hagedolim" entry on him, vol. I, Os Ches, Siman 21
5. "Shem Hagedolim" ibid
6. "Shaar Hagilgulim" vol. II, p. 10 (Premiszlan)
7. "Shivchei R' Chaim Vital" p. 5
8. "Shem Hagedolim" under R' Chaim Vital, Os Ches, Siman 21
9. "Shivchei R' chaim Vital" p. 35
10. "Divrei Yoef" p. 228
11. "Shailos Utshuvos Maharit," Siman 82
12. "Shivchei HaArizal" p. 14; "Maase Nisim" Chapter 4
13. "Chezyonos R' Chaim Vital" (Jerusalem 5714) p. 219 14. "Otzar Yisrael" vol. III, p. 232, see index 'Gallico'
15. "Sefer Hachezyonos" p. 113
16. "Reshis Chochmah" Shaar Kedushah, Chapter Two
17. "Shivchei R' Chaim Vital" p. 22
18. "Shaar Hakavanos" "Pesora d'Abba" Vol. I, Siman 139
19. "Shivchei HaAri" p. 5; "Maase Nisim" Chapter One
20. "Kav Hayashar" Chapter 92, p. 124 (Livorno 5603)
21. "Shivchei HaAri" p. 35
22. "Divrei Yosef" p. 264
23. Ibid
24. "Shem Hagedolim" Vol. I Os Mem, Siman 9
25. "Ashmores Haboker" (Mantua 5384) p. 248
26. "Eden Tzion" (Jerusalem 5716) under 'Ari', quoted from "Shivchei HaAri"
27. "Shivchei HaAri" p. 50
28. Ibid p. 24
29. Ibid

CHAPTER TWENTY
THE ARI'S WRITINGS AND HIS SPIRITUAL LEGACY

The Ari himself did not leave over much in writing of the vast wealth of wisdom which he taught. Among the few works which he did produce, we find the commentary to the *Sifra DiTzniyusa* which he wrote as a young man, during his period of seclusion in Egypt.

Sifra DiTzinyusa, one of the oldest works of *Kabbalah* in existence, is attributed to Yaakov Avinu. The *Zohar*, in the end of *parashas Terumah*, quotes from it. It is a difficult book, closed to the general reader. When the Ari, in his youth, began to study *Kabbalah* he labored over it and attempted to explain it, so that others might more easily understand it. This commentary is probably his first creation in the area of *Kabbalah*, which is why it aroused controversy. The truth is that many errors crept into its text because of careless transcription.

One of the giants of Torah in the generation of the Ari's disciples, R' Menachem de Lunsano, wrote a work which challenges them and their teacher's commentary on *Sifra DiTzniyusa*. Before he presents his criticisms and arguments, he showers praise upon and expresses his submission and self-negation before the greatness of the Ari. However, he maintains that the Ari wrote this composition when he was freshly initiated into *Kabbalah* and, therefore, could not help erring here and there. Had he reviewed it later, when he was blessed with divine intuition, he would surely have corrected his misconceptions or hidden the book away altogether. But he could not do so, says R' Menachem, since, as soon as the book appeared, his admirers and followers pounced upon it and copied it over in many editions and it spread throughout the world in that form. By then, it was too late to recall the volume.[1]

Upon the appearance of R' Menachem de Lunsano's critique, R' Avraham Monson, a disciple of R' Bezalel Ashkenazi, author of the *Shitah Mekubetzes*, leapt to the master's defense.

And when R' Binyamin Halevi undertook the task of copying it and winnowed out all of the chaff — the inaccuracies and errors which had become incorporated into it — everything fell into place and the questions dissolved of their own.[2]

Shitah Mekubetzes

During the period that the Ari studied in seclusion with his teacher, R' Bezalel Ashkenazi, he assisted him in writing that monumental work, the *Shitah Mekubetzes*, and took a major part in producing the commentary on *Zevachim*.

His Poems

Aside from these writings, we also possess several *piyutim* (sacred poems) which the Ari produced in times of exaltation and spiritual ecstasy, when his soul soared to its highest peaks. The *Shabbos zemiros* which he wrote are especially popular. The first letters of the verses combine to form his name. These *zemiros* are:

Azamer bishvachin — some sing it on Friday evening before *kiddush*,[3] others, after *kiddush* and *netilas yadayim*.[4] It is written in Aramaic.

Asader liseudasa, also in Aramaic, is sung during the *Shabbos* morning meal.

Bnei heichala, a song for *seudah shlishis*, is also in Aramaic.

Aside from these commonly known *piyutim*, there are others which are less familiar: *Yom ze dar bamromim; Mah lach yitzri, tamid tirdefeni;* (a liturgical poem for *shacharis shel Rosh Hashanah* according to the Sefardim) and *Keli, Keli, Keli* which is attributed to the Ari.

His songs are based upon deep *Kabbalistic* concepts from the *Zohar*.

A Hasty Transcription

It will be recalled that the Ari strictly forbade his disciples, with the exception of R' Chaim Vital, to write down his teachings. He, himself, did not record his thoughts in writing since he found it difficult to constrict his vast knowledge and transfer it to paper. This is why he assigned the task of writing and editing to R' Chaim, his greatest disciple. Nevertheless, others occasionally tried their hand at surreptitious writing. After the Ari passed away, R' Chaim demanded that all of these scholars submit their notes to him. Those who considered him as their master, did so, knowing that it had been the Ari's express wish that only R' Chaim produce his writings.

R' Chaim held on to these writings tenaciously for fifteen years — copying, annotating, compiling and arranging them, incorporating *chiddushim* attributed to the Ari, which he had heard from other disciples. He organized the notes according to topics, each 'gateway' subdivided into chapters. He called this comprehensive work *Etz Chaim*, though others referred to it as *Kisvei HaAri*. But he still was not ready to publish it.

Throughout this period, the Tsefas scholars tried to get their hands upon the Ari's writings, so that they could study their teacher's works. But they were unsuccessful; R' Chaim guarded them jealously for he was not ready to publish them.

After many attempts, R' Yehoshua bin Nun finally succeeded in gaining access to the writings. It happened when R' Chaim Vital became seriously ill. He was bedridden for an entire year, hovering between life and death. At the end of the year, R' Yehoshua felt that the time was ripe. He approached R' Moshe Vital, R' Chaim's brother, and begged him to lend him the writings for three days in return for a huge sum of money. R' Moshe secretly unlocked the chest which contained the precious writings, removed them and brought them to R' Yehoshua bin Nun. By Heaven's will, not all of the writings were handed over. The missing ones contained especially profound secrets which were not yet to be revealed.

R' Yehoshua had possession of the writings for a mere three days, but in this brief time he hired one hundred efficient scribes to copy them over. Each one was assigned six scrolls; they worked diligently. During this period R' Chaim's health took a turn for the better, so that it was urgent to replace the writings, lest he discover their absence. But the transcription was completed on schedule.

Now that R' Yehoshua possessed these copies, he was able to lend them out to privileged individuals. The great *mekubalim* of Tsefas studied them thirstily and learned their contents.[5]

At this time, other disciples of the Ari also began to write down that which they had heard, overriding R' Chaim's vehement opposition; they did not want these teachings to be forgotten with the passage of time. And before long, these writings, also, received widespread circulation among the seekers of *Kabbalah*.

However, these various copies contained errors. Those in the copies which R' Yehoshua bin Nun had produced were the result of the great haste in which they had been made. In the other copies, it was the shortcomings of those who wrote them which caused the errors — faulty memory or lack of comprehension. R' Chaim comments on this in *Etz Chaim*:

> "Some of the colleagues wrote books on what they heard from my master... all of them with additions and omissions, depending on the abilities of the writer. Their limited understanding gives rise to some questions. These works are unreliable and should be avoided.

As a result, Jewish leaders, especially the *mekubalim* of Jerusalem, gathered together and imposed a strict ban upon these copies and forbade people to study from them, since they did not truly represent the Ari's teachings. Over the years, they abolished the ban, but the truly pious continued to refrain from studying those works which had aroused the censure of the *gedolim*.

Etz Chaim

R' Chaim himself revised his master's teachings several times. He passed first editions on to his son, R' Shmuel, while the latest revision, *Mahadura Basra*, the clearest, best annotated and most organized version, was buried along with him. Among the scrolls which R' Shmuel Vital inherited, he found one 'gateway' of the book actually written in the Arizal's own hand! R' Shmuel revised the comprehensive work, rearranged it into eight 'gateways' and published it in this form under the name *Etz Chaim*.

These are the eight gateways (or sections):

The First Gateway: *Shaar Hahakdamos* — this contains all of the prefaces necessary for the understanding of *Kabbalah*, its precepts and concepts. The introduction to this gateway of prefaces contains R' Chaim's description of the Ari's greatness and of his practices.

The Second Gateway: *Shaar Maamarei Rashbi* — this contains the Ari's commentary on the essays of the saintly *tana*, R' Shimon bar Yochai. This gateway is constructed according to the order of the *Zohar*, *parashah* after *parashah*.

The Third Gateway: *Shaar Maamarei Chazal* — this contains the Ari's commentaries on the Talmud and the various *Midrashim* — *Rabbah and Tanchuma, Sifri, Sifra* etc.

The Fourth Gateway: *Shaar Hapesukim* — the Ari's commentary on the Torah and the *Nach*.

The Fifth Gateway: *Shaar Hamitzvos* — the Ari's commentary on the 613 commandments, arranged according to their appearance in the Torah.

The Sixth Gateway: *Shaar Hakavanos* — explains the Ari's approach towards the meaning of the daily, *Shabbos* and festival prayers as well as the *kavanos* (thoughts) and *yichudim* (unities) which one must concentrate upon when performing *mitzvos*.

The Seventh Gateway: *Shaar Ruach Hakodesh* — the Ari's teachings concerning the preparations which are necessary prerequisites for attaining divine intuition. This gateway also includes *yichudim* (unities) and *azharos* (instructions) for *tikkun hanefesh* (the perfection of souls), which the Ari outlined for those who wish to do *teshuvah* for their sins.

The Eighth Gateway: *Shaar Hagilgulim* — this deals with the concept of souls in the World-to-Come and the punishment of the wicked for their sins. It also deals with the essence of nature and all creations upon this world. It speaks about the rebirth of souls into other people or in other forms.[6]

Jewish sages who studied *Kabbalah* avidly sought to acquire the final edition, that which was buried along with R' Chaim Vital. R' Avraham Azulai, author of *Chesed LeAvraham* and R' Yaakov Tzemach, a great *mekubal*, two of the saintliest figures of their generation, purified themselves, prepared special *yichudim* and prayed to receive an answer in a dream. They wished to obtain permission from R' Chaim to open up his grave and remove those buried writings. To their joy, they were told to proceed. With trepidation, they unearthed the *Mahadura Basra* of the Ari's writings, in its final, annotated form by R' Chaim.[7]

This edition, which remained in the possession of R' Yaakov Tzemach, eventually reached the hands of his disciple, R' Meir Papirsh-Katz, but R' Shmuel Vital did not possess such a copy. R' Meir went to Damascus and received from R' Shmuel the writings that he still possessed. From these combined works, he made a new revised edition, which he also called *Etz Chaim*.

These writings, by R' Shmuel Vital and R' Meir Papirsh, received the stamp of approval of Jewish leaders everywhere. For they were said to be the most authentic ones and truly reflected the teachings of the Arizal and his approach. The Chida writes:

> "And therefore, whoever wishes to study from more exact versions, should use that of the eight gateways systematically arranged by R' Shmuel, and *Derech Etz HaChaim* arranged by R' Meir Papirsh, named *Mahadura Basra*, which is a section within the work."[8]

The Ari's Impact upon Posterity

The Ari's approach in *Kabbalah* was very innovative and radical, compared to those which preceded it. As we noted above, the Ramak, before his death, predicted that one of the wise men of Tsefas would arise and illuminate the entire world with his innovations in *Kabbalah*. And even if his approach proved to be altogether different, it would not constitute a contradiction to what he himself had taught. Indeed, in the beginning, the Ari's teachings did arouse considerable opposition because it was felt that he was contradicting what the Ramak had taught. But when his ideas became more familiar, people were able to differentiate between the secrets of 'the world of futility', to which the Ramak referred, and the 'world of improvement',[9] with which the Ari dealt. In other words, there really was no disagreement between the two; each addressed a different plane.

R' Chaim Vital, who was a disciple of both, explained that R' Moshe Cordovero paved the direct road for beginners while the Ari made an inner and deeper road.[10]

The Ari's approach rapidly became widespread, in the main through the efforts of his closest disciple, R' Chaim Vital. In Italy, it was promoted by R' Yisrael Saruk and by his disciple, the Rama of Pano.

It soon became the most widely accepted method of study for the *Kabbalah*. R' Shlomo Shlumil testified in 5367 (1607) that *mekubalim* explained the *Zohar* according to the Ari's mode, regarding this as incomparably superior to any other — like "the sun is superior to the moon." When R' Yeshayah Halevi Horowitz, the *Shelah (Shnei Luchos Habris)*, a significant *Kabbalist* himself, first saw R' Shmuel Vital's copy of *Etz Chaim* he said, "From the day that Torah was given, there has not been the like of this book. This book explains the study (of *Kabbalah*) according to topics in chapters. No mortal eye has yet beheld anything to compare with it. These are the very secrets of the Heavenly Chariot."

The influence of the Ari's teaching was so far-reaching that the rabbis of Cracow wrote to R' Moshe Zakus, a famous *mekubal*, asking him to teach them how to write a *sefer Torah* according to the precepts of *Kabbalah*. This set an unparalleled precedent. He replied with a detailed outline on how to write the holy Names of *Hashem* and how to sanctify the quill used for writing, according to the teachings of the Arizal.[11]

The disciples of R' Moshe Zakus continued to study and teach the Ari's Torah in Italy. They were: R' Binyamin Kohen and his disciples, the Mahari Basan and the Ramchal. The Ramchal explained the words of the Ari in depth through the help of a *maggid* angel which appeared to him.

The *Gaon* of Vilna, who was born about a century and a half after the passing of the Ari, also dealt with the secrets of *Chen*. According to his son, R' Avraham, the *Gaon's* strength in *Kabbalah* was even greater than his prowess in the revealed Torah![12] When he was only nine, "he already had a full grasp of works in *nigleh* (the revealed) and *nistar* (the hidden). He completed his study of the entire *Etz Chaim* in half a year." He dealt with the teachings of the Ari in depth and even taught them to his disciples. For example, the *maggid* of Vilna reported that the *Gra* studied "*Zohar* and *Sefer Yetzirah* with him and explained everything which he found difficult in the writings of the Gurei Ari."[13]

Sifra DiTzniyusa, it will be remembered, was the only work which the Ari wrote himself. The *Gra* regarded this work highly and wrote a lengthy commentary on it, saying that the Ari had left blanks for him to fill.[14]

In the commentary, the *Gaon* showed that all the aspects of Creation and the Heavenly Chariot which are dealt with in the *Zohar, Idros, Tikunim* and the writings of the Ari are alluded to in that work. He invested great effort in weeding out errors in the Ari's writings which had crept in through carelessness and the additions of disciples which had not been verified by R' Chaim Vital. "These disciples," he said, "did not truly understand the meanings of the master's essential thoughts. Only R' Chaim Vital truly understood the inherent truths in his words in their source, as the Ari himself testified."[15]

R' Yisrael of Shklov, author of *Pe'as Hashulchan* and one of the *Gaon*'s most famous disciples, wrote: "I know of one other (the *Gaon*) to whom Yaakov Avinu appeared to explain what eluded him in the writings of the Ari."[16]

The strong bond that existed between the *Gaon* and the soul of the Arizal can be seen through one of the stories which his closest disciple, R' Chaim of Volozhin, tells in his introduction to *Sifra Ditzniyusa*:

There was once a man in Vilna who was able to tell each person what his thoughts were and about his most private actions. People were terrified of him. When he was brought before the *Gaon*, he said to him, "Rebbe, allow me to tell you something. Two weeks ago, on Thursday, you sat in such and such a place and said a *chiddush* on *parashas Haazinu* on such and such a verse. R' Shimon bar Yochai sat with you on that occasion, he on the right and the Ari on your left." Everyone present was astounded and even the *Gaon* murmured in surprise, "How can a mortal know such things?" He turned to the man and nodded, "That is true. I did think of truly amazing things then!" His face was radiant with light in the joy of reminiscence.

The Sefardic scholars were greatly devoted to the study of *Kabbalah* for many generations. In *Eretz Yisrael*, Turkey, Syria, Persia, Yemen, Egypt and in the more western lands of Morocco, Algeria, Tunisia, the greatest Sefardic sages studied *Kabbalah* following the Ari's approach; they adopted his *kavanos* in prayer and his other customs. We have already mentioned the *Beis El beis midrash* under the direction of R' Gedalyah Chayun which devoted days and nights to the study of the Ari's teachings. The Rashash, R' Shalom Sharaabi, spent years of his life in this *beis midrash* which produced other great *Kabbalists*. To this very day, that academy remains a stronghold of the study of *Chen*.

Its Influence on Chasidus

R' Yisrael Baal Shem Tov, who revealed the great light of *Chasidus* to the world, founded the principles of his teachings on the *Zohar* and the Ari's commentary.

Just as the Ari had placed special emphasis upon humility, so did this movement establish that "the more a person truly belittles himself, in greater measure does the *Shechinah* come to rest upon him... One cannot become elevated spiritually without being genuinely lowly and insignificant in his own eyes."[17]

The Ari's teachings are not only evident in *chasidic* thought, but also in the day-to-day life of its adherents. The *tzaddikim* and their followers preferred to adapt the customs of the Ari even where these ostensibly conflicted with the *halachah* as ruled in the *Shulchan Aruch*. They altered the text of the prayers, the familiar *nusach Ashkenaz*, which was a centuries-old tradition throughout Jewish communities, in favor of the Ari's text, today referred to as *nusach S'fard*. R' Chaim Halberstam of Sanz, in his *Divrei Chaim* writes:

> "After that holy angel, the Baal Shem Tov, descended from heaven,. he understood that his soul had not emerged from the gateway of *nusach*

Ashkenaz... therefore whoever adheres to the precepts of the Baal Shem Tov and his disciples has embraced the version of the Arizal."[18]

Chasidus laid particular emphasis on *kavanos* (intentions) in prayer. The Baal Shem Tov and his followers prayed according to the *kavanos* of the Arizal and adopted additional customs practiced in the Ari's *beis midrash*: these include frequent immersions in a *mikveh* in preparation for *Shabbos* and festivals; immersions before the daily morning prayer and prior to any concerted effort in service to *Hashem*; an additional verbal consecration before prayers and the performing of *mitzvos* through a *"leshem yichud Kudsha Brich Hu uShechintei..."*; reciting *Tehillim* in all difficulties, with a special *"Yehi ratzon"* at the end of each 'book' of *Tehillim* recited or 'day' (section of *Tehillim* recited on that day of the week); prohibition against shaving the beard or cutting off the *payos* even in the permissible ways; wearing white garments on *Shabbos* (this practice fell into disuse, though silken garments have remained the traditional *Shabbos* garments); laying out twelve loaves for each of the three *Shabbos* meals (the original disciples were most particular in keeping this). All these practices of the Ari were followed by the leaders of *chasidus* and by their *chasidim*.

1. "Rav Pe'alim" by the Gaon's son, p. 91
2. "Shem Hagedolim" Os Samech, Siman 60
3. The Beis Yaakov siddur (Emdin) — laws of kiddush
4. The Or Hayashar siddur, Kodinov
5. "Shivchei HaAri" p. 35
6. "Shaar Hakavanos" (Jerusalem)
7. "Shem Hagedolim" II (Sefarim) Os Ayin, Siman 70
8. "Shem Hagedolim" under R' Chaim Vital Os Ches Siman 21
9. "Emek Hamelech" Shaar Olam Hatohu, Chapter 55
10. Sefer Hachezyonos, vision from 5333; "Shivchei R' Chaim Vital" p. 13
11. "Lechem Hapanim", last Kuntres, p. 72
12. Introduction to "Shnos Eliyahu" on Zeraim
13. Introduction by the sons of the Gra to his commentary on Shulchan Aruch Orach Chaim
14. The preface of the Gaon's commentary to "Sifra DiTzinyusa"
15. R' Chaim Volozhiner's introduction to the Gaon's commentary on the Zohar
16. The introduction to "Pe'as Hashulchan"
17. "Avodas Yisrael' by R' Yisrael of Kozhnitz, Parashas Ekev
18. "Orach Chaim", part II, Siman 9

CHAPTER TWENTY-ONE
LOCATIONS TELL THEIR TALES

A man and woman were waiting in the communal offices of the Jewish quarter in the Old City. He was holding on to several bundles while she stood behind him bashfully, coddling a tender, sleeping infant in her arms. Both looked hopefully up at the official.

He was shaking his head, "No, I am sorry but I cannot give you that apartment."

"Why not?" the man pressed his case. "It is small but it is most suitable for us. We will try to take very good care of it."

"Impossible!" he said with finality. "It is not meant for a family."

The man looked at him in surprise, "Why not? Didn't so-and-so live there until a short time ago?"

"Yes," the clerk replied impatiently, "but he lived there alone, which is a different story. You are a family and we cannot permit it. It is a holy site, the birthplace of R' Yitzchak Luria, the Ari Hakadosh!"

Their crestfallen expression turned to one of excitement,

"Really? We did not know that!"

The people of Jerusalem treated the house where the Ari was born with great respect. They were careful not to behave lightheadedly when visiting. The communal officials did not allow families to live there; only single people were permitted to reside there. The building itself was owned by Arabs, but the Jews of Jerusalem made a special effort to rent it, at a prohibitive price, and erected a *beis midrash* for the study of *Kabbalah* and for prayer in the fashion of the Ari.[1]

There is a small alley leading off from the *Beis Knesses Hachurvah* in the Old City. After crossing Chabad Street, it goes up a few steps towards Jaffa Gate. This steep winding lane is called *Rechov Or Hachaim* though it used to bear the name "Chana and Her Seven Sons", since, tradition has it that these eight martyrs are buried below. On this street stands that historic landmark in which a son, Yitzchak, was born to R' Shlomo Luria Ashkenazi in 5294 (1534).

In 5502 (1742), one hundred and seventy years after the passing of the Ari, a holy man came to Jerusalem together with his followers: R' Chaim ben Atar, the Or Hachaim Hakadosh. He chose this very spot for his home and his *beis midrash*, *Knesses Yisrael*, today known as the *Beis Knesses Or Hachaim*. His heart was drawn to this sacred place where the sun of the godly Ari first rose.

The Ari's Sefardi Synagogue

In Tsefas, the Ari always prayed together with the Sefardim in their ancient *beis knesses*, which later became known as *Knesses shel Eliyahu*. Tradition has it that

Eliyahu Hanavi prayed there. On the three festivals of *Pesach, Shavuos* and *Succos*, and on the *Yamim Noraim*, he joined the Ashkenazic congregation. His followers wondered about this and asked him, "Why does the master pray together with Sefardim when he is Ashkenazi by birth?"

He explained, "The format of the prayers of either Sefardim or Ashkenazim contain the words of *Hashem*. I find that the Sefardic manner of prayer, with its *bakashos* and songs, and with its *vidui* at *minchah*, suits me during the week while I prefer the Ashkenazic format for festivals."[2]

The *beis knesses* where the Ari prayed so intently and studied the secrets of the Torah is truly splendid and magnificent. Here, it was, apparently, that his *talmidim* gathered to hear his lectures. Anyone descending along the southwestern slopes of Tsefas, in the winding road which passes by the slaughterhouse, will not be particularly impressed at first glance. He will not realize that he is approaching such a famous landmark. Built on a steep incline, it does not stand out on the city skyline; its roof rises a mere five or six feet from the ground. But someone coming up from the valley from the west will immediately be struck by the impressive sight of the Sefardic *Beis Knesses HaAri*, which stands before the first row of houses. One cannot stand before it and not feel the powerful impact of this structure with its hewn stones and their floral engravings. And upon entering the building, there is the stirring sight of the huge, unique *aron kodesh*. It is artistically carved and supported at its sides by two gorgeous towering marble pillars. There is the large marble *bimah* upon which the Ari summoned the Seven Shepherds to read from the Torah: Aharon as *kohen*, Moshe as *levi* and the Patriarchs — Avraham, Yitzchak and Yaakov, Yosef Hatzaddik and David Hamelech. Who does not feel a thrill in beholding the small niche in the eastern wall with its eternal light — the very place where the Ari Hakadosh would sit and pray, where Eliyahu Hanavi appeared to him and revealed deep secrets of sublime subjects being studied in the *mesivta d'rakiya* (Heavenly Academy).

After his passing, a new popular name was given to this ancient *beis knesses* — Beis Knesses HaAri shel HaSefardim. Each year on the Ari's *yahrzeit*, the 5th of *Av*, the residents of Tsefas gather here and pray for the elevation of his soul.

His Home

In times gone by, the Ari's home stood not far from the *beis kensses*. After his death, the people of Tsefas consecrated it and would not allow anyone to live there.

R' Simchah ben R' Yehoshua, who came with a caravan of *chasidim* in 5525 (1765), told a tale about what had occurred on that very site, as he heard it from the elders of Tsefas:

A wealthy man who came to settle in Tsefas purchased the house and wanted to restore it for his own use. The townspeople warned him not to dare live in such a holy place, but he ignored them. One old man approached him and said, "Let this be a warning to you: the ground upon which you are standing is sacred. It was the residence of the Ari. How can you defile a holy site by using it for general purposes?! 'One rises to a higher level of sanctity and does not descend!'" But he ignored the old man's warning as well and invested huge sums of money to renovate the building. He hired workers and craftsmen who labored until the finished product was a credit to their efforts.

He was happy with the final changes and he invited all of his friends and acquaintances, Jews and gentiles alike, to the housewarming. In the midst of the festivities there was a shattering explosion. The ground shook, the walls crumbled and several of the participants were buried in the debris while others were burned in a fire that broke out.

It was learned, later, that during recent military skirmishes between the government and warring factions, a shell had landed on the house. But it had not exploded until the precise time of the rich man's party...

The people of Tsefas were so moved by this event that they razed the building altogether. And since then, that site has remained in ruins. Nor does anyone dare to rebuild it for fear of defiling that holy residence.[3]

The Ashkenazic Beis Knesses of the Ari

The Ari and his disciples would *daven minchah* in the *Beis Knesses Eliyahu Hanavi* (the Sefardi one) every Friday together with the entire congregation. Upon conclusion, they would sing, "*Lecha Dodi*, let us go out to the field." And the entire congregation would rise and go out, up the hill to a field outside the city which faced the Rashbi's tomb in nearby Meron, to greet the *Shabbos* Queen. The area was paved with hewn stones and encircled with a stone hedge. People called it *chakal tapuchin* (an apple orchard — a euphemism for *Gan Eden*).

What a magnificent sight they were, the master and his disciples. Each one would be wearing four garments, corresponding to the four letters of the name of *Hashem*. The Ari in his white garments, his inner ecstasy visible to all, appeared like an angel.[4]

On that very site where the Ari had been wont to greet the incoming Queen, a *beis haknesses* was built and it was named after him. There were special rules to preserve the reverence and sanctity of the place. Eating and drinking were forbidden.[5] This Ashkenazic *Beis Knesses HaAri* was also called *Chakal Tapuchin Kadishin*.

With the expansion of the community, this *beis knsses* became too cramped and an adjoining one was built next door. It, too, was named after the Ari.

The Galilee suffered a series of earthquakes in the past. The one that occurred in 5597 (1837) hit Tsefas in particular and destroyed the Ashkenazic *beis knesses* almost entirely. Only its southern wall facing Jerusalem where the *aron kodesh* with its scrolls stood, miraculously remained intact. The renovation took twenty years to complete. Above the lintel of this structure is the inscription: "How fearful is this place, this *beis knesses* of the Arizal, in the year of *'Umikdashi tirau* — You shall be in awe of My sanctuary (the year 5617 — 1857 —) in which the renovation was completed.

When the Ashkenazic communities in the Diaspora learned about the devastating earthquake that laid waste to Tsefas, they rallied to help, through funds and actual labor. One skilled carpenter from Galicia offered to carve a huge olive wood *aron kodesh*. He labored at this task for fourteen years, producing a truly magnificent work of art, complete with pillars and intricate carvings.

These carvings included figures of animals in relief

which drew the criticism of the rabbis of Tsefas. They thought that these might be a transgression of the commandment of "You shall not make graven images." We find, for example, the chief rabbi of the Ashkenazim of Tsefas of that time, R' Shmuel Heller, writing as follows: "I testify that there are many pure wise men who know for a fact that from the day that those images were installed there, the sanctity of the *beis knesses* was defiled, so that it is no longer the wondrously holy place, the gateway to heaven, of yore. Some even refrain from entering it."[6]

The Ari's Mikveh

As you descend along the slopes of the Jewish quarter of Tsefas and turn to the cemetery, you can make out the upper edges of the Ari's *mikveh*. This stands above a fresh spring and is the place where the Jews of Tsefas have immersed themselves from time immemorial. They came here each Friday to purify their bodies in preparation for the holy day.

His Grave

No Jew visits Tsefas without going to pray for Jewish salvation at the grave of the Arizal and the other great sages buried nearby.

That same traveler, R' Simchah ben R' Yehoshua, decribed the Ari's tomb:

> "From the *beis knesses*, down the mountain slope, bearing north, is the grave of the Arizal. It is not covered with a structure but is open like the tombs in Poland. It has a three feet high stone wall upon which

rests a large whitewashed stone the length of the tomb. This bears the inscription: 'This marks the grave of the Mekubal R' Yitzchak Luria.'

We have traveled along the historic path of the wondrous life of R' Yitzchak Luria Ashkenazi, the Ari Hakadosh. Ever since his revelation, his name has been spoken with reverence by the greatest leaders of all kinds: Sefardim and Ashkenazim, *chasidim* and *misnagdim*. The customs which he instituted, based upon *Kabbalah*, have spread throughout Jewish communities and left their impression upon great and small. *Chasidus*, founded by R' Yisrael Baal Shem Tov, is based upon his teachings. Yet, at the same time, R' Chaim of Volozhin (from the camp of *misnagdim*) tells us that when his master, R' Eliyahu of Vilna, spoke about the Ari, his entire body would tremble with deep reverence. And the Sefardic communities also produced many great *mekubalim* who carried on his legacy.

The study of *Kabbalah*, as the Ari explained, taught and disseminated, brought comfort and dispelled the darkness of the Exile.

LIBRARY
Manhattan Day School
310 West 75 Street
New York, N.Y. 10023

1. "Toldos Chachmei Yerushalayim", Part I, Chapter Five, Os Ches, p. 101, footnote 2
2. "Sheluchei Eretz Yisrael" p. 841, quoted from an ancient Yemenite manuscript
3. "Maasos Eretz Yisrael" (Tel Aviv, 5706), p. 402
4. "Otzar Hamasaos" Eisenstein, p. 246
5. "Eden Tzion" on the Arizal
6. "Tsefas" Nasan Shur, p. 227